EUROPEAN MONETARY UNIFICATION

European Monetary Unification

GIOVANNI MAGNIFICO

A HALSTED PRESS BOOK

JOHN WILEY & SONS
New York – Toronto

Published in the United Kingdom 1973 by The Macmillan
Press Ltd

Published in the U.S.A. and
Canada by Halsted Press, a
Division of John Wiley & Sons, Inc.,
New York

Library of Congress Cataloging in Publication Data

Magnifico, Giovanni.
 European monetary unification.
 "A Halsted Press book."
 Includes bibliographies.
 1. Currency question—European Economic Community
countries. 2. Monetary policy—European Economic
Community countries. 3. Euro-dollar market.
I. Title.
HG930.5.M26   332.4'94   73-303
ISBN: 0-470-56525-X

Printed in Great Britain

To my children
Katia, Roberto and Giovanna

Contents

Foreword

THE formation of a monetary union is likely to be the dominant theme in the process of European unification during the current decade and the next, just as the implementation of the Treaty of Rome as it concerned the customs union and the common agricultural policy has been the main achievement of the sixties. In the monetary field, some steps have already been taken to further the partial approach to unification that has basically been followed since the first European community was set up. The attraction of this approach is that, as long as the measure of support needed for political unification is not forthcoming, it allows progress to be made by small, but definite steps. According to one (the dominant?) school of thought, monetary union would lend itself to a treatment of this sort well beyond the initial stages. The narrowing of the margins of fluctuation of intra-E.E.C. exchange rates and the attendant intervention and settlement rules, the creation of the European Fund for Monetary Co-operation, together with other measures which may be taken in the near future, would not require the formation of a political body to formulate economic policy for the Community as a whole.

But the creation of a common monetary framework, if it is to mean anything, will put constraints on the use of policy instruments–directly in the monetary field, indirectly in other fields. And this will affect the process of growth favourably in some member countries; but not in others. Unless Community economic policies can be evolved and implemented which meet the needs of all parties concerned, the monetary framework now being built may prove for a time too fragile a construction.

The merit of Dr Magnifico's book is that it stresses the link between the mechanism of monetary unification and its implications for the process of growth in the regions and countries of the Community. He makes a set of proposals hingeing on the early introduction of a common European currency and tries to show in detail how they would work in practice. One may or may not agree with him; but, in the face of the difficulties that are upsetting our endeavours to unify money in Europe, no one can deny the need for exploring all the different ways and means likely to make our task both feasible and acceptable. Moreover, different approaches may at some stage of the unification process prove to be complementary, rather than alternative.

This is why the ideas put forward by the author with great skill and with convincing force command the attention of all those who are in search of the way towards European Union.

GUIDO CARLI

Preface

This book comprises four essays. The first was originally published by the International Finance Section of Princeton University. In the main I have added a few footnotes and have omitted the postscript – a commentary on the portentous flare-up in exchange markets in the spring of 1971. I have felt that the readers of this book, who are presumably interested in the problems of European monetary unification and perhaps in the 'new approach' which I have put forward, should have, to begin with, the text in which the ideas leading to it were developed and first set out.

Essay 2 delves into the theory of optimum currency areas and relates to it the proposals I have made. In writing the Princeton Essay, my principal concern had been to draw attention to the far-reaching implications of monetary unification for the process of growth in the different economic regions of the Community and to show the need for a new approach. I felt that the immediate task was to present a set of proposals in a fashion which, however embryonic and tentative, would allow readers to form an opinion as to whether they could be made to work advantageously. I left it for a later occasion to elaborate the theoretical basis of my proposals. The occasion arose some months afterwards when I was asked to submit a paper to the meeting of the List Gesellschaft, held in Basle in February of · this year. Essay 2 is a somewhat revised version of that paper. It dwells mainly upon the concept of national propensity to inflation, which it indicates as a more suitable criterion for defining the optimum domain of a currency area. It concludes that the Community does not form as yet *one* optimum currency area; and suggests the need for limited internal flexibility of exchange rates during the intermediate stage of the integration process, when gaps between the economies in their propensity to inflation would be gradually closed.

The nucleus around which I have developed Essay 3 is an address I delivered to a committee of European parliamentarians last March. On that occasion I expounded my ideas principally on the link between monetary unification and regional growth, on the measure of intra-group exchange rate flexibility I was envisaging, and on the narrowing of the margins of fluctuation, which was implemented last April. I have expanded these points in Essay 3, which is largely new because I have also dealt with all those other aspects to which my mind has turned time and time again since at the end of the winter of 1971 I completed the manuscript of the Princeton Essay, and which I could not fit into Essay 2. Thus it includes an attempt to explain why policy harmonisation has eluded us so far and to show what might be done to make it effective; the 'blueprint' of a European monetary convention; a series of steps to be taken in order to get the new European currency established. It also tackles the objection, sometimes raised, that the Community would acquire an inflationary bias if it harnessed the machinery of monetary unification to help finance a policy of balanced growth. And it points to the usefulness of defining and implementing a European money supply policy.

Having considered the problems of 'official' monetary unification, in Essay 4 I have turned mainly to its market aspects. I have appraised the past and future of the Euro-currency markets and what chances a new European currency has of standing up to competition from the dollar, in its Euro-variant, and from some of the national European currencies. I have indicated the steps that need to be taken in order to make the Common Market truly common, from the viewpoint of money and capital markets. Finally, I have engaged in speculation concerning the future of the European financial centres, illustrating the conditions which are likely to help them to rise to a position of primacy in the Community. I have concluded that a polycentric structure would be better suited to the achievement of a set-up in which markets would not just communicate through the intermediation of a super-centre, but would be fully integrated with one another. As part of this set-up, I have suggested a pattern of specialisation for the leading E.E.C. financial centres. I have also referred to steps which banks and other financial institutions would have to take to foster the establishment of a closely-knit polycentric structure. Essay 4 was written for this book. Having originally written these essays independently of each other, to suit particular occasions, I had to integrate them into a whole for this book. Repetitions, however, could not all be eliminated; this would have implied rewriting them almost entirely. Also it soon became clear to me that when points are taken up in various essays, they are each time shown from a different angle. Partly, this reflects progress in my own thinking during the process of evolving the 'new approach' to monetary unification, at so eventful a time for the European and international monetary scene.

In the book is also reproduced the Federal Trust report on European monetary integration. This resulted from the work of a study group, but Professor J. Williamson and myself, as co-rapporteurs, are responsible for the report itself. It accepts the thesis that a European common currency should be created alongside the existing national currencies, at an early stage of the unification process. In adopting this proposal the study group chose to motivate it primarily with considerations of external monetary policy, whereas I feel that monetary unification should be pursued with the primary object of solving the internal problems of growth and balance within the participating countries and regions. A stronger and healthier Community will be in a better position to make valuable contributions to overcome world monetary and economic hardships.

The damage to Europe's fragmented monetary sovereignty and the re-moulding of the international monetary system under the pressure of crises on exchange markets and of policy measures, often taken unilaterally, have increased the sense of urgency for the achievement of a united stand by the E.E.C. countries. But Europe cannot be united externally while remaining divided on internal issues. Progress towards monetary unification will be a fragile achievement as long as member countries have conflicting perceptions of the attendant benefits and dangers. It would be wrong to ignore that conflict and its causes. What is needed is an approach whose logic must be aimed chiefly at minimising the area of conflict and, for the rest, can offer an acceptable and credible trade-off between the constraints which *must* be accepted to make policy harmonisation against inflation effective, and the commitment to a centrally-financed European management of growth. Clearly, countries will be less reluctant to renounce whatever freedom they now have to use important policy instruments, if the Community itself possesses the power and the means to help them in a meaningful way to overcome inflation and to solve their growth problems, which monetary unification along conventional lines might in fact aggravate.

This is the task I set myself in evolving a new approach to European monetary unification. Briefly, I have been guided by the awareness that inflation is and will remain for a time a most serious problem in Europe, and outside it; that regional disparities have dominated Europe's history of conflicts; and that economic growth ranks uppermost among the objectives pursued by governments, as being essential for improving the quality of life. I am aware that I have made, more or less explicitly, a number of value judgements in this volume. I had to be forceful, at times perhaps letting feelings harden into arguments, in order to make my points in a way that would start a full-blooded debate. In the light of the reactions I have received, both privately and publicly, to the proposals made in the Princeton Essay it would appear that my aim is being achieved.

I owe thanks to Dr Paolo Baffi, M. Raymond Bertrand, Sir Alec Cairncross, Mr Peter Coffey, Professor Richard Cooper, Dr Paul Einzig, Dr T. E. Josling, Professor Harry G. Johnson, Professor Fritz Machlup, Mr Christopher McMahon, Dr Rinaldo Ossola, Mr John Pinder, Professor Edgar Salin, Mr Charles Siegman, and Professor John Williamson, as well as to the Reader of the International Finance Section of Princeton University, for stimulating comments and criticisms they have made in writing or in the course of conversations I have had with them. With one or two exceptions, however, their remarks were confined to the draft of the published text of Essay 1. None of them is, of course, responsible for the arguments and opinions expressed there or elsewhere in this book.

I wish to express my gratitude to the Governor of the Banca d'Italia, Dr Guido Carli, not only for having written the foreword to this book, but above all for having shown by his own example that imagination and courage are among the qualities worth cultivating by central bankers and monetary experts.

I also wish to thank the International Finance Section of Princeton University, the Banque Nationale de Belgique, the List Gesellschaft, the Monte dei Paschi di Siena and the Federal Trust for having kindly authorised me to use for this book material already published by them.

Finally, the staff of the Banca d'Italia office in London deserves my warmest thanks. Dr Luigi Marini has efficiently assisted me by supervising the work of preparing typescript, arranging the bibliography and helping with the indexes. Towards the end Dr Alessandro Manzelli helped in that work. Mrs Ruth Malagodi, Miss Anne Dougary, Miss Nadia Iacovazzi and Miss Paola Andreanelli have patiently deciphered the manuscript and unstintedly typed drafts, revisions as well as the final version. I am grateful to Mrs Malagodi and Miss Dougary also for having helped to polish my English.

1 September 1972 G. M.

List of Abbreviations

B.I.S.	Bank for International Settlements
ECU	European currency unit
E.E.C.	European Economic Community
E.I.B.	European Investment Bank
E.P.U.	European Payments Union
G.N.P.	gross national product
H.M.S.O.	Her Majesty's Stationery Office
I.M.F.	International Monetary Fund
I.P.I.	industrial propensity to inflation
M.E.B.	Multi-role European Bank
N.P.I.	national propensity to inflation
O.E.C.D.	Organisation for Economic Co-operation and Development
O.E.E.C.	Organisation for European Economic Co-operation
R.P.I.	regional propensity to inflation
S.D.R.	Special Drawing Rights
U.A.	European unit of account

1 European Monetary Unification for Balanced Growth: a New Approach

Outline of the New Approach

IN this essay I surmise that, sustained and regionally balanced growth being ultimately the main economic goal of integration, progress towards economic and monetary union in Europe ought to be enhanced by defining a number of large economic regions and regrouping them on the basis of their ability to realise their full growth potential. Although each group might include whole member countries, the border between the two would cut across national frontiers. Instead of having one general economic policy for the whole Community, with piecemeal measures for the weaker regions tacked on, twin 'regional' policies should be defined and pursued at all times for the high-activity and the low-activity grouping respectively. Policies for the former would continue to be implemented, in much the same way as up to now, mainly by national institutions. For the latter group, instead, existing machinery would be reinforced by setting up an *ad hoc* body: the Multi-role European Bank. As implied by the name, the M.E.B. would be empowered to carry out a very wide variety of operations; it would be endowed with resources on a scale adequate to play a major role in raising the rates of growth in the laggard regions. Gradually, the M.E.B. could be developed into the Community central banking system and co-exist with the national systems. Its

First published in August 1971 by the International Finance Section, Princeton University (Essays in International Finance, No. 88).

liabilities would serve as money and be issued in the form not only of deposits, but also of notes: the European Currency Units (ECUs). These would circulate alongside the national currencies and thus meet the need for a common monetary standard in those economic sectors which by the nature of their activities are most open to integration.

It will appear from what follows that the arrangements here proposed should allay the fear that some countries, or parts thereof, may become large depressed areas as a result of the loss of freedom to change their exchange rates. This will make the commitment to rigid rates and absolute payments freedom acceptable to countries, and credible to markets. A differentiated regional policy will reduce the need for intra-Community flexibility of exchange rates. But resort to Community-supervised flexibility of all or some Community currencies might also not be ruled out altogether at the outset. Flexible exchange rates within the Community would after all mean only *partial* internal flexibility, since in each and every member country European Currency Units would circulate. While flexible national currencies, if and when necessary, would add room for adapting demand-management policies to local needs, the ECUs would be the instrument for maximising benefits from freedom of trade and factor movements in the Community. Finally, the ECUs might, or might not, have a fixed parity in terms of dollars, gold and/or Special Drawing Rights.

Summary of the Werner Report

It is of the essence of an economic union that goods and factors of production should be allowed to circulate freely within it. As long as it remains a multi-currency area, total interconvertibility and irrevocably fixed rates help to secure unhampered freedom of circulation. Transactions across national borders are thereby assimilated, in character and risk, to domestic ones: in neither case is a forward-exchange cover necessary.

It is therefore understandable that the authorities of the European Economic Community should be so much concerned with the monetary aspect of integration, as the emphasis put on it by the Werner Report suggests. [21]

The *Report to the Council and Commission on the Realisation by Stages of Economic and Monetary Union in the Community* was drafted by a group of experts presided over by the Prime Minister and Minister of Finance of Luxembourg, Pierre Werner, by whose name the group and the report are usually designated. The Werner Group was set up in March 1970, in accordance with the directives issued by the Conference of E.E.C. Heads of State and of Governments which took place at The Hague on 1 and 2 December 1969. In the report which the Werner Group submitted to the Council of the E.E.C. in October 1970, the conclusion is reached that economic and monetary union is an objective attainable in the course of the present decade, and that a plan to that effect should be implemented by stages. At the end of the process, the principal decisions of economic policy would be taken at Community level, with consequent transfers of responsibility from the national governments to Community organs. The creation of a centre of decision for economic policy, which would be politically responsible to a European Parliament, and of a Community system for the central banks are deemed indispensable. The steps to be taken would be interdependent and reinforce one another: standardisation and, finally, unification of economic policies would accompany the process of monetary unification. For the latter, the Report states that it implies 'the total and irreversible convertibility of currencies, the elimination of margins of fluctuation in rates of exchange, the irrevocable fixing of parity ratios and the total liberation of movements of capital'.

The Report does not lay down a rigid timetable, nor does it indicate in detail the measures to be taken during any but the first stage. This will cover the three years from 1 January 1971 to 31 December 1973 and will entail *inter alia*:

(*a*) Compulsory prior consultations in matters concerning principally medium-term economic policies, cyclical policy, budgetary and monetary policies.

(*b*) Establishment of procedures for regular 'concertation' at the Community level between the E.E.C. Commission and the social partners (associations of employers and trade unions).

(*c*) Formulation of the general lines of economic policy at Community level and determination of quantitative

guidelines to be applied to the main components of
public budgets; preparation of a Community survey
before member governments draw up and adopt their
budget proposals; synchronisation of national budget
procedures.

(d) Fiscal standardisation, and in particular adoption by *all*
member countries of the value-added tax system, with
'assimilation' of national rates; alignment of excise duties
sufficient to allow suppression of controls at intra-
Community frontiers.

(e) Abolition of residual exchange controls and discriminatory administrative practices which still restrict capital
movements between member countries; co-ordination of
policies concerning current problems and structural
aspects of capital markets.

(f) Standardisation of the instruments of monetary policy;
obligatory consultations to be held by the Committee of
Central Bank Governors, which will scrutinise at least
twice a year monetary and credit conditions in each
member country, and will issue guidelines concerning
principally interest rates, bank liquidity and the granting
of credit to the private and public sectors.

Finally, the Report recommends that, from the start of the
first stage, the central banks limit the fluctuations in the intra-
group rates of exchange within bands narrower than those
resulting from the application of the margins in force for the
dollar. This would be achieved by concerted action on the dollar
and, after an experimental period, would be announced
officially.

Narrowing of the margins would be accompanied by interventions on exchange markets in Community currencies.
During the first stage, the mutual-credit facilities to which such
interventions may give rise should not exceed those laid down
for the mechanism of monetary support at short term. But it
is proposed in the Report that possibly during the first stage, or
in any event the second, a European fund for monetary co-
operation should be created as a forerunner of the Community
system of central banks to be established in the final stage. The
fund would absorb the existing E.E.C. mechanism for monetary

support, and for financial aid at medium term. It would gradually become the organ for common management of the reserves of external liquidity.

The Resolution and the two Decisions, which were adopted on 22 March 1971[1] by the Council of Ministers of the Community concerning economic and monetary unification, embodied the substance of the proposals made in the Werner Report. Among other things, it was decided that, from 15 June 1971, member countries would narrow from 0·75 to 0·60 per cent the margins of fluctuation for intra-group exchange rates. Furthermore, a mechanism for the granting of financial aid at medium term (two to five years) was set up in the form of mutual-credit facilities adding up to the equivalent of $2,000 million (the French and German shares amount to 30 per cent each; Italy's to 20 per cent; Belgium–Luxembourg and the Netherlands participate with 10 per cent each). Finally, it was decided that the creation of the European Fund should again come up for consideration by the Council by mid-1972, with the aim of setting it up before the expiration of the first stage.

However, on a point of principle the decisions taken by the Council did not follow Werner. In the Report's philosophy the transitions to the second and third stages were to be automatic. Acceptance of the Report was assumed to imply a commitment to participate in the whole process, leading eventually to the introduction of a common currency and the creation of a policy-making body to manage it. But at least one member country, France, was not willing to undertake that commitment, and argued that for the time being countries should commit themselves for the first stage only. Although the French request met with considerable opposition, in the end it was agreed to – but with an important proviso. It was laid down that the agreement on the narrowing of the margins, the machinery for medium-term financial aid and the European Fund would at first be limited to five years from the beginning of the first stage. The life of the agreement would be extended for an indefinite period – as was originally intended – at the time of the transition to the second stage, the extension being contingent upon the progress made towards the 'convergence' of national economic policies and the readiness to accept the constraints put upon

[1] For later developments see Essay 4, pp. 168-9.

them by the measures proposed in the Werner Report for the second and third stages.

The inclusion in the above-mentioned Resolution of the E.E.C. Council of the 'precautionary clause', as the proviso is now known, is meant to give the right to opt out of the venture to those countries which, in the absence of measures to check differentials in national propensities to inflate, might be called upon to make good other members' inflationary gaps. These latter, on the other hand, would not accept a firm commitment to the Werner Report *in toto*, being aware that rigid adherence to a common monetary standard could, under certain circumstances, and failing adoption of adequate counter-policies on the part of the Community, thwart their process of growth.

The solution was (not!) found by postponing the ultimate decision on the issue – while not questioning the basic assumptions in the Werner Report.

Growth as the Ultimate Economic Objective of Integration

One should not lose sight of the fact that unrestricted freedom of trade and factor movements is not the be-all and end-all of economic union. Because that freedom is not a sufficient condition for full employment and growth, it cannot be considered as more than an intermediate objective and it should be treated as such. Consequently, in the process of achieving the goal of economic union more attention should be paid to matters, other than freedom of circulation, which will secure for the Community a better employment and growth performance. There is, of course, growing awareness of the costs that growth involves for society and the individual, so that the growthmanship *à outrance* which has been fashionable for the past twenty years appears now to be almost obsolete. Yet the better 'quality of life' towards which the emphasis has shifted is hardly to be attained without full employment of resources, progress of productivity, and growth. By offering its members better prospects of performing well on that score, the Community will be better placed to overcome the centrifugal forces which no doubt will time and again threaten progress towards unification. These prospects will have to measure up against the unprecedented achievements of Europe as a whole during the post-war period.

The growth of the European economy after 1945 was steeper and smoother than at any other period in modern times. The advance was not equally rapid in all countries, yet even the economic performance of the laggards represented an improvement when set against their record in the late nineteenth century and the first four decades of the twentieth. The O.E.E.C. itself contributed to this result. It has recently been argued that the relevant trade and output statistics supply no substantial evidence that the E.E.C. countries have become more competitive, more specialised or faster-growing by reason of their membership, and that if anything the evidence points the other way. But what would have happened both in member and non-member countries if the Community had not been created could not be shown by these statistics ([14] pp. 29-43). Be that as it may, there is scarcely any doubt that the E.E.C. will not only have to keep overall growth rates high by international standards, but also see to it that no member country or large economic region lags too far behind.

There is, however, no built-in mechanism that would work quickly enough to prevent underemployment of resources and economic decline in some regions of a unified area, while the area as a whole was experiencing a period of rapid growth. In fact, one of the outstanding empirical regularities to be observed in the process of growth of countries which have long been unified is that some regions have persistently had higher unemployment and/or grown more slowly than others. And there is a school of thought that holds that regional inequalities, which may have at their origin an exogenous, accidental change, tend to perpetuate themselves. Gunnar Myrdal, among others, argues that:

In the centres of expansion increased demand will spur investment, which in its turn will increase incomes and demand and cause a second round of investments, and so on. Saving will increase as a result of higher incomes but will tend to lag behind investment in the sense that the supply of capital will steadily meet a brisk demand for it. In the other regions the lack of new expansionary momentum has the implication that the demand for capital for investment remains relatively weak, even compared to the supply of savings which will be low as incomes are low and tending to fall. Studies in many countries have shown how the banking system, if not regulated to act differently, tends to become an instrument for siphoning off the savings from the poorer regions to the richer and more progressive ones where returns on capital are high and secure. ([16] p. 28)

For today's mixed economic systems, in which governmental influence and intervention are so far-reaching, the relevant question is not whether the tendency to perpetuate regional inequalities is inherent in the play of market forces, but whether suitable policies are being pursued to prevent a region from falling behind. Europe's integration could not succeed if it promised to make the strong regions stronger and the weak ones weaker.

Payments in Semi-integrated and in Fully Merged Economies

It should also be borne in mind that balance-of-payments problems of the traditional inter-country type continue to be difficult to solve only as long as the process of integration is only half accomplished. Once that process has gone as far as to bring about an effective merger of the national economies, such problems will generally recede into the background. For one thing, the formation of surpluses and deficits is the result of discrepancies in national economic trends. But in fully merged economies the economic cycle would no longer coincide with national frontiers; economically homogeneous regional groupings would emerge with common cyclical trends. Discrepancies would tend to form between the more dynamic regions on one side, and the weaker ones on the other.

Moreover, the settlement of payments would be made smoother, since, as in the case of imbalances within one and the same country, there would be much wider scope for inflows and outflows of *securities* to offset a country's excess of exports or imports. Given an adequate supply of marketable *securities* in people's and firms' portfolios, and fully integrated markets for monetary and financial securities, small changes in prices can bring about movements of securities sufficiently large to offset current-account imbalances. Thus the adjustment process via changes in relative costs, employment and income is made more gradual. Indeed, the achievement of economic and monetary union might be rendered less painful if already during the transition period the mechanism of equilibrating capital movements could be relied upon. Had that mechanism worked satisfactorily so far, balance-of-payments problems within the E.E.C. would not have acquired quite the disturbing connotation that they did. In fact the liberalisation of capital movements made remarkable progress, but did not go far enough to create a unified market, nor did it elicit, at least until recently, the follow-up of initiatives in the private sector needed to create truly integrated and efficient security markets. Furthermore, the size of external payments problems which one or two countries had to face at times compelled them to suspend and partly revoke capital-liberalisation measures. Finally, fixed exchange rates came to be equated in people's minds with an adjustable-peg system, that is, a system in which rates are subject to revisions taking place at long irregular intervals and resulting in large parity changes. Had there been no grounds for expecting such changes, and had the margins of fluctuation around the parity been done away with, small interest-rate differentials would have brought about equilibrating short-term capital movements which, as under the classical system, would have been an important element in the adjustment process.

Under fixed exchange rates, faltering credibility deprives the system of the mechanism which tends to smooth out payments in a unified market. In fact, that mechanism's working can be made to swing in a perverse direction, and this may of itself force a change of parity or restrictions to freedom of payments, or both. It is therefore essential, *if a system of regulated, internal flexibility is held to be incompatible with Europe's economic integration*, that the commitment to irrevocably fixed rates and absolutely free capital movements be at all times beyond doubt. Rightly it is pointed out in the Werner Report that the firmest guarantee to that effect could be given by replacing national currencies with a European currency:

Monetary union . . . may be accompanied by the maintenance of national monetary symbols or the establishment of a sole Community currency. From the technical point of

view the choice between these two solutions may seem im-
material, but considerations of a psychological and political
nature militate in favour of the *adoption of a sole currency which
would confirm the irreversibility of the venture.* [The italics are
mine.] [21]

Before adoption of a European currency is within reach, that
commitment will be taken in earnest if member countries can
be satisfied as to the prospects for growth of their economies.
But countries with a higher vulnerability to inflationary
pressures and/or to shifts of overall demand away from certain
products will tend to lose competitiveness and payments equilibrium. In order to restore them, without parity changes of the
type that has been resorted to in recent years or a succession of
small downward rate adjustments, a more severe restriction
of demand will be necessary, which in turn will discourage
investment activity. Given full convertibility, there will be an
outflow of capital in search of profitable investment elsewhere.
The process tending to slow down the rate of growth in some
member countries could go on long enough to transform them
into industrially depressed areas, such as are still to be found at
present within certain member countries. But the process of
integration today simply cannot afford to repeat old *laissez-faire*
patterns and, as Kaldor has recently commented, 'nations do
not commit hara-kiri for the sake of international treaties,
however solemnly and sincerely entered into'([12] p. 35).

*Different National Propensities to Inflation as an Obstacle to an
Acceptable Pattern of Unified Policies*

Under the rules of the International Monetary Fund, measures
relating to exchange rates cannot be taken as isolated acts of
national sovereignty, those rules resting on the lessons drawn
from inter-war experience that individual exchange rates will
not automatically add up to an equilibrium system. The I.M.F.
system of fixed rates and freedom of trade and payments
benefits from a built-in adjustment mechanism. A strong
demand pressure in one country will tend fairly promptly to
spill over; in the inflating country prices and costs will not rise
to the full extent of the excess demand, while prices abroad will
by the same token be pulled upwards. As a result, prices and

cost levels in mutually trading countries should be prevented from getting too far out of line, and balance-of-payments problems from becoming unmanageable.[1]

The mechanical element in the adjustment process needs, however, the support of appropriate policies.

But countries having broken loose from the gold standard would not readily accept being bound by a new set of rules. No matter how much of an improvement the latter may represent, the co-ordination of policies aiming at a mutually acceptable equilibrium in each member's balance of payments has proved an elusive goal. No doubt the task of maintaining domestic and external equilibrium has been made more intractable by the fact that, while not much has been added to the range of effective institutions and policy instruments, there has been a multiplication of objectives. Full employment and growth have been throughout the post-war period the major objectives of governmental policies, but they have been pursued along with a number of other objectives, each being sought in turn with important qualifications. Growth should be smooth over time and space; the economic and social costs of heavy congestion in certain areas find less and less acceptance, while the raising of the tempo of economic activity in the weaker regions has come to be recognised as a primary objective. Growth policies should not be pursued at the expense of, but rather should promote, a more equitable distribution of income and wealth; they should bring forth an adequate supply of social goods and services, and

[1] With reference to Italian monetary developments in the years 1958–65, Dr Paolo Baffi, Director-General of the Banca d'Italia, has described the working of that mechanism as follows:

'If the country is strongly integrated in the world market through foreign trade, this condition will prevent it from falling too far out of line with its trade partners in terms of unit costs, since the balance-of-payments effect of any such tendency will be prompt and massive. Therefore, action to reabsorb a foreign imbalance will not meet the obstacle of a long-standing, rigid cost structure.'

He has also remarked that, in conditions of generalised inflationary trends, the maintenance of fixed exchange rates by a country which has got out of line does not require absolute price and wage deflation, but only the containment of its rate of inflation below its trading partners' and competitors' average. ([1] pp. 139–41)

secure the desired balance between the private and public sectors in today's mixed economies, and so on.

The increase in the number of objectives, without a corresponding one for policy instruments, has augmented the possibility of conflicts among them. When conflicts have arisen, a certain goal has been attained by not fully achieving others. In other words, the partial sacrifice of the latter has been accepted, or 'traded-off' against the attainment of another goal.

Because the readiness to sacrifice related objectives differs from country to country, as does the trade-off relationship between G.N.P., unemployment and prices, it is not surprising that in actual fact discrepancies in the national price and cost levels have become so large as to require parity changes. And since the parities of E.E.C. currencies have undergone changes of opposite sign vis-à-vis the dollar, it would appear that such discrepancies grew larger within the Community itself, *at any rate in relation to the imbalances that member countries could sustain.*

The functional relationship between the rate of change of prices and changes in aggregate demand relative to potential output, as measured by the rate of change of unemployment, is emphasised in the approach based on the 'Phillips curve'.[1] But, given the multiplicity of forces which combine and alternate to bring about changes in the price levels, the trade-off relationship between inflation and unemployment does not emerge from empirical analysis as consistently as some tend to assume. In fact, recent experience suggests that the trade-off is not stable and may not be of much help in certain circumstances, such as when forcing 'changes of gear' in economic activity to fight an inflation in which the cost-push element has become predominant.[2]

---

[1] A. W. Phillips put together statistical evidence which led him to the tentative conclusion that, except when import prices are rising rapidly, 'the rate of change of money wage rates can be explained by the level of unemployment and the rate of change of unemployment'. ([19], p. 299)

[2] For alternative explanations of the departures from the 'Phillips curve' shown by recent experience, see A. G. Hines, 'The Determinants of the Rate of Change of Money Wage Rates and the Effectiveness of Incomes Policy', and M. Parkin, 'The Phillips Curve: A Historical Perspective, Lessons from Recent Empirical Studies and Alternative Policy Choices'. Both papers have been published in H. G. Johnson and A. R. Nobay (eds.), *The Current Inflation* (London: Macmillan, 1971).

But experience seems also to indicate that countries possess to different degrees what I shall call *national propensity to inflation* (N.P.I.).[1] Differences in N.P.I. would seem to depend *inter alia* on historical and social factors, on the system of industrial relations and the militancy of trade unions, on the structure of industry and its regional deployment, as well as on the building into the general public psychology of expectations of inflation or price stability generated by demand-management policies, which in the past may or may not have aimed consistently at guaranteeing the full-employment level of monetary demand, with little regard to changes in external competitiveness and payments balance. In other words, historical patterns may not tell us what level of unemployment would be necessary for a given country to attain the desired degree of price stability, but they would indicate that, in order to prevent prices from rising faster than at a specified rate, higher unemployment would be needed in certain countries, less of it in others.

The foregoing argument suggests that member countries fail to keep broadly in line as regards the rate of inflation not just because governments decide in favour of different policy options, but perhaps more importantly as a result of the economies themselves having a different inflation–unemployment trade-off relationship. If that is so, readiness to agree on a common order of priorities among the main objectives will not suffice, and no pattern of unified economic and financial policies is going to be both practicable and acceptable within an area where N.P.I.s vary considerably. To contain price increases within the same range would mean either stagnation and waste in the economies which would have to bring about higher unemployment than the economies with a lower N.P.I., or a relatively high rate of inflation in the latter – which, not being needed, would hardly be accepted.

Differentiated Regional Policies as a Way out of the Deadlock

The way out of the impasse ought perhaps to be sought by gradually closing the gaps in the member countries' trade-off patterns and by following two different policies tailored to the needs of the two categories in which countries, or rather the

[1] I have developed the concept of N.P.I. more fully in the essay on the theory of optimum currency areas (see below, pp. 62-81).

homogeneous economic regions of the Community, would be regrouped.

Advances on the path to integration should of themselves help to restrain some of the elements responsible for the gaps in the trade-off pattern. Since we are today as much on a labour standard as on any monetary standard, wage trends have strategic importance. The growing integration of the economies will help to bring more uniformity in these trends *inter alia* by increasing labour mobility, as well as making the pressure of competition stronger and thereby setting more effective limits to cost divergences.

As a result of this and of the fact that a growing share of consumption in each member country will be made up of goods and services supplied by other members, it is likely that trade unions will adopt a common approach in their wage and other claims, even while striving for pay parity.

Further, to the extent that national inflation propensities incorporate lessons from past inflationary experience and the expectations that they breed, a more uniform pattern should be brought about also by the shrinking room for national auto-nomous demand-management and employment policies. These policies have often shown an inflationary bias in countries with sizeable regional problems. As with a regional unemployment gap the national average of unemployment tends to be low only when the high-activity regions experience pressure of excess demand, accompanied by rising costs and prices, governments have been inhibited in their fight against inflation lest un-employment in the weak regions should rise to socially and politically intolerable levels. 'Fine tuning' in particular has been made nearly unworkable, since the disinflationary impact of restrictive measures tends to concentrate in the weak regions, where unemployment is already high, and to affect high-activity regions less and later. But while in the latter wage rises are, however loosely, correlated to the demand for labour, as measured by the level and rate of change of unemployment, in the high-unemployment areas wage increases depend largely upon those in the former group. Thus the wage spiral, which starts where there is a labour shortage, eventually extends to the low-activity regions, as a result of external cyclical conditions.

If, therefore, a more even pattern of demand and employment could be brought about, the unemployment–inflation trade-off would be improved. In other words, less unemployment and more price stability would be attained by countries which, suffering from large regional problems and being inflation-prone, have run into payments difficulties because they have tended to get too much out of line with the Community's external payments equilibrium. Thereby the gaps in the trade-off pattern of member countries would tend to close.

In the United Kingdom, the case for a fully-fledged regional policy was recently set out as follows:

Regional policy has a key role to play in the achievement of faster growth. One of its major aims is to make use of the reserves of unused labour in some regions of the country and so speed up industrial growth where it is lagging. . . . National unemployment has only been relatively low when the prosperous areas have been experiencing pressure of excess demand and all the disadvantages of shortages, delays and inflation of costs and prices. When measures have been taken to reduce this inflationary pressure, unemployment in the less prosperous regions has risen to high levels, leading to a waste of resources. This loss to national output would be avoided if the levels of unemployment in the less prosperous regions were nearer the national average. . . . A policy of stimulating economic growth in regions with under-employed resources will therefore help to avoid regional concentrations of excess demand which set the pace in driving up costs and prices. . . . ([17], p. 84)

For most of the time since the war manpower has been a scarce commodity in Britain as a whole. If it has been in surplus supply in the Development Areas, that is because of the uneven distribution of demand for labour. When the level of national economic activity has been relatively high, the pressure of demand for labour in the centres of maximum employment, especially in the South and the Midlands, has built up from time to time to very high levels, with consequent and well-known inflationary effects and damage to the balance of payments. Even at these times the degree of

B

unemployment in the Development Areas has represented a waste of scarce human resources. When action has become imperative to restrain the pressure of demand in the areas of high employment – and because this has involved measures affecting the whole economy – then unemployment in the Development Areas has been pushed up to an extent which has not proved acceptable for any length of time. This has led to a reaction against the measures of restraint and to pressure for relaxations. ([7] p. 11)

The notion that a more balanced pattern of employment helps to attain both more growth and monetary stability underlies also the analysis in the report concerning Italy's national economic programme for 1971–5 ([15] p. 82).

The foregoing argument points to the advantages of a regionally differentiated policy of demand management. Such a policy conceived and implemented at the European level would help to raise the overall rate of growth in the Community and fight inflation, which is bedevilling governments in their pursuit of expansion. It would afford an escape from the trade-off mechanism implied by the Phillips curve, or at least bring about a shift of that curve by improving the terms of the trade-off (a result which some governments and some economists also expect from incomes policy). The process of economic integration would be more likely to take place in conditions of expanding output and monetary stability, which would be of great assistance from the political point of view. In a perspective which gives economic integration the role of a launching-pad towards political unification, it is difficult to envisage the effective acceptance in the meantime of unified economic policies, if those policies have to aim at unemployment for attaining and maintaining internal and external equilibrium: indeed, it can hardly be envisaged without the backing of democratic Community institutions.

Regional problems have dominated the history of Europe's development. In *Growth and Stagnation in the European Economy*, Svennilson convincingly argues that, in all likelihood, the arbitrary combination of resources within the national units slowed down not only the growth of less favoured countries, but also the general development of Europe's joint resources after the First World War. Moreover, Europe would have been unable to maintain its still prominent place in the world economy, because of the failure to achieve a redeployment of industry offering the backward peripheral regions sufficient opportunities to industrialise in an open system. In the absence of a European regional policy, the far-reaching reorientation of production and industrial structure required by the changing structure of the world economy did not take place in the inter-war period ([20] p. 26).

The fact that a very high proportion of the trade of European countries is with one another does not suffice to bring about a geographically balanced pattern of development and growth. In the inter-war period, in fact, countries turned away from free trade and an open economic system, because the mere absence of obstacles to trade and payments was not enough to provide Europe's economy and each of its constituent parts with adequate opportunities for full employment and growth. As it was, intra-European trade fell more sharply than trade with non-European countries.

Limited Scope for 'Locally' Financed Expansionary Policies in a Fully Integrated Area

Today growing strains are appearing in the post-war fabric of free trade and payments. Lately that fabric could not be spared the contradictory reintroduction of however subtly disguised administrative controls, nor the jolts of devaluation and re-valuation of member currencies. Not surprisingly, countries are loath to surrender the right ultimately to decide in matters of exchange-rate policy. They regret the already mentioned in-adequacy of the available instruments in view of the proliferation of policy objectives; and it has been forcefully argued that, by using the exchange-rate weapon too sparingly, countries with a high national inflation propensity have hindered their process of growth. Main reliance on management of internal demand for dealing with full employment and growth problems, which should be treated – so it is argued – as problems of international competitiveness and thus centre on export performance, would have led to the formation of an economic structure involving a slower rate of growth of productive potential [13].

By permanently relinquishing the right to resort to exchange-rate changes *and* by adding to full interconvertibility of their currencies the undertaking to eliminate totally all sorts of obstacles to freedom of trade and capital movements, countries see the scope for autonomous policies substantially reduced. The more open an economy, the greater the balance-of-payments effects of an autonomous expansionary policy financed 'locally'. As far as an autonomous fiscal policy is concerned, the multiplier effects on income and employment of government spending tend to leak into other regions of the integrated area. Autonomy in taxation meets a limitation in the mobility of people and enterprises.

In fact, because of contiguity in the industrial heart of Europe, where industry closely adjoins industry and the social and cultural environment is fairly homogeneous, that limitation would soon start to be felt. As to monetary policy, since the cost of interregional transfer of monetary and financial assets is negligible, the pervasive opening of the national markets is bound to equalise prices for the same categories of risk. The creation of monetary base by a *national* central bank in excess of a 'common norm' would have little effect on securities prices and interest rates within the country, because it would quickly spread over the whole integrated area; the impact on the balance of payments would be very strong.

It should, however, be noted that the speed and pervasiveness with which these mechanisms work depend on the degree of integration reached, that is, on the success in transforming national economic entities into an interregional system, with a highly developed institutional and operational linkage network for impulse transmission through space. It is this type of integration that sharpens the sensitivities of member regions to changes in credit, tax and fiscal policies in any of them. But it cannot be attained at one stroke, and the E.E.C. will for some time still operate as a semi-integrated system, in which it will not be impracticable and pointless to pursue autonomous policies – to a certain degree.

The loss of autonomy will tend to vary from country to country according to size and strength; some of them will be in a position, say, to raise or lower the interest rate and see the increase or decline gradually spread to the rest of the

Community. People and businesses in the weaker areas will have
to adjust to this rate level, and if the country happens to be
in current-account deficit, they will have to offer fractionally
higher rates in order to activate an offsetting capital inflow. As
pointed out above, this tends to make the settlement of payments imbalances smoother. But, although spread over time,
the adjustment process still takes place via income and employment changes. Higher interest rates tend to depress the prices of
capital goods, investment activity and production, and this
would lead in the end to a worsening of the terms of trade. The
fact that settlements would take place in a more automatic
fashion does not make the plight of members with prospective
payments and growth problems less serious.

Because effective integration is unavoidably going to be
accompanied by a reallocation of economic-policy powers, the
real issue is actually whether one or two countries should emerge
from it with the ability to influence the rest of the Community,
or whether the basic economic strategy – the priority which from
time to time is to be given to the main objectives – should be defined and agreed upon collectively, by means of Community procedures and organs. In the latter case, the scope for autonomous
policies allowed by imperfect integration could be harnessed
in favour of a Community policy for the low-activity regions.

*Twin Economic Policies for the High- and the Low-Activity
Regional Groups Respectively*

To this end, a number of major economic regions should be
defined, which would be divided into two different groups.
One group would embrace the high-activity regions, where
demand for factors of production has tended to outrun supply,
while in the other the low-activity regions would be brought
together. The latter would include regions experiencing difficulties in feeding a self-sustaining full-employment rate of
growth, and therefore failing to maintain the actual rate close to
the potential rate over a period of time. The contour line
between the two groups would cut across national frontiers, but
might at times include whole member countries; it would be
kept flexible in order to allow for the passage from one group to
the other (and eventually back again) according to a region's,
or country's, growth performance.

As countries with experience in regional development policy have found out, it is far from easy to define unambiguously criteria for allocating a region to either group, and to apply them neatly. Some countries have had to change the yardstick (rate of growth of G.N.P., rate of unemployment, and so forth) and have deemed it opportune to introduce a third category: the grey areas. The suggestions made here are intended to provide only an indication of the criteria that might be followed.

A differentiated policy for each of the two groupings should at the limit imply that two different policies would be formulated and implemented at all times. One indiscriminate policy for the whole Community might be as prejudicial to growth and the integration process as six or ten inconsistent national policies would be. One general economic policy with some regional measures tacked on would not measure up to the task envisaged here.

The usefulness of the two-policy device lies in the fact that it would imply a radical departure from old-style regional policies, a 'jump from quantity into quality'. With a few exceptions, these policies have been inadequate to meet (reasonable) expectations, largely because they have been relegated to an ancillary role vis-à-vis general economic policies. If some economic policy measures are tagged 'general' and others 'sectorial', subordination of the latter to the former follows almost by definition. Yet the measures taken as part and parcel of overall countercyclical policies that can be said not to have a regionally differentiated impact are very few.[1]

---

[1] With reference to the United States, Borts and Stein argue that:

'. . . many Federal policies have a differential effect on regional growth in the areas of agriculture, natural resources, public power, transportation, and housing, to name a few. . . . In a sense, all governmental economic policies have a regional impact. Some laws and regulations are consciously designed to stimulate the growth of one or two regions at the expense of others. Public power projects are an example. Other policies have an implicit regional effect because of the varying geographical location of economic activity. Examples of the latter might be a tight-money policy pursued by the Federal Reserve System or the favourable Federal tax treatment of mineral property depletion. The impact of tight money is likely to be greatest in those regions where a large proportion of resources is devoted to construction. The tax policy will affect the regions where mineral production is located.' ([6] pp. 188-9)

The differential regional impact is implicit even in monetary measures of 'quantitative and general' character, depending *inter alia* on the varying geographical concentration of different industries. *Ceteris paribus*, a tight-money policy is likely to affect most seriously regions where building represents a higher share of overall economic activity. Measures taken in order to deal with changes in 'general business conditions', that is, with the business cycle over time, tend to disregard changes through space.

Because in the arrangement proposed here the Community policy for the low-activity regions would constitute a policy in its own right, it is more appropriate – if 'regional' is to be retained – to think and speak in terms of twin regional policies. They would be placed on an equal footing, and possible conflicts between them would not be settled by having the same one usually yield to the 'general' needs of the other.

The two policies would not need to be harmonised in actual detail. They might even diverge, for achievement of a common strategic aim might require action in opposite directions. In conditions usually described as 'overheating of the economy', it might be appropriate to switch to restriction in the high-activity group while pursuing more or less moderate stimulation in the group in need of economic invigoration.

Still, the danger of conflicts arising from the policy dichotomy would be there. As far as objectives are concerned, the Community might be faced with the choice between fast growth on one side and regionally balanced development on the other. However, in the light of what was earlier pointed out, it would appear that the trade-off between different objectives might be improved: if a more uniform pattern of employment tends to curb inflationary tensions, then it should be possible to carry policies of expansion further than is possible under policies which do not discriminate as between regions.

It should be noted in passing that politically the task of co-ordinating the two policies would be facilitated by the growing solidarity of interests that would link the economic regions of different countries belonging to the same group, and by not having to argue the case for or against certain measures in a context which would see countries as a whole in the position of supporters or opponents.

*Means of Implementation of a Centrally Financed Policy for the
Low-Activity Regional Group*

As far as the implementation of the twin regional policies is
concerned, the problem is one of the inadequacy of the instruments available to carry out the policy for the low-activity
regions. National governments can avail themselves of a well-
diversified armoury, which includes administrative controls.
They make large use of measures such as regionally differentiated payroll taxes, unemployment-compensation payments,
interest-rate subsidies, and other income-transfer payments, in
order to mitigate the tendency of incomes in the weaker
regions to lag or fall. In addition to *ad hoc* measures, there are
built-in stabilisers. In a system of progressive taxation, as
incomes fall, the share absorbed by taxes falls more than
proportionally, while that part of government expenditure in
these regions that is not linked to the level of economic activity
will remain unchanged. If any action is taken, it will very likely
be in the direction of raising it. The experience of countries with
a federal political structure shows that there is no need to unify
national systems of taxation *in toto* and centralise public expenditure. But fiscal instruments can be used in a meaningful
and effective way to promote regional balance if the central
authorities share adequately (say from one-third to one-half of
the total) in the proceeds of taxation and in the process of expenditure.

The existence of a centralised share helps to create room for
'local' autonomy: a region receiving fiscal aid through the
central bodies, because of a fall in its level of employment and
income, is thereby enabled to lower its taxes and/or increase
expenditure. Furthermore, uniformity of federal income-tax
rates dilutes the importance of discrepancies in national tax
rates and weakens their disruptive effects. This perhaps explains
the excessive tendency to ask for detailed harmonisation of
national tax systems in cases such as the European Economic
Community, where an important centralised fiscal share cannot
be reckoned with, in a short-term perspective. This will be so
until further substantial progress towards outright political
unification introduces some form of effective democratic
representation and control in the Community. In this paper

it is assumed that the political thrust behind the drive for unification will not be strong enough to bring about such progress in the near future.

As to monetary and credit instruments, the difficulty of implementing by these means a regionally differentiated counter-cyclical policy lies with the tendency of money created for the low-activity regions to flow into the high-activity areas, thus defeating the very object of a differentiated policy. It is often held that this difficulty cannot be surmounted without introducing control on interregional capital flows. But this would not be necessary, since it would appear that even in countries which have long been unified, compartmentalisation of regional markets allows room for a regionally differentiated management of money. A scholar of regional economics has questioned, with reference to experience within the United States, the general assumption that open-market operations have pervasive and uniform effects throughout the entire American economy, and argued in favour of a regionally orientated monetary policy. According to him:

Reserves put into or drawn from the central money market are postulated to flow out to or away from every Reserve area both automatically and uniformly. Yet experience suggests that this assumption is invalid, that lags of different magnitudes exist, and that regional effects are not of the same intensity. These findings imply that open-market operations are offset by other factors to different degrees in the several Reserve districts. . . . Furthermore, in view of the imperfect mechanism by which funds flow from one district to another, and in view of the unique characteristics of each regional organism, it would seem that a more effective national discount-rate policy ought to embody differentials in discount rates among districts. This hypothesis finds support in empirical materials. For example, the existence of excess reserves nationally is not typically associated with the existence of the same amount of excess reserves in each district. Rather, at any given time the extent to which excess reserves are present in each district varies considerably; and in some instances a district's reserves may be under pressure when substantial excess reserves persist nationally. This suggests that a policy based on national aggregates alone is an inferior one. ([11] pp. 76-7)

Compartmentalisation of money and capital markets exists, of course, also within the countries that are members of the E.E.C. (especially those with substantially different regional economic structures), as well as between them. These imperfections, which are typical of semi-integrated economies, are not going to disappear overnight. As was pointed out earlier, they represent a drawback for the smooth working of the mechanism of interregional settlement; but they also tend to check leakages.

Leakages might still represent a major problem if a differentiated policy were to be pursued by purely *monetary* means; that is, with injections of liquidity by a lender of last resort through advances against the security of bills of member countries' governments, through open-market operations of the conventional type, and so forth.

But that would not be so if the differentiated policy were implemented through credit operations and instruments of the type used in various countries by regional and interregional banks. In fact, territorial specialisation in credit-granting was a feature of banking long before governmental regional policies were developed. Banks, including large ones, have tended to establish a special connection with locally based industrial and commercial firms, and that connection has been an important factor in determining the availability of credit for those firms. In Italy, regional and multiregional banks in the North, the Centre and the South have represented a very substantial part of the banking system. Although there was no administrative control over interregional money flows (these banks could do business with residents outside the regions covered by their network of branches), leakages do not seem to have represented a problem. In the case of the two ancient Southern banks (Banco di Napoli and Banco di Sicilia), which until 1926 shared with the Banca d'Italia the privilege of issuing notes, the limit to the contribution they could make to the development of economic activity in that part of Italy was set instead by factors such as the dearth of entrepreneurial resources, the low volume of local savings and the absence of an outside supply of (sub-sidised) funds.

In more recent times Italy has been endowed with regional, multiregional and national industrial-credit institutions. Their territorially directed credit-granting, and financing extended by the 'Cassa per il Mezzogiorno', have tended to secure for economic activity in the Southern regions of the country a larger amount of financial resources, flowing at a steadier pace, or at any rate one less sensitive to changes in the country's overall economic trends and policies. In this connection, it is worth quoting the following passages from the annual reports of the Banca d'Italia for the years 1962–4, which embrace an unusually strong cyclical fluctuation – an inflationary outburst accompanied by a serious balance-of-payments crisis having been followed by internal stabilisation and large surpluses in external payments:

From a territorial aspect, in 1962 the salient feature of the activity of the system of industrial-credit institutions was a larger injection of funds into the process of industrialisation of the South. These credit flows, already significant in the two preceding years, have produced a marked increase in the share of the Southern and Insular regions in the outstanding total of such loans: 24·8 per cent at the end of 1962, while three years before the share was 20·4 per cent. During the same period the share of the North-western regions has been static (40·1 per cent), while those of the North-eastern and Central regions have decreased respectively from 20·9 and 18·6 to 18·2 and 16·9 per cent. ([2] pp. 387-8)

The influence of the credit-control authorities on investment has become somewhat more important through the regulation of the activities of industrial-credit institutions and their co-ordination with the security issues floated directly by companies. The directives to be followed have been more closely defined in geographical and sectorial terms, but within these directives the institutions remain free to conduct their credit business according to their own judgement. Geo-graphically speaking, the results would appear satisfactory.

. . . Credits to Southern industry expanded about twice as fast last year as in 1961. ([3] p. 110)

In 1963 loans to productive activities in Southern and Insular Italy also grew considerably. . . . Out of 623 milliard lire of new loans, 246, that is nearly 40 per cent (35 per cent in 1962), were allotted to the South, where the process of development is being stimulated in an increasing degree by the system of industrial credit and by the large institutions with a national field of action . . . the North-western and North-eastern regions have received new loans in amounts considerably lower than those of the year before . . . the intensity of the financial flows which have been directed towards the South through the industrial-credit system becomes evident. ([4] pp. 383-6)

In 1964 the activity of the industrial-credit institutions has been directed, more than in the two preceding years, to accelerating the process of industrialisation of the South; the large institutions with a national field of action have contributed more than in the past to this objective. . . . ([5] p. 325)

The three Southern institutions (Istituto per lo Sviluppo Economico dell'Italia Meridionale, Istituto Regionale per il Finanziamento alle Industrie in Sicilia and Credito Industriale Sardo), having increased their receipts from bond issues and having received, albeit in a smaller measure than in 1963, fresh government funds and loans from abroad, show an increase in the loans they granted that is larger than in 1963 in absolute value, but not in relative terms. None the less, their loans show a rate of growth (32·4 per cent in 1964 and 40·5 per cent in 1963) much higher than the average of the system. ([5] p. 329)

. . . Industrial-credit operations both increased and underwent some change in geographical distribution, in so far as the share of credits extended to industries within the regional competence of the Cassa per il Mezzogiorno rose from 48 per cent in 1963 to 61 per cent in 1964. ([5] p. 497)

Finally, the Italian Central Bank's Report for 1970, a year which was again marked by money and credit tightness, points out that the loans by the special credit institutions continued to rise considerably. The largest single share in the increase was accounted for by loans to the South, mainly to finance industrial investment.

While tax and fiscal measures would appear to be in principle more suitable instruments for a differentiated regional policy (in combination with administrative controls, they have been largely used by the United Kingdom for coping with its regional problems), Italy is a case in which territorial direction of credit has played a salient role. Government subsidies have also been dovetailed into the system of 'directed credit'. Although they have been an important factor in its working, differential availability *per se* should not be underrated.

The Federal Republic of Germany, where of course regional disparities represent much less of a problem, seems to have followed an approach similar to Italy's. There the Kredit-anstalt für Wiederaufbau has also been used, at least since the mid-1950s, as an instrument of regional policies. The Kredit-anstalt für Wiederaufbau has channelled considerable resources towards investment in areas where regional development schemes have been in operation. And it is interesting to note that the Kreditanstalt für Wiederaufbau has tried to manage its affairs in close harmony with the Bundesbank, its objective being to establish itself as the nation's 'second central bank'. W. Hankel has in fact suggested that a second central bank should be set up as a 'market solution' for the problems of long-term financing in Germany ([9] pp. 132ff.).

The directional manoeuvring of credit (*Kreditsteuerungs-funktion*, as it is called in Germany) is a device with which Continental Europe is perhaps best acquainted. It can be resorted to in order to implement a differentiated policy for the Community's low-activity regions, until the time when political unification permits resort to tax and fiscal instruments.

Credit can be directed to particular regions of a unified area by financing local firms and projects to be carried out in these regions, and it can also be linked to the finance of investments in housing and economic and social infrastructures being under-taken by local authorities. If operations are on a large enough scale, they will have a *conjunctural* impact and will thus lend themselves to use as an instrument for a differentiated policy of demand management. This means that dynamic firms happening to need an expansion of their productive capacity while investment activity is being discouraged by restrictive credit policies will have the option of getting the necessary finance by building new plant in the low-activity regions. Furthermore, if there are reasons to assume that the supply of credit for the current needs of industrial plants located in these regions will be shielded from the restrictions enforced periodically for fighting inflationary tensions generated by the high-activity regions, then this of itself might be an incentive for big and old-established companies to move some of their operations into the low-activity regions. Community credit-granting in those regions would not, therefore, have to be confined to medium and small firms, nor to 'lame ducks', large or small.

The tied loan and other technical devices would curb, not totally prevent, leakages. Such leakages as still took place would not be likely to jeopardise the effectiveness of restrictive policies in the high-activity regional group: at most, authorities would have to take into account their impact when deciding the degree of restrictiveness. After all, national money and credit markets have been fairly widely open for over a decade now; their interdependence is lop-sided because of the huge differences in size, and yet monetary authorities have managed, except during a few periods of unusual stress, to keep a degree of autonomy in their policies, even vis-à-vis the influence of conditions in the United States.

Finally, an autonomous policy of support of levels of production and employment would put an unbearable burden on interregional payments balance, if it were to be financed out of local resources. That would not be the case, however, if a large-scale credit institution were set up with funds contributed by all member countries and empowered to tap the Community's monetary and financial markets. The availability, through the intermediation of a European credit institution, of an external supply of funds would go a long way towards solving payments difficulties due to leakages filtering through a 'directed credit' system. And of course, the payments problem would be felt still less, once the status of that institution had so evolved as to allow its liabilities not to be 'withdrawn' in any conventional sense. In other words, they would remain outstanding in circulation in order to serve as money in the Community. At that stage it would no longer have to worry about its liquidity in the way an ordinary commercial or industrial-credit bank does.

Structure and Operations of a Multi-role European Bank

The institution envisaged here for making a start towards a differentiated demand-management policy for the low-activity regions would represent a departure from anything so far achieved or attempted in the European Community, both because of the size of the resources with which it would be endowed and the range of operations in which it would be allowed to engage.

The initial resources, in gold, would have to be of an order of magnitude comparable with the average amount of external liquidity reserves held by the major central banks in the Community. They would form the basis on which, by applying in a flexible fashion the fractional-reserve principle, a credit pyramid would gradually be created. The credit-granting activity would mainly take the form of loans which would be 'directed' in the sense outlined in the preceding section, and would be carried out with the help of branches – at least one would have to be set up in each of the regions belonging to the group – as well as through the network of branches of the national central banks. It is generally held that an *ad hoc* credit policy for the less favoured regions needs an element of subsidisation in order to work. This might be done in the case of the European credit institution by having the governments create for it an 'endowment fund' out of which subsidies on interest-rate account would be paid. But it will be seen from what follows that the envisaged credit institution may be able to raise funds on cheaper terms than the going market rates, and in turn channel them on preferential conditions towards the low-activity regions. Furthermore, it should be noted that the differentiated policy for these regions would hinge mainly on differential *availability* rather than on *cost* differential.

The new European credit institution would naturally have to operate in harmony with national central banks to fulfil its basic function of giving the extra stimulus needed to secure full

use of productive resources in the regions which would otherwise fail to do so. But it would not be subordinate to them and it
would have as a matter of principle full access to national money
and capital markets. Indeed, the objection so often raised in
different contexts, that the operations of an 'outsider' are bound
to upset monetary and financial markets, except as they may
have previously been agreed upon (i.e. authorised) by national
authorities, would be very hard to justify here. That objection
would make a mockery of the undertaking, envisaged in the
Werner Report, to maintain full and unhampered freedom of
money and capital flows within the Community. Honouring
that undertaking implies that individuals and business firms
would be allowed to make massive shifts of funds across national
frontiers within the Community, if they so desired, in response
to changes in the economic and political outlook of member
countries. In view of this, there would be little room for concern
that an accountable institution could cause disruption with its
day-to-day operations.

The new European credit institution would bring under the
same roof the operations of commercial and development banks,
as well as certain operations more typical of central banking. In
many ways it would resemble the 'universal' central banks
which developing countries all over the world have discovered
they need.

It would absorb the existing European Investment Bank, as
well as the proposed European Fund for Monetary Co-operation. If it should be decided to create, as a further tool for
enhancing integration in a general context of balanced growth
and stability, a 'Community fund for conjunctural stabilisation',
more or less along the lines of those existing in some countries,
the new European credit institution could be entrusted with its
management.

Among E.E.C. member countries, the Federal Republic of
Germany in June 1967 passed a 'law for promoting stability
and growth of the economy', by virtue of which the Federal
Government and those of the *Länder* may be called to constitute
'reserves for conjunctural equalisation' (*Konjunkturausgleichs-
rücklagen*), in the form of deposits with the Deutsche Bundesbank. These deposits can be withdrawn only after overheating
of the economy has disappeared.

The amounts paid into the conjunctural fund by member countries, on the basis of a formula which would take into account the degree of 'overheating' in their economies, the payments position of the central government and local authorities, and the current requirements of public-debt management, would be credited to them in a special interest-bearing account. Against these liabilities the account would show loans and investments in the regions where it was appropriate to stimulate economic activity.

For the purpose of this essay, I shall call the credit institution I am suggesting the 'Multi-role European Bank'.

The Multi-role European Bank would be entitled to accept deposits from Community, governmental and other public bodies, banks, industrial and commercial companies, and perhaps from individuals – provided each account and/or depositing and withdrawing operation did not go below a minimum amount, to be established and varied in accordance with the Bank's organisational development. The deposits might be expressed in units having their own parity directly linked to gold or to any other suitable non-currency yardstick. They would be transferred for settlement of debts among holders of such deposits, as well as of debts expressed in national currencies, on the basis of respective cross-rates. Banks would be authorised to use and deal in them. Companies, especially those with large export business, would be allowed to use them for paying salaries. Eventually they would generally be used alongside member countries' currencies and enter circulation in the form of notes: the M.E.B. would issue European I.O.U.s.

Indeed, this might be the sequence for the creation of a European currency unit (ECU). Its main strength would lie in the fact that the institution issuing it would have a functional role in the differentiated credit policy for the low-activity regions, the monetary functions emerging as an outgrowth of that role. Since new means of payments need creation of the demand to hold and use them, the M.E.B. would have the advantage of being able to put them into the payments circuit through its own lending operations to businesses. Furthermore, by extending rediscount and other credit facilities to regional banks, and to other banks in a form that would not jeopardise the fulfilment of its institutional role, it would encourage the banking systems to hold ECUs.

By circulating alongside the national currencies, a gradual process of acclimatisation would take place, during which markets in ECUs would be started, develop and settle down. The ECUs would not have the character of a monetary artefact, as would be the case if the creation of a European currency were to take place as a sort of one-act play, in which a new, ready-made, perfect monetary symbol was bestowed upon the Community to replace at one stroke the old-established national currencies.

As already implied, the ECUs would at some stage be declared legal tender; anyway, they would be backed by the initial gold subscriptions to the M.E.B.'s capital, as well as by the bank's access to national central-bank credit, which would have to be regulated as warranted by circumstances. Their direct link to gold would of course not imply a gold guarantee for holders; but the undertaking to maintain a given parity if the present fixed-exchange-rate system were to continue would very likely carry more weight than would be the case with the currency of any single member. If on the other hand external flexibility were chosen, the ECUs would crawl in a more predictable way, as they would be less liable to jerky variations than single national currencies, which these days have their parities threatened increasingly by the consequences of sudden outbursts of social unrest.

The European Currency Unit and National Currencies: the Management of a Dual Monetary System

The ECUs would therefore afford a diversification of the risk inherent in any one national currency, and ultimately this would in many cases minimise exchange risks. This *might* make them attractive to hold, in preference to members' currencies and to Euro-dollars. The 'pull' exerted on residents would be regulated by means of variable interest-rate differentials; but at the height of a fully-fledged social or political crisis in a member country, interest differentials would not be of much use. The occurrence of such emergencies has at times compelled countries to suspend exchange liberalisation, with noticeable damage to the credibility of integration as an irreversible process. The only alternative to suspension of freedom of payments might be afforded by recycling of funds. In this respect, the M.E.B. and its I.O.U.s might be of great help. Easy access to a Community-based, stable monetary asset would prevent, or at least reduce, an outflow of hot money outside the Community altogether; it would thereby facilitate recycling. The recycling of funds which flowed into the M.E.B. as a result of a 'flight' from a member currency would be easier also than in the case of a member country's central bank being the main recipient. For in a Community institution the crisis-stricken country would be represented and there would be less reason for excessive displays of national loyalty.

A number of alternative intervention techniques and procedures can be envisaged for managing the sort of dual monetary arrangement considered in this essay. It would appear, however, that the task of maintaining the parity of the European currency unit would have to be assigned to the M.E.B., while responsibility for the currencies of member countries would rest primarily with national monetary authorities. Starting from the present position, in which operations in support of exchange rates are conducted in U.S. dollars, central banks would gradually diversify interventions by adding Community currencies and ECUs. They would have to acquire a supply of one another's currencies, which would be done through setting up a network of swap agreements centralised in the M.E.B. They would also have to obtain an adequate supply of European currency units from the M.E.B. The gradual shift from the dollar to the members' currencies and ECUs as means of intervention would contribute to the assimilation of trade and payments between member countries to 'internal transactions'. Indeed, the fact that the E.E.C. has gone in several respects beyond the customs-union stage, while the ultimate media of settlement within it are dollars and (less and less) gold, means that parts of a semi-integrated area use a currency external to them to manage internal exchange rates, and settle balances not cleared by transfers of assets on private account. This arrangement, which may have been the only practicable one to date, has of course had a number of advantages; but it would become more and more an anomaly as the Community proceeded towards full economic union.

As the ECUs came into full use, the M.E.B. would continue to be responsible for the ECU–dollar rate, by intervening in accordance with current international arrangements. On the other hand, member countries would now fix the parities of their currencies in terms of ECUs and central banks would find it practical to conduct their interventions in ECUs, for maintaining rates in narrow bands or 100 per cent fixed.

Distribution of responsibility between the M.E.B. and national central banks could not ignore the facts that (a) the latter's gold and foreign-exchange reserves would be depleted by the amount each would have to contribute by way of subscription to the M.E.B.'s capital, and (b) the payments position of each member country would be affected by the M.E.B.'s operations. This means that the M.E.B. would have to make its resources available to support member currencies, in principle, it would try to improve the payments position of a country through its credit operations in the low-activity regions. Because the M.E.B. would not be primarily a reserve fund, it would help to prevent formation of deficits and thereby reduce the scope for official settlements.

In so far as this was not practicable, the M.E.B. in deciding the amount of balance-of-payments assistance would take into account, among other things, (a) the impact of its own operations in that country, (b) the Community's overall external payments position, and (c) the degree of restrictiveness that would appear appropriate for the policies pursued by the national monetary authorities concerned.

An overall Community deficit vis-à-vis third countries would of course be the algebraic sum of members' surpluses and deficits towards those countries, and would be met jointly by the M.E.B. and the national central banks. But once the stage was reached when the latter would intervene in support of national currencies using exclusively ECUs, their holdings of gold, foreign exchange and Special Drawing Rights would be centralised in the M.E.B. The settlement of balances vis-à-vis third countries would then become the responsibility of the M.E.B., which in parallel to that external function would organise and run a system of intra-Community clearing, possibly along the lines of that existing in the United States. The Inter-district Settlement Fund, formerly known as the Gold Settlement Fund, is the instrument through which the Federal Reserve System operates an efficient system of clearing payments between the twelve districts, each of which has a distinct regional orientation. Each day the district banks wire to the Fund's management the total of their claims against one another, arising for example from the sale in one district of goods produced in another, or from a shift of funds by a corporation to the district where the plants producing goods sold all over the United States are located, or from 'migration' of notes issued by a district bank and spent in other districts.[1] Clearing takes place through credit and debit entries on the books of the Interdistrict Settlement Fund, with which each Federal Reserve Bank has to maintain a certain amount of reserves in the form of gold certificates.

It seems safe to predict that, in a framework of the type sketched in this essay, policies relating to the Community's overall payments equilibrium would give rise to the most questions. By contrast, situations in which national monetary authorities would get too far out of line with one another will become less and less likely to arise. Because the M.E.B.'s main domestic task would be to take care of the problems of the low-activity regions, an important cause of gaps in member countries' inflation–unemployment trade-off patterns would subside. With the M.E.B. pursuing appropriate demand management in these regions, a central bank having to cope with overheating in the high-activity regions and showing a tendency to lose reserves would be expected to cut credit – or slow down its expansion. In general, central banks would now be expected to pay more regard to the principles of private banking. Their behaviour would have to draw gradually closer to that of commercial banks, which are not allowed by market reactions to create money in violation of the rules of the game.

To put it in another way: if countries can be satisfied as to the ability of a Community institution, such as the proposed

---

[1] Federal Reserve notes bear the name of the issuing bank in the seal which appears on the left-hand side of the front surface; in addition, a letter and a figure identify each of the twelve Federal Reserve Banks: the letter is printed in the centre of the bank seal and prefixes the serial number, the figure in each of the four corners.

M.E.B., to meet their growth problems, their behaviour can be expected to be consistent with the requirements of a multi-currency area based on a rigid exchange-rate system. This has been the general assumption so far in this essay. But parity changes of member countries' currencies in terms of each other (and of ECUs and third currencies) are not ruled out from the outset even in the Werner Report. The Report states in this regard:

> Progress in the convergence of economic and monetary policies should be such in the course of the second stage that the member States no longer have to resort on an autonomous basis to the instrument of parity adjustment. In any case, it will be necessary further to reinforce the consultation procedures laid down for the first stage. *Only at the moment of transition to the final stage will autonomous parity adjustments be totally excluded.* [The italics are mine.] [21]

The method and scope of parity changes in the E.E.C. will be discussed in the following and final section.

Partial Internal Flexibility of Exchange Rates in the Process of Integration

The many distinctive features of the European case recommend caution when drawing upon the experiences of other nations. And yet one can hardly ignore the fact that economic and monetary union was not free from tensions in the case of the United States, where for a number of reasons one would have expected adjustment and settlement mechanisms to be at work effectively and smoothly. The stream of bank failures and suspensions in the troubled years of 1891–7, which were regionally concentrated among national, state and private banks mainly in the West and the South, could be regarded as the outcome largely of imbalances which the built-in equilibrating mechanism could not rectify.

Again, the insistent demand in the last decade of the nineteenth century, by restive political organisations such as the American Populist Party, for free and unlimited coinage of silver was an attempt by silver-producing regions and by

agricultural regions in deficit vis-à-vis the Eastern regions to
improve their terms of trade within the Union and to regain a
degree of monetary independence. Still, it is worth recalling that
prior to the Civil War notes of different banks circulated at
premiums or discounts that varied according to whether they
happened to be nearer to, or further from, the issuing banks;
and that the economy coped with the phenomenon by employ-
ing 'bank-note detectors' to determine the value of such notes.
Finally, flexibility of internal rates was again experienced in the
United States in 1893 when currency and bank deposits were
for a period no longer interchangeable at a fixed rate. And this
was followed by no less interesting episodes in the first years of
this century,[1] until the assumption of growing monetary powers
by the United States Treasury and finally the creation, in 1913,
of the Federal Reserve System.

It is not surprising that the appeal of internal-rate flexibility
should keep lurking in so many minds when considering ways
and means of furthering the process of economic integration in
Europe.

It is felt that, as long as the integration process of both
official policies and market structures is only half accomplished,
too rigid a system of exchange rates would cause breakdowns
which, even if they were of a temporary nature, might do
permanent damage psychologically to that process. And if
exchange-rate changes are bound to be part of the adjustment
process anyway during the transitional period, it is argued that
moderate Community-supervised flexibility could be better
accommodated into the mechanism of integration than the
spasmodic parity changes that have recently taken place in the
E.E.C. Those who oppose regulated internal flexibility fear at
bottom that what is recommended as a temporary measure
might last for ever, that regulated flexibility might drift towards
widely floating rates, and that, as a result, the trend towards
growing intra-Community trade and payments might be
checked and even reversed.

The monetary arrangement outlined in this essay could

[1] During the panic of 1907, currency again went to a premium over
deposits as a result of restriction of payments on the part of banks anxious
to stop the drain on their reserves. For an account of these episodes,
see [8].

perhaps make it possible to adopt a compromise solution, in that internal flexibility would find only partial application. It would be left as an option open at any time to national monetary authorities; but disincentives would be built in against its abuse.

When considering internal flexibility of member countries' currencies, the hypothesis in which an irrevocably fixed-rate link would be provided to a partial extent by a common monetary medium circulating alongside them has never been made. But this is exactly the situation which would obtain once the ECUs came into their own. They would circumscribe the operational area in which flexible national currencies would continue to be used and where freedom of circulation, which at any rate should be viewed as a means to the end of achieving fast and balanced growth, might possibly be affected. They would do so because their use would quickly spread to sectors and categories of transactions where the need for a stable and widely based monetary standard is strongest.

The large industrial corporations and business firms, whose operations with companies in other member countries (and third countries) represent a large share of total turnover, would find a suitable monetary medium in the ECUs. They belong to sectors of the economy which are most exposed to competition from outside. They tend on the whole to move together as regards technological innovation, evolution of costs, and changes in prices and profitability, because the markets for their products and their inputs truly cut across national borders. They are most in need of a common monetary standard, and in fact they already use one to the extent that it is vital to them. Large companies manage their operations in national currencies – and in U.S. dollars. They therefore are already on a dual monetary standard. If in the meantime national currencies experience some degree of rate flexibility vis-à-vis the dollar, the change would simply be a switch from the dollar – or one of its market variants – to the European currency units. European companies would be using a monetary standard in whose management they – through the Community and their governments – would participate and whose reliability would in the end depend on their own performance.

Thus the impact of a national currency resorting to regulated flexibility would fall mainly on sectors and firms more closely geared to local economic conditions. These are less exposed to outside competition and are the ones where so often divergent trends arise, making the maintenance of a rigid monetary link in the long run very difficult, unless in the meantime full integration, with the accompanying high mobility of products and productive factors, has been achieved.

The option to choose flexibility would be open to governments, as well as to people and businesses. The latter would be in a position constantly to optimise the ratios in which holdings of (actually or potentially) crawling national currencies would be combined with holdings of ECUs, a stable asset easily accessible to them. This means that the kind of partial internal flexibility of exchange rates envisaged here would itself be governed by flexible criteria. In addition, the easy ECU option for the markets would build a powerful factor of discipline into the system. Governments could not overlook the fact that the use of a national currency, as against ECUs or other members' currencies, would tend also to increase or decrease depending on the performance of the currency itself as a stable standard. Because that performance might be the decisive differential in determining the fate of national currencies (and central-banking systems), it is likely that member countries would not abuse flexibility in a context in which the dual articulation of policies in the Community would in fact reduce the need for it. In addition, the increasing share of goods and services supplied by other member countries will make it difficult, as hinted earlier, not to take fully into account their price variations in national currencies when negotiating wage increases. 'Money illusion' is going to count even less than it now does. The wage link to a cost-of-living index, in which Community goods and services would weigh heavily, would on the one hand reduce the usefulness and attraction of exchange-rate depreciation, and on the other would tend to equalise rates of wage increases in member countries and thereby facilitate the task of sticking to a given rate.

For these (and other) reasons it is also unlikely that partial internal flexibility would constitute the centrepiece of the adjustment mechanism. But it would make an addition to the instruments for dealing with stubborn imbalances, such as

might persist for a time while discrepancies in national propensities to inflation have not narrowed and effective integration of markets has not been fully achieved. By official fiat one
can change overnight the ritualism of policy-making, but one
cannot do away with the constraints placed on policies by the
different ways in which the national economies themselves, with
their long-standing segmentation and deeply rooted differences
in habits and attitudes, would react to unified policies. Realism
requires that allowance be made for differential behaviour of
the economies by not excluding altogether available market
mechanisms. The integration process needs to be nursed by the
markets to a larger extent than is often allowed for; in fact, one
could envisage it as a succession of official measures and market
responses interacting. And this is the reason why integral
monetary unification in the sense of one country, one currency
only, does not lend itself easily to accommodation into a rigid
timetable. Yet, once under way, that process might quickly
gather momentum and meet the Community's internal and
external monetary aspirations sooner than one would now be
inclined to expect.

The design I have ventured in the preceding pages is only
sketched: many points still need to be hammered out. But the
main purpose of this essay is to start off exploration of the
possibilities for a novel approach. There seems to be too strong a
tendency to what basically amounts to transposing in a European key procedures, methods and institutions which have
successfully been resorted to in the post-war period on a world
scale. But to propose for Europe a miniature, albeit strengthened,
version of the solutions tried by general international co-
operation in the economic and monetary field will be of
diminishing avail as integration progresses. Truly to break
through the national diaphragms, new trails need to be blazed
and the prerequisite for that is, to paraphrase the nineteenth-
century nonconformist economist, a frame of mind which
does not allow opinions and experiences to crystallise into
dogmas.

REFERENCES

[1] BAFFI, P., 'Italian Considerations and Experiences', in *Fundamentale Fragen künftiger Währungspolitik*, Frankfurter Gespräch der List Gesellschaft (Basle: Kyklos-Verlag, 1965).

[2] BANCA D'ITALIA, *Assemblea Generale Ordinaria dei Partecipanti – Anno 1962* (Rome, 31 May 1963).

[3] BANCA D'ITALIA, *Abridged Version of the Report for the Year 1962* (Rome, 31 May 1963).

[4] BANCA D'ITALIA, *Assemblea Generale Ordinaria dei Partecipanti – Anno 1963* (Rome, 30 May 1964).

[5] BANCA D'ITALIA, *Assemblea Generale Ordinaria dei Partecipanti – Anno 1964* (Rome, 31 May 1965).

[6] BORTS, G. H., and STEIN, J. L., *Economic Growth in a Free Market* (New York and London: Columbia U.P., 1964).

[7] DEPARTMENT OF ECONOMIC AFFAIRS, *The Development Areas* (London: H.M.S.O., Apr 1967).

[8] FRIEDMAN, M., and SCHWARTZ, A. J., *A Monetary History of the United States* (Princeton U.P., for National Bureau of Economic Research, 1963).

[9] HANKEL, W., *Die zweite Kapitalverteilung* (Berlin: Knapp Verlag, 1961).

[10] HINES, A. G., 'The determinants of the Rate of Change of Money Wage Rates and the Effectiveness of Incomes Policy', in H. G. Johnson and A. R. Nobay (eds.), *The Current Inflation* (London: Macmillan, 1971).

[11] ISARD, W., 'The Value of the Regional Approach in Economic Analysis', in National Bureau of Economic Research, *Regional Income*, Studies in Income and Wealth, vol. XXI (Princeton U.P., 1954).

[12] KALDOR, N., 'The Price of Europe: 3, The Truth about the "Dynamic Effects" ', *New Statesman*, vol. LXXXI, 12 Mar 1971.

[13] KALDOR, N., 'Conflicts in National Economic Objectives', Presidential Address to Section F of the British Association at the Annual Meeting in Durham, Sept 1970, in *The Advancement of Science*, vol. XXVII, no. 133 (Mar 1971).

[14] MAJOR, L. R., and HAYS, S., assisted by CRUMBERGER, A., 'Another Look at the Common Market', *National Institute Economic Review*, no. 54 (Nov 1970).

[15] MINISTERO DEL BILANCIO E DELLA PROGRAMMAZIONE ECONOMICA, *Rapporto Preliminare al Programma Economico Nazionale, 1971–75* (Rome, Apr 1969).

[16] MYRDAL, G., *Economic Theory and Underdeveloped Regions* (London: Duckworth, 1957).

[17] 'NATIONAL PLAN, THE', Cmnd 2764 (London: H.M.S.O., Sep 1965).

[18] PARKIN, M., 'The Phillips Curve: A Historical Perspective, Lessons from Recent Empirical Studies and Alternative Policy Choices', in H. G. Johnson and A. R. Nobay (eds.), *The Current Inflation* (London: Macmillan, 1971).

[19] PHILLIPS, A. W., 'The Relation between Unemployment and the Rate of Change of Money Wage Rates in the United Kingdom, 1861–1957', *Economica*, vol. xxv (Nov. 1958).

[20] SVENNILSON, I., *Growth and Stagnation in the European Economy* (Geneva: United Nations Economic Commission for Europe, 1954).

[21] WERNER, P., *Report to the Council and Commission on the Realisation by Stages of Economic and Monetary Union in the Community* (Oct 1970).

2 The Theory of Optimum Currency Areas and European Monetary Unification

In a pioneering article published in 1961, Professor Mundell endeavoured to lay the foundations of a theory of optimum currency areas; a few important contributions have been made subsequently, notably by Professors McKinnon and Kenen. Mundell warned the reader not to regard the exercise as purely academic: 'Certain parts of the world are undergoing processes of economic integration and disintegration, new experiments are being made, and a conception of what constitutes an optimum currency area can clarify the meaning of these experiments' ([33] pp. 65-7). Now, about a decade later, it so happens that monetary unification has been pushed in the forefront of the process of economic (and political) reorganisation of Europe. And yet the promising start of the optimum currency area theory does not seem to be living up to expectations – so much so that already in 1968 Professor Ingram could comment:

I do not think the question of an optimum currency area is any longer a very interesting one . . . it seems to me that the

This is a revised version of a paper prepared for the meeting of the List Gesellschaft in Basle, 11-12 Feb 1972. Its theoretical parts have been published in the June 1972 issue of the *Bulletin de la Banque Nationale de Belgique* [28].

geographic extent of a currency area – including in that term
national currencies rigidly linked by fixed rates and full
convertibility – can be whatever we want it to be, large or
small, although I do agree that when the currency area
becomes very small we lose the advantages of the use of
money. . . . When we attempt to analyse payments-relation-
ships among advanced industrial countries which are connected through fixed exchange rates, but proceed by
assuming that no capital movements occur (or, indeed, that
capital does not even exist), that net investment is zero, that
we have one factor (labour) and one, or perhaps two, products, and that we can ignore the accumulation of wealth
and the forms in which it is held, I think we have little hope of
saying anything useful. Such analysis seems to leave little
room for money at all. It is virtually equivalent to barter,
with prices expressed in real terms of trade and full adjustment occurring on current account. The other functions of
money and most of the interesting issues seem to have been
excluded altogether. ([18] pp. 97-8)

And Ingram's scepticism is not an isolated voice.[1]

The concern with the waste of time and effort involved in the
pursuit of sterile theories is of course justified. One does not
have to search far afield for instances of discussions which
tended to be an intellectual game. But it would be ironical to
drop the optimum currency area theory now that the time may
have come for it to be put to perhaps the most important test:
Europe's monetary unification. What is needed is to make good
the inadequacies of the theoretical analysis, and to use a good
dose of imagination in devising the monetary arrangements,
which we need and which we can afford, in the age of advanced
computer technology, of instant communications and of
sophisticated economic and financial know-how.

International Trade Theory and the Theory of Optimum Currency Areas

In Mundell's formulation, everything hinges upon factor
mobility. In defining the optimum domain of a monetary union,

[1] M. De Cecco, among others, applies tools of the theory of second best to
prove the ambiguity of the optimum currency area theory ([4] pp. 94-108).

one should see whether there is full mobility of factors of production between the regions which it would comprise: inter-regional factor movements can substitute changes in regional exchange rates. If between A and B, assumed to be regions of the same monetary area, mobility is low, a shift of demand from the products of B to those of A will cause unemployment in B and inflation in A. Unemployment in B could be prevented by expanding money supply, but by the same token inflation would be fed in A. Conversely, inflation could be checked in A, at the expense of employment in B; or, finally, both A and B could contribute to the adjustment process, the former by allowing some inflation, the latter by tolerating some unemployment. But both inflation and unemployment could not be avoided.

The adoption of a flexible exchange rate for the currency common to A and B (or resort to external flexibility in the case of A and B each having its own currency, but being linked through a fixed rate of exchange), while it would work in favour of payments equilibrium with the rest of the world, would not help to correct the imbalance between A and B. Flexibility would be of no great avail for the purposes of domestic stabilisation policy. While, on this basis, the world is not an optimum currency area, if it could 'be divided into regions within each of which there is factor mobility and between which there is factor immobility, then each of these regions should have a separate currency which fluctuates relative to all other currencies' ([33] p. 663).

Thus what Mundell in fact does is to relax for monetary theory the assumption on which Ricardo built the theory of international trade as a body distinct from the general theory of exchange; namely, that productive factors are mobile internally but immobile internationally. Ricardo argued that 'the difference . . . between a single country and many is easily accounted for by considering the difficulty with which capital moves from one country to another, to seek a more profitable employment, and the activity with which it invariably passes from one province to another in the same country' ([40] p. 83).

The Ricardian assumption was exploded – as Mundell him-self points out – by international trade theorists, writing in the first decades of this century. Williams, among others, argued that:

the question whether we have, have ever had, or are ever likely to have the same mobility of factors between as within trading countries ceases to be *the* question on which the entire analysis must turn and takes its proper place as one, only, among a number . . . it is not Ricardo's *immobility* premise that stands most in need of defence, but rather his *mobility* premise, the assumed free movement of factors *within* countries. . . . For us, the theoretical question raised is as to the adequacy of a method of analysis which, taking a cross-section view in that moment of time, to fit those conditions so created, assumes as a first fact national entities, economically organised, internally mobile and coherent, and then attempts to study contacts between them on the assumption that international mobility of factors is so imperfect that for value purposes it may be ignored. ([45] pp. 197, 209)

The decisive step forward was taken when the emphasis was shifted from the law of comparative costs to the factor-proportion theory. The latter was formalised by Ohlin, who argued that a country's comparative advantage lies with those products which use more intensively the country's more abundant factor [37]. Building on the work of Heckscher and other economists, he pointed to the link between a country's foreign trade and its factor endowment – or economic structure – and surmised that even in the total absence of international movements of productive factors, factor prices would *tend* towards equalisation as a result of free international trade in goods.

There are two basic points in the new approach which are relevant to this paper's argument. The first is the relaxation of Ricardo's assumption about internal mobility and external immobility. 'Factors command varying prices in different parts of the same country, and these differences in local factor cost and supply affect the location of production and interregional trade within countries in the same way as international differences affect foreign trade' ([37] p. 159). The second point is that mobility was discarded as the cornerstone in the equilibrating process.

If internally, instead of the hypothesised one-market factor mobility, there are the immobilities of a multiple-market system, in which factors are confined to certain locations, and hence the latter are quasi-given, there may simply not be enough mobility altogether for it to play *the* dominant role. It is commodity trade which will compensate for the prevalent immobility of factors and *under certain conditions* equalise both commodity and factor prices.[1]

Now it seems to me that Mundell only goes as far as to extend to monetary theory the former of the two points just mentioned. He points out that the optimum currency area is not necessarily conterminous with national boundaries:

> The optimum currency area is the region. . . . If factor mobility is high internally and low internationally a system of flexible exchange rates based on national currencies might work effectively enough. But if regions cut across national boundaries or if countries are multiregional, then the argument for flexible exchange rates is only valid if currencies are reorganised on a regional basis. ([33] pp. 660-1)

But he does not seem to accept the implications for monetary theory of the second point. He keeps factor mobility in the key role; he defines the (regional) optimum currency area in terms

---

[1] Ohlin argued that free trade would not entirely equalise factor prices, as he considered it a partial substitute for factor movements. Samuelson [41, 42] instead proved that free trade would bring about full equalisation, under certain conditions. These have been so stated by Professor Haberler [19]:

'(1) Free competition in all markets; (2) absence of transportation costs, hence equality of all commodity prices as between different countries or regions; (3) all commodities continue to be produced in both countries after free trade has begun, in other words, that specialisation is incomplete; (4) the production functions in both countries are identical and homogeneous in the first degree, that is, a given uniform percentage change in the quantity of all inputs results in an equal percentage variation in the resulting output; (5) in addition, the production function must be such that one commodity is always labour-intensive and the other always capital-intensive whatever the relative supply of factors and the ratio of factor prices; (6) the factors of production are qualitatively the same in all countries, although they are available in different quantities; and (7) the number of factors is not greater than the number of commodities'. [11, p. 18]

These conditions are so restrictive that they have prompted the comment that they could be regarded as proving the opposite thesis.

C

of internal factor mobility and external factor immobility. Having upheld in the substance Ricardo's approach, he only differentiates his position by not regarding political frontiers as necessarily marking optimum currency domains.

Openness and Diversification as Conditions for Optimum Monetary Areas

The criteria for defining the optimum currency area, offered by McKinnon [27] and Kenen [23], refer on the other hand to elements of the economic structure. McKinnon classifies, for analytical purposes, the goods produced by a country into tradable and non-tradable. By tradable goods he means exportables (i.e. goods produced domestically, and exported) and importables (i.e. goods produced domestically, and imported). He argues that if the ratio of non-tradables to tradables is high, primary reliance on monetary–fiscal policy reducing domestic demand in order to maintain external balance will bring with it higher unemployment. 'The optimal currency arrangements may be to peg the domestic currency to the body of non-tradable goods . . . and change the domestic price of tradable goods by altering the exchange rate to improve the trade balance. . . . The desired effect of the relative price increase in the tradable goods is to stimulate the production of tradable compared to non-tradable goods and thus improve the trade balance' ([27] p. 720). If, on the other hand, the ratio of non-tradable to tradable goods is low, fixed exchange rates would be more appropriate:

. . . external exchange-rate fluctuations, responding to shifts in demand for imports or exports, are not compatible with internal price-level stability for a highly open economy. . . . In a highly open economy operating close to full employment, significant improvements in the trade balance will have to be accomplished via the reduction of domestic absorption, i.e. real expenditure. . . . In the extreme case where the economy is completely open, i.e. all goods produced and consumed are tradable with prices determined in the outside world, the only way the trade balance can be improved is by lowering domestic expenditures while maintaining output levels. Changes in the exchange rate will necessarily be completely offset by internal price-level repercussions with no improvement in the trade balance . . . if we move across the spectrum from closed to open economies, flexible exchange rates become both less effective as a control device for external balance and more damaging to internal price-level stability. ([27] p. 719)

In turn, domestic price instability would undermine the liquidity value of individual currencies; residents would tend to shift their financial assets to other currency areas, in order to stabilise their purchasing power; and the process of saving and capital accumulation would be hampered.

While McKinnon stresses the degree of economic openness, Kenen emphasises diversification:

In my view, diversity in a nation's product mix, the number of single-product regions contained in a single country, may be more relevant than labour mobility . . . a well-diversified national economy will not have to undergo changes in its terms of trade as often as a single-product national economy . . . when, in fact, it does confront a drop in the demand for its principal exports, unemployment will not rise as sharply as it would in a less diversified national economy . . . the links between external and domestic demand, especially the link between exports and investment, will be weaker in diversified national economies, so that variations in domestic employment 'imported' from abroad will not be greatly aggravated by corresponding variations in capital formation. ([23] p. 49)

Kenen himself qualifies his thesis in several important respects. He points out that production and export diversification cannot guarantee internal stability, even where external shocks tend to average out, unless there is sufficient occupational mobility to reabsorb labour and capital made idle by external disturbances. Again, he acknowledges that when changes in export demand arise from business-cycle swings, the whole range of exports will be hit, and therefore export diversification cannot be expected to protect in this case against imported instability. And he also grants the main counter-argument to his conclusion that the more diversified an economy, the more appropriate are fixed exchange rates: namely, that in a large, highly diversified economy, the use of monetary–fiscal policy, in spite of the smallness of the foreign trade sector in relation to total G.N.P., would imply greater internal instability (rather like the tail wagging the dog).

A feature of the optimum currency area theory, as developed so far, is that it has been largely developed in terms of demand; the criteria suggested for defining the optimum domain of a currency area are intended to secure an optimum condition under which monetary–fiscal policy is used for purposes of stabilisation against shifts in demand. Another feature is that those criteria fail to offer guidance as to the size, at the lower and upper limits, of an optimum currency area. Mundell's factor-mobility criterion would easily lead to the establishment of micro-currency areas, if not restrained in its application through some other criteria. Kenen's economic diversification comes short of indicating an upper limit to size: Mundell, for instance, has argued that it could be stretched to imply that the world is the optimum currency area ([34] p. 111).

Finally, the currency area is defined as one in which a single currency is in circulation. When a multiple-currency area is considered, it is assumed that currencies are linked on the basis of fixed exchange rates. This latter monetary arrangement is then regarded as a very close substitute, from an economic viewpoint, of the single-currency area. But the assimilation of the two definitions, which in abstract may be innocuous, can in fact be misleading; for when several currencies are in circulation, a 'credibility gap' may form as to the irrevocably fixed-rate link, and there is also the likelihood of all kinds of more or less thinly disguised controls and obstacles to the free flow of funds being resorted to, for supporting the exchange rate. Therefore, while the optimum currency area theory has so far revolved round the fixed or floating exchange-rate dilemma, there is now a need to pay more attention to the convertibility aspect, and to investigate possible forms of intermediate monetary arrangements, representing a sort of half-way house towards the establishment of a fully fledged monetary union, with one currency, one central banking system, one monetary policy.

An Unsuitable Criterion: Factor Mobility

The concept of factor mobility, while possessing great intellectual appeal, is elusive. International trade theorists had good reasons for discarding it as *the* condition for achieving factor-price equalisation, and developing a theory in which commodity trade reduces interregional discrepancies in factor prices, interregional factor movements are thereby made less compelling, and the movement of goods takes at least partially the place of factor movements. There are good reasons – it seems to me – which also apply against making it *the* criterion for the determination of optimum currency areas. As Williams questioned Ricardo's mobility premise – the assumed free movement of factors within countries – so can one do for Mundell's assumed intra-regional mobility, if one thinks of regions as consisting of a system of sub-regions, each of these comprising in turn a myriad of micro-districts. Only when these smaller components of a region have a similar distribution of natural resources, production factors and environmental facilities can the consideration of factors which determine the intra-regional location of industry, the intra-regional distribution of production and trade, be disregarded.

Whether it is justified or not to repeal the Ricardian assumption about internal mobility and external immobility in relations among countries, but then retain it for the definition of the region, it seems to me that elements in the very nature of factor mobility make it unsuitable as a basis for a durable arrangement – which of course a currency area has to be, lest it resemble an industrial or commercial conglomerate expanding or contracting, selling a business and buying another without any too great toil.

Mobility is a behavioural quality, the readiness to respond to stimuli imparted by market conditions, by the changing supply–demand relationships for production factors and commodities. Labour will move when an excess demand for it will tend to bring about a differential in remunerations high enough to overcome the attitudes which make for immobility. True, it may have an equilibrating effect in an area which has both high- and low-activity regions, and it tends to move in parallel to the cycle: mobility is as a rule higher during the upswing than in the downswing, when uncertainty arises as to the ease of finding employment. But it is during the cyclical troughs that the relationship to one another of even geographically contiguous labour markets turns out to be a remote one. In periods of less than full employment, workers feel the lack of security. The greater difficulty of finding a job in the high-activity regions, coming on top of the private opportunity costs usually associated with the transfer from one geographical area to another, reduces the ability of the market to allocate labour efficiently and distribute unemployment in an even fashion throughout the system.

Also, geographical mobility often implies occupational mobility, although the latter may reduce the need for the former. Occupational mobility confronts the worker with hardships of its own, which in some respects are even weightier than those associated with geographical change. In conditions of swift and huge shifts in demand, or when during recessions a few areas manage to expand into new fields of production thanks to a conversion effort, both geographical and occupational mobility would be required to prevent, or reduce, unemployment in some areas, inflation in others. But the combined hardships of the two heighten immobility.

The intensity of mobility fluctuates in the course of the cycle, as well as in response to changes in trends. When mobility remains high throughout, its direction will change. If the area as a whole happens to go through a prolonged period of slack in economic activity, then the migration of labour will be to outside areas, where economic activity may be booming: labour mobility will be low internally, very high externally. To draw upon Italy's experience, in the 1950s labour migrations from the South to foreign countries were by far more important than internal movements – a pattern which was reversed in the 1960s when the booming North proved to be a magnet for Southern unemployed and underemployed manpower. Should the domain of Italy's currency area have been changed before internal mobility emerged, only to be restored afterwards?

The same experience was made on a larger scale. While European countries were industrialising, migration within Europe itself never developed into a mass phenomenon comparable with migration overseas – with the large emigration waves of Italians, Scandinavians, Poles and other East Europeans which took place in the five decades prior to the First World War. This trend did not continue; some signs of its reversal appeared in the 1920s, when 2 million Europeans migrated into France; and intra-European migration came eventually to dominate the scene in the post-Second World War period. Finally, an interesting case is represented by the United States, which at present is the country with perhaps the highest internal mobility. They did not seem to possess this quality some decades ago, when the huge inflow of foreign labour met with very imperfect internal distribution, to such a point that some scholars spoke of external mobility producing internal immobility ([45] p. 201).

World-wide mobility is still more marked with other productive factors. In contrast with Ricardo, J. S. Mill emphasised the world vocation of capital:

> A tendency may, even now, be observed towards such a state of things: capital is becoming more and more cosmopolitan: there is so much greater similarity of manners and institutions than formerly, and so much less alienation of feeling, among the more civilised countries, that both population and capital now move from one of those countries to another on much less temptation than heretofore. ([32] p. 348)

It is not just financial capital which can move swiftly on a world-wide basis. With regard to enterprise capital, mercantile and industrial, Adam Smith, who shared with Ricardo a lack of enthusiasm for investment abroad, remarked that:

> The capital . . . that is acquired to any country by commerce and manufactures is all a very precarious and uncertain possession. . . . A merchant, it has been said very properly, is not necessarily the citizen of any particular country. It is, in great measure, indifferent to him from what place he carries on his trade, and a very trifling disgust will make him remove his capital, and together with it all the industry which it supports, from one country to another. ([43] p. 373)

If by definition mobility tends to stay unfettered, it cannot be assumed to remain constant as to intensity, breadth and direction; *ergo*, it cannot provide the criterion for defining a currency area, if this is meant to be a durable arrangement, or unless it comprises the whole world. Indeed, from this point of view one might argue that the world *is* the optimum currency area.

Assuming that controls were introduced along the perimeter of the area, to prevent capital from flowing to third countries, internal capital mobility would not *necessarily* contribute to achieving payments equilibrium and minimising both unemployment and inflation. In a recent analysis, Fleming has concluded as follows: 'Altogether it will be seen that mobility of capital among the members of the group is as likely to aggravate as to mitigate the losses and frictions that would otherwise result from the inability to adjust par values in the face of disequilibria arising among members of the area' ([8] p. 474).

Fleming's analysis applies to economies which are only semi-integrated, so that, as between them, cost-push factors are unequally strong, prices rise at different speeds, as a result also of policy choices made on the basis of a different trade-off between unemployment and inflation, and gaps in interest-rate levels may emerge, or widen. The analysis is relevant, however, since this is the scenario in which newly unified currency areas have probably to be managed for a number of years. It shows that, under such conditions, mobility of capital can be a hindrance at least as much as a help.[1]

Factor Mobility and Regional Development

To pursue somewhat further aspects relating to the working of mobility in the longer term, let us assume that between districts of a currency area there obtains a fairly constant pattern of factor mobility, in the sense of a one-way movement of labour and/or capital from one district or group of districts to another – a pattern which has in fact been observed in a few countries. The long-term implications of this, however, might well be unacceptable. Of course, industrial growth cannot be pursued in every district, however improbable a location. Development policies have to be geared to the needs of larger areas in order to have a meaningful choice between suitable and unsuitable industrial locations. But it would hardly be realistic to appraise the suitability of countries, with old cultural and industrial

---

[1] Onida, on the other hand, has argued that factor mobility offers neither a *necessary* nor a *sufficient* condition for the determination of a currency area ([38] p. 4).

national traditions, to form an economic and monetary union, on the basis of a criterion and a mechanism which, at the limit, might denude their whole territory, or very large regions, of people and capital, and push them back to the stage of declining subsistence economies.

The process can go that far, since differential rates of growth tend to be self-perpetuating. They may arise as a result of accidental changes; and, as Myrdal among others has argued, unless such changes are immediately cancelled out in the stream of events, a process of circular causation may be started, with capital leaving regions where it would be needed most ([35] p. 28). In Myrdal's theory of cumulative regional disequilibrium, the 'spread effects' of expansion emanating from the growth poles cannot be relied upon alone to neutralise the 'backwash effects', which tend to increase regional inequalities. 'By themselves, migration, capital movements and trade are rather the media through which the cumulative process evolves – upwards in the lucky regions and downwards in the unlucky ones' ([35] p. 27).

Moreover, the external economies which a central location affords, though real, seem to be overrated by entrepreneurs. This attitude, 'which is healthy for the consolidation of economic growth at its beginning but may represent irrational prejudice and clannishness at a later stage' ([16] p. 185), helps to explain why established industrial centres survive, and so continue to attract production factors, even when the causes that originally favoured them as industrial locations decline or subside. As Estall and Buchanan have pointed out:

Often the survival of an old-established industrial area rests on geographical inertia. This is a 'built-in' resistance to decline and it is sometimes extremely strong in preserving the location of industry. For various reasons – a raw-material supply, a power supply, a nodal location for existing transport services and so on – an area may have become an important centre of industrial production. The factors that initially caused industry to settle at this point may decline in their importance, or even disappear, but the industrial centre often remains. . . . There is therefore strong resistance to the abandonment of an established industrial area from all the vested interests concerned, including capital investments, jobs held, skills attained, social capital and all the impedimenta of industrial life and work.[1] ([7] p. 98)

If one considers allocative efficiency in a dynamic setting, in which the availability and quality of productive factors are no longer assumed to be given as in static analysis, but change over time as does the efficiency of production processes, the rise of internal and external economies is allowed for, and deviations of market prices of factors and products from their opportunity cost are taken into account, then conflicts between the indications of development policies and those of efficiency (which largely reflect conflicts between growth and trade theories) are less likely to arise. By the same token, the objections would apply that are made against measures such as the differential availability and cost of loan funds. These measures influence directly resource allocation as between the countries and regions of a unified area, tend to reduce the degree of specialisation within it, but mainly affect the *static* benefits to be derived from economic and monetary union.

Finally, those objections would appear still less justified if appraised within a theoretical framework integrating economic efficiency and distributional equity effects. Conventional economics has in the past understandably avoided involvement in equity issues and in the consideration of their effects, given the special difficulties of placing a value upon these effects that would make them commensurable with costs and benefits. But the attitude of regarding economics as an abstract, value-free science is losing ground, given the yearning for more realistic measures of welfare; the emphasis now being placed on the 'quality of life' is the most conspicuous illustration of the dissatisfaction with traditional criteria and instruments of measurement. Meade argued several years ago that we need a framework for appraising simultaneously the efficiency and equity aspects of economic changes ([31] p. 79). In other words, we need an integrated efficiency–equity social welfare function, in order more realistically to extend the notions of costs and

---

[1] A cause of geographical inertia is the higher cost of constructing a new plant on a new site. In the case of steel, the authors refer to estimates according to which a new plant on a new site costs about three times as much as adding the same capacity to an existing plant; the additional cost would be still greater for a new site in an entirely new location ([7] p. 98).

benefits to the total disadvantages and advantages of economic policies. We would then get a notion of 'grand efficiency', as a more appropriate yardstick for measuring the benefits of policies aiming at goals such as regionally balanced growth.[1]

If within countries a case can be made, also on economic grounds, in favour of regionally balanced growth, that case is stronger when different countries set about to merge their economies. All the more so since, while national economies are a mixture of geographically concentrated dynamic poles and of 'passive' locations dependent on the former for their growth, whole large countries tend in fact to behave as if each were one homogeneously favourable industrial location. This is a distortion, which – as Perroux has suggested – is largely due to the fact that every state tries to exploit for the exclusive or principal benefit of its nationals the poles on its territory, thereby causing waste and hindering growth ([39] pp. 307-20).

In an attempt to explain governments' protectionist attitudes, Johnson makes recourse to the ingenious device of hypothesising a 'preference for industrial production', instead of assuming that welfare depends on private consumption of goods and services, a standard assumption of international trade theory and welfare economics. But he also warns that the economist should not be prevented 'from asking whether industrial production yields the economic benefits believed to flow from it, from calculating the real product cost of protection and asking whether the benefits repay this cost' ([20] p. 282). Clearly, the answer would have to be different for the case of countries which in the process of forming an economic union tried to secure a 'fair share' of industrial production, and for the case in which large economic units (firms, industries, growth poles), whose economic influence does not coincide with political boundaries, continued to be used, in Perroux's words, as 'instruments of prosperity and *weapons for the power* of the national state' ([39] p. 319) (my italics).

[1] Of course, the mere existence of external effects, or externalities, in so far as it implies that in a pluralistic economic order profitability calculations do not allow for social costs and benefits, or rather for part of them, is a reason why competitive markets may fail to attain a Pareto optimum. However, as Buchanan and Stubblebine have shown, there is not a prima facie case for public intervention every time external effects are observed ([2] pp. 371-8).

Even if the tendency for the location of economic activity to polarise, which as we have just seen can be and is at times reinforced artificially, did not have adverse effects for the union as a whole, it would affect the interests of some member countries favourably, those of others unfavourably. Such re-distributional effects could hardly be neglected; indeed, in a multinational context the spatial aspects of the process of growth deserve in policy-making no less attention than the problems of the business cycle over time.[1]

Some of the economic gains which can be expected to accrue to the area as a whole as a result of regional policies leading to a definite location of any increase in demand for output and labour assume that mobility would not mop up unemployment altogether. This will be the case when production processes show widely differing labour intensities. Also, natural growth of population may more than offset the effects of emigration. One might perhaps argue that there is a relationship between the two, in the sense that net emigration may push under-utilisation of private and social capital, such as houses, schools, hospitals, to a point where, in the age of social security and welfare, it elicits a higher birth rate. This may help to explain why in certain areas high mobility and persistent unemployment co-exist. Furthermore, the size and speed of changes in demand, technology, industrial organisation and deployment may be such as to outweigh by far the working of the mobility mechanism. Referring to conditions in Great Britain during the inter-war period, Professor Cairncross has written:

. . . the new and growing industries, such as motor-car manufacturing, instead of expanding alongside the older and declining industries and absorbing unemployed workers in the vicinity of their homes, grew up in the very parts of the country where there was least unemployment, and created a major problem of labour transference from contracting to expanding areas. No group of workers suffered more from

[1] In what is now a long tradition, time is given special consideration. Marshall, although he dealt at some length with the (natural) causes of concentration of specialised industries in particular locations, wrote that time requires more careful attention, because its influence is more funda-mental than that of space ([30] bk. v, chaps. i and xv).

these changes than the coalminers. Employment fell from 1,212,000 in June 1923 to 638,000 in June 1932, and since mobility was low in comparison with other industries, and opportunities of alternative employment rare, a serious problem of long-term unemployment came into existence in the mining areas. . . . In pre-war Britain, the changed balance between export and home markets, between capital and consumption goods, and between north and south, put a heavy strain on the adaptability of industry. Structural unemployment, therefore, was unusually high. ([3] p. 419)

Mobility and Stabilisation Policies in a Currency Area

The foregoing analysis points to the conclusion that for policy purposes it is necessary to acknowledge, no matter how small the area considered, the existence of immobility as well as mobility. That the two concepts are not mutually exclusive is implied by the standard statement that mobility is not perfect. What should be pointed out, however, is that rather than making everything hinge upon mobility and then dismiss as an empirical question whether or not it passes the threshold, a more fruitful approach would be for stabilisation policies to take into account both factor movements and rigidities. If the rate of unemployment in the area as a whole is also a function of the locational pattern of the labour force, increases in demand which differentiate as to location would be required: factor immobilities themselves could be turned to advantage for the enactment of differentiated policies.[1]

The role of mobility has generally been examined in relation to shifts in demand, just as the theory of optimum currency

[1] To quote again from Cairncross:

'. . . The heaviest unemployment that Britain has suffered in the past half century has been concentrated in her export industries. Had those industries been diffused over different parts of the country and made use of a wide range of skill and technical experience, much of this unemployment might have been made to yield to a general increase in the level of demand accompanied by restrictions on imports. . . . In fact, however, the export industries were highly localised and highly specialised, and this reduced the effectiveness of a general increase in demand. To take the extreme case: it was of little help to unemployed shipbuilding workers in Glasgow, if people spent their extra earnings on beer, or, for that matter, on imported meat.' ([3] p. 643)

areas has mainly been developed in terms of the instruments best suited to adjust to fluctuations in demand. In Mundell's model, the disequilibrium emerging between East and West follows a shift of demand from eastern-produced cars to western lumber products. However, the disequilibrium will not develop if the increased demand for western products and the West's rising demand for labour are met by an inflow of workers from the East. Thus mobility will help to fight (demand-pull) inflation in the West and unemployment in the East. A flexible exchange rate between the eastern and western regions is not required for purposes of stabilisation policy; they comprise an optimum currency area.

Of course, even in the case of demand-pull inflation the adjustment may not be as simple as that, when *countries* happen to be parts or regions of a currency area. National authorities may still have sufficient power to aim at different employment and growth targets; prices may show a tendency to increase at different rates.

While experience has repeatedly shown how difficult it is to harmonise governmental policies as to the order of priorities, membership of the same currency area would tend to force alignment of priorities. In this respect the contention of the 'monetarists' that monetary unification would itself be a powerful instrument for bringing about overall consistency of national policies in other fields also, thus fostering the process of economic integration, contains a grain of truth. A stance in demand-management policy which happened to differ too much from that in most constituents of a currency area might not be sustainable for any length of time. Because leakages affecting the regional multiplier are as a rule larger than in a closed economy, the addition to employment and income which can be expected from differential local demand management would tend to have a high cost, in terms of the payments imbalance which would arise vis-à-vis the rest of the area. The case would be different if expansion could be fed with resources attracted by, or channelled into, a region from elsewhere in the area. This need not give rise to a payment and/or inflation problem. Thus for open regions it is reasonable to assume no specific 'warranted rate of growth'. The supply of savings, and of productive factors generally, which for closed economies represents the exogenous variable determining the equilibrium growth paths, as in the Harrod–Domar model of growth [12, 5], must be treated as an endogenous variable in the case of an economy becoming part of a larger area. And this could be the other side to the set of constraints which the harmonisation of priorities among the main objectives of economic policy would require member countries to accept.

The crucial dilemma for stabilisation policy within a monetary area arises when national authorities agree on the same employment and growth-rate targets, but costs and prices keep rising at different rates. Although there has been a tendency to assume, through unqualified application of the Phillips-curve analytical framework, that countries would have less inflation if only they were ready to accept higher unemployment, in fact lower unemployment/lower inflation, higher unemployment/ higher inflation are often to be found together. In Europe, some countries have had more success in attaining monetary stability and low unemployment, in the context of an expanding labour force; some others have had less success both in fighting inflation and in securing full employment. In terms of the Phillips curve this may be taken to mean that some countries have a more favourable inflation-unemployment trade-off than others.[1]

[1] In Phillipsian terms, Fleming writes:

'Where tendencies towards progressive relative disequilibrium existed within a unified exchange-rate area because some of the participating countries had more favourable unemployment/inflation relationships than others, the following situation would tend to emerge and persist. Much the same rate of price inflation would prevail over the area as a whole, a rate somewhat higher than that preferred by the surplus members. The deficit members would be able to keep their rates of inflation down to the common level only by tolerating indefinitely a level of unemployment higher than they would prefer if they were free to change their exchange rates and adopt their preferred positions on the unemployment/inflation curve.

'The argument in the foregoing paragraph assumes the existence in each country of an inverse long-term relationship (given the rate of productivity growth and the rate of change in terms of trade) between the rate of unemployment on the one hand and the rate of price inflation on the other. In the short run this relationship will be affected by such dynamic factors as past rates of change of prices and the rate of change of unemployment, but this does not preclude the existence of steady-state relationships linking levels of unemployment with the corresponding long-term equilibrium rates of price increase.' ([8] pp. 468-9)

While it is plausible, in the first instance, to apply to the price of labour the general principle that changes in the demand for a commodity or a service relative to supply will change its price, so that one might expect money-wage rates to increase when demand for labour increases, a deeper insight into the dynamics of inflationary processes shows that one cannot take the trade-off for granted. The inflation-unemployment trade-off implies that price stability and employment are two alternative policy goals, a theorem which I believe to be wrong *as a general proposition*. Under certain conditions it is possible to improve both stability and employment. Equally, and escalation of inflation may worsen (or leave unchanged) unemployment. It seems to me that for every economy there is a given degree of price stability (or instability) which is most conducive to employment and growth maximisation.

At any rate, inflation is not just the result of demand management, or rather mismanagement. Not only governmental stabilisation policies are involved in inflation; for the economies themselves may be said to possess a different ability to build up inflationary pressures and a different vulnerability to them.

The National Propensity to Inflation and its Determinants

In the previous essay I found it helpful to introduce the concept of *national propensity to inflation* (N.P.I.).

If countries showing the same rates of utilisation of productive factors systematically show different rates of cost and price increases, they can be said to possess a different N.P.I. The concept of N.P.I. is akin to that of cost-push, but differs from it in some important respects. In both concepts the functional relationship between the changes in aggregate demand relative to potential output and the rate of change of prices is looser.

The relationship of aggregate demand to potential output as measured by the level and rate of change of unemployment may be the same in countries belonging to a currency area; and yet cost and price trends may diverge as between such countries, owing to differentials in trade union militancy, and ability to bargain for money-wage rises, or to resist increases in the prices of wage-goods. Contrary to the view held by some that trade unions cannot affect wages independently of the state of demand, it has been found that changes in trade union 'pushfulness', measured by the rate of change of the labour force unionised (a measure not correlated with the demand for labour), can help to explain the total variation in wage rates. For the United Kingdom, Hines has found trade union pushfulness to be 'the most powerful of all the explanatory variables' since the end of the First World War ([15] p. 221).

Because it is true of most industrialised countries that unions can push up wage rates in a way which is, albeit to different degrees, independent of the state of the markets, money tends to accommodate itself to changes in wages, rather than the other way about. As Professor Hicks stressed some years ago, 'instead of actual wages having to adjust themselves to an equilibrium level, monetary policy adjusts the equilibrium level of money wages so as to make it conform to the actual level. It is hardly an exaggeration to say that instead of being on a Gold Standard we are on a Labour Standard' ([14] p. 88).

And while the gold standard was an international standard, so that 'there was some sense in saying that there was an "equilibrium wage", a wage that was in line with the monetary conditions that were laid down from outside' ([14] p. 88), the labour standard is, or at least tends to relapse into, a *national* standard. To build it firmly into a consistent standard for a currency area embracing several countries, intergovernmental harmonisation of demand management is not a sufficient condition, nor is factor mobility.

More generally, gaps in N.P.I.s are – to paraphrase Keynes when describing the subjective factors in the propensity to consume – also a matter of attitudes, of habits formed by education and convention, of social practices and institutions which, *though not unalterable, are unlikely to undergo a material change over a short period of time*. Prices are fixed and changed against given institutional and social backgrounds. To make these converge implies a sort of *'gesellschaftliche Integration'*, which is indeed one of the conditions often named for giving solid foundations to Europe's process of integration.[1]

Different attitudes are one of the factors responsible for the uneven pace of diffusion of technological progress even among

[1] See, for instance, Emminger ([6] p. 677).

modern industrial countries. They lead to the acceptance of innovations in some of them earlier than in others, and therefore to differences in the actual production functions. This in turn makes for different rates of productivity growth; where that rate is lower, the margin by which the growth of money incomes exceeds the increase in real terms of G.N.P. *tends* to be larger, and inflationary tensions *tend* to be stronger.

Furthermore, the inflationary bias affects the different national economies to different degrees, because the mixture of competition and monopoly differs from country to country. I have referred above to trade union militancy and their monopoly bargaining power as the factor which seems to exert the most powerful upward push on costs today. But to the divergences in N.P.I.s the organisation of markets for factors as well as goods contributes, according to the measure by which the competitive elements prevail on the monopolistic ones in each and all of those markets. In a wider sense this can be meant to include also the institutional and administrative restrictions which shelter certain groups or sectors from competition. To them accrues a surplus income, the 'institutional rent', which does not substantially differ from the surplus profits made under conditions of monopoly.

If there is a feeling that actual income shares are too much out of line with a 'fair pattern', this is likely to impart an inflationary bias. As Ackley has put it:

> the competition for incomes – the pressures for and against a redistribution – creates inflation, usually without any significant redistribution occurring. The important conclusion to be drawn is not that whatever income distribution exists is correct or cannot be changed, but rather that attempting to change income distribution through the process of pushing up prices or wages in the market is (*a*) likely to be ineffective, and (*b*) almost sure to be inflationary. Other means are available, and far more effective, should a society conclude that its income distribution needs to be changed. ([1] p. 36)

Again, the gaps between actual shares and the '*Vorstellungen*' of people as to what they should be may not differ from country to country, and yet the pressure on costs and prices may be more or less strong, depending on the instruments which are available to pursue the aim, and the ability of people to use them.

Expectations play an important role. Governments have for some decades now aimed at maintaining the full-employment level of monetary demand. But some have had more success than others in attaining internal and external equilibrium; some have paid more attention than others to changes in external competitiveness and payments balance. As a result, expectations of price stability or inflation have been embedded into the public psychology. The behaviour of people as producers and users of income, as organised workers and entrepreneurs, as savers and investors, is more inflationary in countries which have a record of persistently higher inflation. In this sense, anticipated inflation is a distributed lag function of past inflation, with expectations tending to be self-fulfilling. Expectations (which diverge consistently as to the degree of inflation) affect the working of stabilisation policies and extract from these differential results, even when the national authorities accept the same order of priorities, with the same degree of determination.

Finally, the existence of persistent regional growth differentials has in the case of certain countries limited policy choices in a quasi-automatic fashion, so that it would be proper to regard such situations rather as putting an *objective constraint* on governmental policies. In the context of European monetary unification, the problem arises from the fact that regional disparities have a different weight in the countries of the Community. And it is worth noting that this should start to find recognition also in a country such as the Federal Republic of Germany, which has no sizeable regional problem and a better record as far as growth with monetary stability is concerned.[1]

The causes of gaps in N.P.I.s are deep-rooted and widespread.

[1] Dr W. Hankel, a director in the Federal Ministry of Economics, responsible for monetary affairs, has recently stated:

'A cause of the different degrees of inflation or stability lies no doubt in the objective feature of structural diversities. In France, and also in Italy, the problem of the weak regions has much more weight than in Western Germany. It creates a difficult political situation internally, as concerns the implementation of a policy of stability. Such a policy meets with internal political difficulties of a quite different nature than in Western Germany, and even here the difficulties are quite great. This is what causes a different order of priorities.' ([11] p. 19)

These gaps cannot be closed except in the long run, through the relentless progress towards true integration and interpenetration of the national economic and social fabrics. What is needed to make cost and price trends converge in the E.E.C. as a whole is not just the harmonisation of governmental policies – which is in some respects the most that one can expect from the creation now of a rigid common monetary framework. Convergent changes in the pattern of behaviour of the masses, individuals and organised groups, are also needed, and these cannot be brought about by an adjustment at the margins. The margin is, of course, the cornerstone in any explanation of the working of markets, where demand is elastic, there is substitutability on the supply side, and prices are flexible both ways. It is at the margin that pressure builds up on exchange values and thence tends to affect those values throughout a whole class of goods and their substitutes. But in the light of the foregoing remarks, it hardly appears reasonable to assume that factor movements – the migration of some hundred thousand workers – can alone work changes in what is ultimately a basic behavioural pattern of the tens of millions. Adjustments through factor mobility will simply allow some extra room for manoeuvre in influencing the rates of price increases and growth, without significantly improving the inflation–unemployment trade-off. To this latter end, the N.P.I. needs to be lowered, through long and all-pervasive processes of adjustment in the fields mentioned above. And to make the slow movements in N.P.I.s converge towards a common pattern, the regions or countries of a monetary area need to be fully, not just semi-integrated as is the case in Europe today.

The National Propensity to Inflation as a Criterion for the Optimum Currency Area

The N.P.I. is the resultant of a number of factors, a few of which have been mentioned in the preceding section. It is a compound concept which is meant to do justice to the complexity of the inflationary phenomenon, and to the national connotations which even in this age of fairly open markets it has maintained. The need for such a concept is suggested by the dissatisfaction with monistic explanations of inflation which the demand-pull/cost-push dichotomy has not quite met.

Dissatisfied with the state of theory on inflation, Professor Machlup produced several years ago a remarkable piece of elucidatory analysis, in which he specifically defined (*a*) types of demand and cost-push inflation, which would occur also in a fully competitive market, and (*b*) types which presuppose monopolistic power [26]. The feeling of dissatisfaction is again expressed in a recent articulate analysis of the inflationary process, from which I quote the following:

> In an important sense, each inflation is a unique historical experience. How prices and incomes will behave responds to a wide variety of conditions and forces – economic, social and political – in the society. And each stage in such an inflationary episode depends not only on what happened in earlier stages of that episode, but also on what has happened during preceding inflationary episodes or what is happening in other countries. For example, the whole character of the inflationary process in an economy that has experienced a runaway inflation will be deeply influenced by that fact . . . simple monistic theories of the causation of inflations – that prescribe simple monistic policies for their control – are wrong or seriously incomplete. . . . [Inflation] will not go away by itself, and it cannot be cured simply by avoiding future 'mistakes' of economic policy. Given the understandable and desirable pressures for full employment in every country, given the increasing aspirations of every group for rising real income, given the tendency everywhere for the fulfilment of people's aspirations (in all areas of economic, political and social life) to be pressed ever more aggressively and insistently, given the inevitable frictions and immobilities that exist in every economy, no country can avoid inflation merely by avoiding 'mistakes'. ([1] pp. 56, 96)

The case for referring to N.P.I.s when deciding about the domain of a currency area is strengthened by the relevance of that concept to present-day conditions. Inflation is at the centre of the economic policy debate. In industrial countries it is generally felt that inflation is the most pressing problem, and that it could become disastrous, to the point where it would prevent the proper working of the market mechanism of allocation of resources, as well as jeopardise the social and political order based on freedom. On the other hand, it is argued that the failure to stop inflation, despite the high price which quite a few countries have had to pay lately in terms of resources made idle by restrictive policies, proves that it has become an endemic feature. Rather than wasting resources on the attempt to undo the inevitable, the task should be to learn to live with inflation, to 'institutionalise' it in the socio-economic structure in a way which will minimise its costs and be politically acceptable. Sometimes reference is made to certain (Latin American) countries which have experienced inflation over several decades, without it degenerating into the hyperinflation of the kind that raged in Germany, Austria and some Eastern European countries in the early 1920s. Professor Johnson, commenting upon the discussions at a conference recently held at the London School of Economics, writes:

> ... the inability of the 'big models' to deal more satisfactorily with wage, and therefore price, behaviour may be less a consequence of the inherent difficulties of the problem than of the probability that, for both government and private business, it is quantities of output rather than the money price tags put on them that it is really important to forecast. If so, the implication is that inflation is by no means as serious an economic problem (I do not say social problem) as the problem of unexpectedly slack demand and high unemployment. ([21] p. x)

Be that as it may, it is generally held that this issue might make or break the construction of a united Europe: the latter cannot afford to be either a community of inflation or one of monetary stability in productive stagnation. In assessing the problem, I think one cannot overlook the fact that, notwithstanding the advance made on the path of integration, fundamental economic processes such as growth and inflation have to date kept distinct national connotations. There are countries which succeed, without great tensions, in establishing and maintaining a rhythm of growth very close to the potential rate. Their N.P.I. is low; prices will not as a rule rise faster than 2–2·5 per cent per annum. They cannot be complacent about inflation, if through some external disturbance it threatened to break through that ceiling. A price rise above it not only would not be needed; it could also do damage since it would not be consistent with the low N.P.I.

On the other hand, there are countries where growth is accompanied by economic and social tensions expressing themselves in a higher N.P.I. Although inflation will not guarantee them growth (those tensions may exist, perhaps even more intensely, in the absence of growth), a relatively higher rate of price increases, from, say, 2·5 to 4 per cent, may be needed to realise their potential rate of growth – as long as the N.P.I. itself remains high.

Thus while it may be true, as it is sometimes argued, that inflation is largely irrelevant to growth, in the sense that satisfactory results have been achieved both by inflationary and non-inflationary countries, the foregoing suggests that the issue is far from irrelevant when considering specific cases. Indeed, one might speak for each country of a rate of price rises consistent with its N.P.I., so that material plus or minus deviations from this 'optimum' rate would hinder its process of growth.

That being so, one monetary policy for a multi-country area only makes sense if members' N.P.I.s have (roughly) equal values. Failing this, no pattern of unified stabilisation policies will be acceptable: in order to keep price increases within a common narrow range, countries with a low N.P.I. would have to accept what to them would be a sterile, possibly damaging, extra dose of inflation, and/or countries with a high N.P.I. would have to bring about more unemployment than would be needed, if they could allow prices to rise to the extent required by their N.P.I.

Thus the condition for countries to form an optimum currency area is that the N.P.I.s have the same value. Being a broadly based concept, a constant for purposes of short-term policy, but carrying essential stabilisation policy implications, the N.P.I. criterion is better suited to define the domain of optimum currency areas.

National, Regional and Industrial Propensities to Inflation

I have so far spoken of *national* propensities to inflation because the case I have in mind is of a group of European countries with a long past as separate political, social and economic entities, which are now striving to merge into an economic and monetary union of some kind. But the questions which the theory on optimum currency areas tries to answer are also relevant, of course, in the case of national states, whose different regions are not thoroughly integrated. In fully integrated economies the business cycle would show no appreciable discrepancy through space, and the ability of the different regions to utilise production factors would over the longer term be uniform. Yet there are countries which have long been unified politically but not integrated economically. In such cases one would evidently have to consider, and speak of, *regional* propensities.

Indeed, to speak of a regional propensity to inflation (R.P.I.) would be more appropriate also on conceptual grounds, since the N.P.I. is the average of a series whose items, in countries that are not well integrated, may have widely different values. On the other hand, the regions could be defined with reference to the determinants of the propensity to inflation; the values of the terms in the series would have to be within a narrow range, as the 'homogeneity' necessary to comprise a region would be established thereby. At any rate, the economic region – whether defined on the basis of its propensity to inflation, or of mobility, openness, or homogeneity of some kind – is the relevant concept for purposes of stabilisation policy; the political and geographical dimensions of that notion are incidental. As Kenen writes by way of interpretation ([23] p. 42) of Mundell's definition, the region which is relevant in this context is not to be found on an ordinary map, because it is a functional concept. If the economic region has a geographical dimension it is mainly because of the (varying) degree of localisation of industries: the extent to which certain industries are concentrated in particular regions gives these latter a structure different from that of the country as a whole. Were it not for this, it would clearly be more useful to speak of an industrial propensity to inflation (I.P.I.), even in an approach which is very much concerned with the spatial balance of integration. Especially if one can abstract from administrative, political and cultural factors, it is the industries, the economic sectors, which present the highest degree of homogeneity: the economic determinants of their propensity to inflation have values which lie within a narrow range internally, while they differ widely individually and in many cases also as a mean in inter-industry, inter-sector comparisons. Industrial specialisation by regions, however, makes the R.P.I. move tendentially towards coincidence with certain I.P.I.s.

That, of course, simplifies matters, for, as McKinnon points out, 'it may not be feasible to consider slicing the world into currency areas along industrial groupings rather than geographical groupings' ([27] p. 724). Undoubtedly, space is still the most straightforward dimension to use for operational purposes (if not for analysis); but contiguity may have to be sacrificed. The elements of a (regional) set, which may have the same propensity to inflation, need the same currency, form an optimum currency area, would not need to be in any sense geographically contiguous, as long as they were part of a larger system, itself comprising more than one optimum currency area.

This is the type of arrangement which would obtain as a result of creating and putting into circulation an (additional) European currency, in terms of which the existing national currencies would be allowed limited, Community-supervised flexibility of exchange rates. Furthermore, an arrangement in which the introduction of a European currency would not imply the adoption of *one* currency alone for the whole Community would also allow a choice consistent with the I.P.I.s. In a multi-currency area, sectors could gear themselves to the common European currency, or to (a group of) existing national currencies. 'Currency specialisation' by industrial sectors could after all prove feasible.

This possibility should be explored, since the integration of the national labour standards seems to proceed, at different speeds, by sectors. Attempts to develop a common European approach are being made by sector industrial unions: in the first place, by those which have to bargain with transnational companies.[1]

---

[1] On the initiative of the E.E.C. section of the International Metalworkers' Federation, several meetings have been held over the past few years between the Federation's affiliated trade unions and the management of the electrical and engineering industries giant, Philips. The discussions, consultative in nature, have concerned the company's E.E.C. plants and have covered *inter alia* production and welfare problems, manpower planning,

The attempts to 'Europeanise' collective bargaining along industrial lines, rather than globally between national labour confederations which as a rule are at one remove from live bargaining, are an auspicious development. Monetary union, and above all the introduction of a common monetary unit, are going in the first place to unleash new pressures towards pay parity in the Community. If the latter should be pursued through a global approach, with no or scant regard for differences in the efficiency of production processes, this would add to the pressures towards industry concentration in the regions with high capitalisation and high productivity (within unified countries, wage drift has mitigated the impact on weaker regions of wage-rate parity). But if in the context of European economic and monetary integration the levelling-out of wages is sought along industry and multinational company lines, then the process might contribute to regionally balanced growth. For it is reasonable to expect circulation of financial and technological resources, as between plants and firms located in different countries but belonging to the same group, to respond to the enforcement of pay parity by raising productivity where it has been lagging.

---

inter-company transfers of profits and profit-sharing. Similarly, the French, German, Italian and American affiliates of the International Chemical and General Workers' Federation have agreed to adopt a co-ordinated strategy in negotiations with Saint-Gobain, the large French-owned chemical and glassmaking multinational company. This includes among other things the setting up of a standing committee and the undertaking not to conclude national negotiations without its approval, as well as the granting of financial and other support to affiliates involved in industrial action. Again, the Transport and General Workers' Union of the United Kingdom announced in May 1971 its intention to ask union leaders of workers in the Belgian, Dutch, French, German as well as British plants of the Ford company to join together in discussing with the European management of the company issues such as production-line speeds, manning, working hours, etc. [10]. Moreover, in June 1971 the first large-scale 'Euro-strike', called by a joint steering committee of shop stewards from Pirelli–Dunlop, took place in protest against closures and redundancies [17]. Finally, an official United Kingdom document reports: '. . . groups of workers in close contact with their counterparts overseas, such as seamen and airline pilots, may increasingly seek pay in the light of an international standard' [35].

Path to the Formation of One Optimum Currency Area in the E.E.C.

When considering the formation of a monetary union in the E.E.C., however, member countries' N.P.I.s are the starting-point. A cursory reading of their record over the past twenty years or so seems to me to point to different N.P.I.s. The gaps which would appear to exist in European N.P.I.s, although not large, do *not* make of the E.E.C. countries (before and after enlargement) an optimum currency area yet.

Their record lends itself to interesting considerations for the operational relevance of the N.P.I. criterion. During the post-war period they have all maintained a historically high rate of growth. But since the general parity realignment of 1949 the currencies of West Germany and the Netherlands have experienced only revaluations. Italy and Belgium–Luxembourg have stayed put up to December 1971. France, which went through a series of devaluations during the 1950s, but subsequently has experienced a long period of payments strength (except for the scare caused by the May 1968 events), might be regarded as a case in which the N.P.I. has changed appreciably within one generation. But then the shift from a high to a low N.P.I. coincided with the transition from the Fourth to the Fifth Republic. Finally, the United Kingdom has had a consistently weak payments position; its growth performance has also been unsatisfactory in comparison to that of most industrial countries in the post-war years.

It is also noteworthy that, as in 1969 the rate of inflation accelerated generally, countries which in the past had shown a low N.P.I. remained on the low side, while those with a high N.P.I. stayed that way. The gap between the two sides remained appreciably stable.

Of course, this does not imply that one should at worst let the European economies drift further and further apart; at best, that the conditions for them to form an optimum currency area would eventually be met in the absence of determinate action on the part of the Community and of national governments. What it means is that if, because of gaps in N.P.I.s, E.E.C. countries would not constitute an optimum currency area, then the *instant formation* of a monetary union, in the sense usually envisaged of an area having one currency (or local currencies linked through irrevocably fixed rates), a common central banking system, and a unified pattern of monetary policy and regulations, is definitely not desirable, and hardly feasible.

If, however, there is the political will to unite, the question arises of how those countries could be made to meet the requirements of an optimum currency area. In my analytical framework, the compact answer would be that European countries would have to close the gaps in their N.P.I.s. This means that the process of effective integration of member countries needs to be pursued much further than is the case today. To second that process, a much wider and deeper opening of national markets is needed; also a series of convergent steps must be taken through the whole range of industrial relations, market monopoly and social exclusionist practices, education and social security, taxation, and general economic and monetary policies.

As far as these latter are concerned, I have put forward proposals with whose implementation a start could be made in the near future. The operations of a Multi-role European Bank could help to relieve an important cause of gaps in member countries' N.P.I.s. The creation of an additional European currency would represent a big step forward towards monetary unification, but in a way that would not do violence to the fact that N.P.I.s differ, that member countries do not yet comprise an optimum currency area. It would make possible a gradual approach to integration, which would start now and be accomplished over a number of years (a quarter of a century?), thus bridging the gap, which is also psychological, between those who would like to see an instant monetary union and those who would prefer as remote a date as possible for departing from the traditional forms of national monetary power.

With the gradual introduction of the new European currency, a common monetary link would be provided for the sectors whose integration was far enough advanced not to make nonsense of one currency. In this new arrangement, the present monetary order based mainly on national currency domains would be reshuffled. Within the Community as a whole a few currency areas would emerge, consisting each of a group of regions/sectors geared respectively to the European currency, to the national currencies which were appreciating, and to those which might have to depreciate. In this set-up, uniformity of rates of appreciation (depreciation) should not be difficult to attain, and might in fact obtain quasi-automatically, given the small annual percentage by which currencies which chose to glide would be allowed, and would need, to do so.

This would also afford the possibility of dealing in a satisfactory way with the problem of size. It seems to me that the solution of this problem is not made any easier by assuming that, as the size of the currency area decreases, the number of areas would have to increase, as would the number of 'independent' currencies. This is the assumption apparently made by Mundell:

If, then, the goals of internal stability are to be rigidly pursued, it follows that the greater is the number of separate currency areas in the world, the more successfully will these goals be attained (assuming, as always, that the basic argument for flexible exchange rates *per se* is valid). But this seems to imply that regions ought to be defined so narrowly as to count every minor pocket of unemployment arising from labour immobility as a separate region, each of which should apparently have a separate currency! Such an arrangement hardly appeals to common sense. ([33] p. 662)

He was considering a world context; the assumption, however, would be misleading in the case of the E.E.C. Here differences in N.P.I.s, while deep-rooted, are not unmanageably large. It is likely that, on the average for a number of years, gaps in N.P.I.s would not imply cost–price discrepancies of more than 2–2·5 per cent per annum compound. Any discrepancies in excess of that would perhaps have to be considered as the result of sheer mismanagement; they could hardly be tolerated for any length of time without causing damage to the economies producing them.

Those discrepancies would possibly be larger as between regions, but again not so large as to prevent their accommodation within a context offering in theory a three-pronged choice. But even if, in actual fact, the choice was limited to two, the national currency and the European currency, it might still help regions or districts, no matter how small, in their process of adjustment. There would not necessarily be geographical contiguity between the various elements of the currency areas; but an undue multiplication of areas and of currencies would be avoided, and so would the problem of illiquidity of currencies, usually associated with the operation of small currency areas.[1] In an arrangement of this type, the usefulness of money as a measure and store value, and as a medium of exchange, would not be impaired.

As to the costs arising from the fact that more than one currency would be in circulation, this would not appear to be a disproportionate price to pay for a mechanism needed to cope with the *dynamic disequilibrium*[2] which different N.P.I.s are apt to generate – a disequilibrium which by its very nature requires a form of gradual, continuous adjustment, rather than a spasmodic one. Professor Sohmen has offered some interesting considerations on the question of 'operating costs' in a multi-currency area [44]. At any rate, these costs would not be eliminated in a multi-currency system which attempted, however, to ossify intra-group exchange rates. Such a system will in addition suffer from the distortions and disturbances – not just in the field of capital movements – caused by the 'credibility gap' which is bound to form if a mechanism is lacking for taking care of the sequence of disequilibrating impulses emanating from different N.P.I.s. Eventually, the undertaking to maintain unimpaired convertibility will come under fire, and in the end may have to be dispensed with. In that case a quintessential ingredient of monetary union will be missed, with effects which usually largely exceed those measured statistically.

I submit that in the initial and intermediate stages of formation of a monetary union less weight than hitherto should be given to fixity of exchange rates and more to the convertibility aspect, as well as to the formation of an *acceptable and regular* pattern of intra-union capital flows. Both these latter objectives should be pursued for the contribution they are likely to make to the achievement of the ultimate objective of economic union: balanced growth.

Absolutely unimpaired convertibility belongs to the essence of monetary union, because exchange controls provoke distortions typical of fragmented markets, imply normally an element of discrimination, and lead to multiple currency practices and to

---

[1] On this point see, for instance, McKinnon ([27] p. 721).

[2] For the notion of dynamic disequilibrium, see Harrod [13].

disorderly cross rates. Since exchange controls and flexible rates represent policy alternatives over a wide range of conditions in which merging economies may find themselves, we have the instrument to avoid backsliding into controls and, indeed, achieve the full convertibility which monetary union pre-supposes. Flexible exchange rates should thus be regarded as a means of maintaining and fulfilling convertibility, rather than as an infringement of it.

It is worth noting in this respect that, although the Bretton Woods system has pivoted on fixed par values, the obligations for members of the International Monetary Fund are stated under Article IV, Section 4, of the Fund's statute, to be in principle the promotion of exchange stability, the maintenance of orderly exchange arrangements with other members, and the avoidance of competitive exchange alterations.

Despite the specific limitations which were laid by the Articles of Agreement on parity changes, the underlying philosophy emphasises *stability* as distinct from *rigidity*. This distinction used to be stressed in the early I.M.F. reports, from which it appears that what the Fund was really concerned for was the avoidance of competitive depreciations: the par-value system was regarded as the best means to that end.[1]

It is worth recalling too that what made the European currencies also formally convertible in December 1958 was the amalgamation of the market for U.S. and Canadian dollars with the market in which eleven European currencies were traded against one another and which through administrative

---

[1] In the Annual Report for 1948, one reads:

'The Fund Agreement makes it clear that the provisions for the regulation of exchange rates are not intended to impose upon the Fund the duty of perpetuating in the name of stability exchange rates which have lost touch with economic realities.

'Stability and rigidity are different concepts. The Fund has never insisted on the maintenance of an exchange rate which was not suited to a country's economy. On the contrary it has always recognised that an adjustment of exchange rates may be an essential element in the measures necessary to enable a country to pay for the goods and services it needs from abroad without undue pressure upon its international reserves. Stability implies that when exchange-rate adjustments are necessary they should be made in an orderly manner and that competitive exchange depreciation should be avoided.' ([19] p. 21)

78 EUROPEAN MONETARY UNIFICATION

controls had been kept separate from the former. Finally, it may be noted in passing that, in view of the restoration of convertibility, discussions were held in the O.E.E.C. to consider the simultaneous introduction of floating exchange rates.

Convertibility does not necessarily imply that currencies are exchanged at a fixed rate. What it implies is the freedom of any holder to exchange them at will and on demand into any other currency (or into gold), no restriction being put on the disposal of the foreign exchange proceeds[1]. If that freedom can be achieved and maintained only with gently moving currency prices, then flexible exchange rates are more likely to bring about the benefits that are commonly associated with rates which, supposedly, are permanently fixed.

Moreover, the rate flexibility which is postulated by existing gaps in N.P.I.s would be kept within very narrow limits – and, as will be indicated in the following essay, would be made to shrink over a period of time, gradually paving the way for the ultimate replacement of the national currencies by a European money. In the meantime we would get as close as logically possible to monetary and economic union by achieving full freedom of circulation; harmonising policies up to the point where discrepancies in cost and price trends would be cut down to the extent implied by the economies' different propensities to inflation; putting into circulation a new currency alongside the

---

[1] Among others, Lieftinck appears to give in a recent article a similar interpretation of convertibility. He does not list fixed rates among the criteria by which convertibility can be said to exist, nor flexible rates as a limitation of convertibility. He concludes:

'If internal or external developments, after convertibility has been established, show that reasonable balance of payments equilibrium cannot be maintained at the existing exchange rate, the rate should be courageously adjusted, and the sooner the better. . . . *Such smaller and more frequent exchange-rate* adjustments are certainly preferable to renewed reliance on trade and payments restrictions, which reduce the degree of currency convertibility and freedom of international trade that has been achieved and should be promoted further. This does not mean preaching laxity in the defence of carefully chosen exchange rates. Stable exchange rates are a precious asset of the international monetary system and most useful for domestic financial discipline. But they should be adjustable and be adjusted in an orderly manner if and when there is sufficient justification.' ([25] p. 7; my italics)

existing ones; and fostering integration and orientating it towards balanced growth through space.

The process of adjustment, however, would not hinge exclusively, or mainly, on regulated internal exchange-rate flexibility. In order that adjustment may take place without hindering growth in some member countries or regions thereof, I have argued that it would be wrong to base policies on Community-wide aggregates, just as it would not be consistent with the aim of realising the economic and monetary union to go on thinking and acting largely in terms of national aggregates. *Community* and member governments' policies should be tailored to the needs of the economic regions. In this respect, it is appropriate to ask whether the Community itself is equipped to pursue, with the national governments, policies suitable to the different needs of different regional groupings: whether in a progressively integrating Community there would be room for policies aimed at preventing regions from falling behind – and some of them, further behind.

The assumption by the Community of direct, albeit partial, responsibilities in this field could be accomplished by wielding the instruments of tax and budgetary policies, which are prominent in the regional policies of many countries and notably the United Kingdom. Professor Kaldor has recently pointed to the regional employment premium, introduced some years ago in favour of the low growth regions of the United Kingdom, as a better substitute for devaluation. Like devaluation it has the effect of counteracting adverse trends in 'efficiency wages' (index of money wages divided by index of productivity); but unlike devaluation it does not bring forth a deterioration in the terms of trade for the beneficiary regions, since the cost is borne by the national taxpayers' community ([22] pp. 346-7). Some of the instruments already available to the Community tend to have a 'favourable' regional impact. And it would appear that the scope for such measures could be expanded somewhat even in the absence of further steps towards strengthening the Community's political institutions; considerably more, if that strengthening did take place ([29] p. 18).

Because economic and monetary union, while benefiting the area as a whole, would distribute benefits and costs unequally as between member countries and regions within them, some of

D

which might be in danger of being left with a net balance of costs, it is quite reasonable to advocate some form of fiscal compensation for them. But, could one also justify large transfer payments in favour of industrial, high-income regions, which happened to be doing less than well, as a result of the constraint to adjust to a rhythm of price increases lower than that postulated, over the medium/long term, by their propensity to inflation? In such cases a combination of regulated flexibility and differentiated demand management would be more appropriate.

I have proposed the creation of a credit institution of the 'universal' type, the Multi-role European Bank, since there seems to me to be room for Community regional policies also in the field of money and credit. The M.E.B. would be an instrument for implementing differential investment policies and demand management.

Increases in demand would be made bearing in mind that the regional distribution of their effects, in markets which will remain for some time only semi-integrated, would depend to a considerable extent on the location at which the injections of demand were made. To implement this policy, the Multi-role European Bank would avail itself of the *immobilities* which exist among member countries, as well as within each of them. Also, in the banking systems which operate on a national rather than a regional basis, there are discontinuities tending to reduce the leakages that might percolate through a procedure of locally tied credits. These imperfections represent a drawback for the smooth working of the mechanism of interregional settlements; but to ignore them, or play down their importance, does not help. While progress on the way to integration works towards the gradual and partial removal of immobilities, the task should in the meantime be to harness them for the need of a differentiated policy, just as mobility is relied upon for the process of adjustment and the mechanism of settlements.

The arrangement sketched here is, of course, meant to apply during the *intermediate* stage of European monetary unification. Steering successfully through that stage is likely to tax most the ingenuity and imagination of those who will be entrusted with the task of merging into *one* optimum currency area a Community which meanwhile would at best comprise three such areas, with the components of each of them not being necessarily contiguous. The measures adopted so far, by differentiating E.E.C. countries from third countries and thus outlining the so-called monetary personality of the Community, have mainly tended towards building the common framework. What is needed now is to concentrate on the internal effects of monetary integration; to introduce with a common European currency the limited amount of internal flexibility and to implement the Community differential policies which will allow a rational set-up for the intermediate period. Within that set-up it will be easier to pursue in the industrial, commercial, banking, labour and social fields the integration of the economies, which will at least roughly equalise the national and regional propensities to inflation, and thus fulfil the requisite for the final transition to a full monetary union, which will also be one optimum currency area.

REFERENCES

[1] ACKLEY, G., *Stemming World Inflation*, Atlantic Papers, no. 2 (Paris: Atlantic Institute, 1971).

[2] BUCHANAN, J. M., and STUBBLEBINE, W. C., 'Externality', *Economica* (Nov 1972).

[3] CAIRNCROSS, A., *Introduction to Economics*, 3rd ed. (London: Butterworths, 1960).

[4] DE CECCO, M., 'La Teoria delle Aree Monetarie Ottime e l'Unificazione Monetaria Europea', *Note Economiche, Monte dei Paschi di Siena* (July–Aug 1971).

[5] DOMAR, E. D., *Essays in the Theory of Economic Growth* (Fair Lawn, N.J.: Oxford U.P., 1957).

[6] EMMINGER, O., 'Die Rolle der Währungspolitik in der europäischen Integration', in H. Giersch (ed.), *Integration durch Währungsunion?* (Tübingen: Institut für Weltwirtschaft an der Universität Kiel, 1971).

[7] ESTALL, R. C., and BUCHANAN, R. O., *Industrial Activity and Economic Growth* (London: Hutchinson University Library, 1970).

[8] FLEMING, J. M., 'On Exchange Rate Unification', *Economic Journal* (Sep 1971).

[9] HABERLER, G., *A Survey of International Trade Theory*, Special Papers in International Economics no. 1 (Princeton University, Princeton, rev. ed. July 1961).

[10] HAND, M., 'International Car Labour Pacts', *Financial Times*, 25 May 1972.

[11] HANKEL, W., comment made in a panel discussion, in H. Giersch (ed.), *Integration durch Währungsunion?* (Tübingen: Institut für Weltwirtschaft an der Universität Kiel, 1971).

[12] HARROD, R. F., *Towards a Dynamic Economics* (London: Macmillan, 1948).

[13] HARROD, R. F., *Money* (London: Macmillan, 1969).

[14] HICKS, J. R., *Essays in World Economics* (Oxford U.P., 1959).

[15] HINES, A. G., 'Trade Unions and Wage Inflation in the United Kingdom, 1893–1961', *Review of Economic Studies* (1964).

[16] HIRSCHMAN, A. O., *The Strategy of Economic Development* (New Haven: Yale, 1959).

[17] HOWELL, NOEL, 'Dunlop–Pirelli Euro-strike Has Mixed Response', *Financial Times*, 10 June 1972.

[18] INGRAM, J. C., 'Comment: The Currency Area Problem', in R. A. Mundell and A. K. Swoboda (eds.), *Monetary Problems of the International Economy* (Chicago U.P., 1969).

[19] INTERNATIONAL MONETARY FUND, *Annual Report of the Executive Directors for the Fiscal Year ended April 30, 1948* (Washington).

[20] JOHNSON, H. G., 'An Economic Theory of Protectionism, Tariff Bargaining and the Formation of Customs Unions', *Journal of Political Economy*, vol. 73 (June 1965).

[21] JOHNSON, H. G., and NOBAY, A. R. (eds.), *The Current Inflation* (London: Macmillan, 1971).

[22] KALDOR, N., 'The Case for Regional Policies', *Scottish Journal of Political Economy*, vol. XVII, no. 3 (Nov 1970).

[23] KENEN, P. B., 'The Theory of Optimum Currency Areas: An Eclectic View', in R. A. Mundell and A. K. Swoboda (eds.), *Monetary Problems of the International Economy* (Chicago U.P., 1969).

[24] KEYNES, J. M., *The General Theory of Employment, Interest and Money* (London: Macmillan, 1936).

[25] LIEFTINCK, P., 'Currency, Convertibility and the Exchange Rate System', *Finance and Development*, vol. VIII, no. 3 (Sep 1971).

[26] MACHLUP, F., 'Another View of Cost-push and Demand-pull Inflation', *Review of Economics and Statistics*, vol. XLII (1960).

[27] MCKINNON, R. I., 'Optimum Currency Areas', *American Economic Review* (Sep 1963).

[28] MAGNIFICO, G., 'À propos de la théorie de la zone monétaire optimale', *Bulletin de la Banque Nationale de Belgique* (June 1972).

[29] MAGNIFICO, G., and WILLIAMSON, J., *European Monetary Integration*, Report of the Federal Trust Study Group (London, 15 Feb 1972).

[30] MARSHALL, A., *Principles of Economics*, 8th ed. (London: Macmillan, 1962).

[31] MEADE, J. E., *The Theory of International Economic Policy*, vol. II: *Trade and Welfare* (Oxford U.P., 1955).

[32] MILL, J. S., *Principles of Political Economy* (London: Longmans, Green, 1904).

[33] MUNDELL, R. A., 'A Theory of Optimum Currency Areas', *American Economic Review* (Sep 1961).

[34] MUNDELL, R. A., and SWOBODA, A. K. (eds.), *Monetary Problems of the International Economy* (Chicago U.P., 1969).

[35] MYRDAL, G., *Economic Theory and Underdeveloped Regions* (London: Duckworth, 1957).

[36] NATIONAL BOARD FOR PRICES AND INCOMES, *Second General Report, July 1966 to August 1967*, Cmnd 3394 (London: H.M.S.O., 1967).

[37] OHLIN, B., *Interregional and International Trade*, rev. ed. (Cambridge, Mass.: Harvard U.P., 1967).

[38] ONIDA, F., *The Theory and Policy of Optimum Currency Areas and Their Implications for the European Monetary Union* (Société Universitaire Européenne de Recherches Finan-ciéres, Tilburg, 1972).

[39] PERROUX, F., 'Note sur la notion de "pôle de croissance" ', *Économie Appliquée*, nos. 1-2 (1955).

[40] RICARDO, D., *The Principles of Political Economy and Taxation*, Everyman ed. (London: Dent, 1964).

[41] SAMUELSON, P., 'International Trade and the Equalisation of Factor Prices', *Economic Journal* (June 1948).

[42] SAMUELSON, P., 'International Factor-Price Equalisation Once Again', *Economic Journal* (June 1949).

[43] SMITH, A., *The Wealth of Nations*, vol. I, Everyman ed. (London: Dent, 1965).

[44] SOHMEN, E., 'Remarks on the Project of a European Monetary Union', in H. Giersch (ed.), *Integration durch Währungsunion?* (Tübingen: Institut für Weltwirtschaft an der Universität Kiel, 1971).

[45] WILLIAMS, J., 'The Theory of International Trade Reconsidered', *Economic Journal* (June 1929).

3 Further Considerations on the New Approach to European Monetary Unification

REGIONAL problems have dominated Europe's development. History, culture, geography, scientific advance and technological change, which have been and are the sources of Europe's material and non-material riches, have also contrived to create regional differences. These persist even today, when unprecedented high levels of income, the relative decline of transport costs, the weakening of locational preferences consequent upon technical progress in the field of energy as elsewhere, the multiplication of links and contacts infinitely varied in their forms, all make for an increase in the 'footlessness' of people, capital and enterprise. In fact, these differences may grow under the impact of increased mobility, and be aggravated if the institutional framework and the policies, in whose context mobility operates, are not adapted to the needs of balanced growth in the wider European area.

Notwithstanding the great progress made in the post-war period on the path to economic integration, the ability fully to realise the growth potential differs considerably and the trade

This is an expanded and revised version of the address I delivered to the Committee on Economic Affairs and Development of the Consultative Assembly of the Council of Europe, Paris, 16 Mar 1972. The address has been published, in its original draft, in the Jan–Apr 1972 issue of *Economic Notes: Economic Review of the Monte dei Paschi di Siena*, vol. i, no. i, pp. 92-110, under the title 'The New Approach to Monetary Unification in Europe'.

cycle continues to show important discrepancies. These phenomena are manifest not only *between* Europe's nation-states, but
also *within* countries, suggesting that the E.E.C. comprises a
system of regions rather than one market. The manifold determinants of regional differences, and the great number of com-
binations to which those determinants give rise, explain why
the nature of regional problems differs. For purposes of stabilisation and development policies it is convenient to distinguish:

(a) regions which manage to show high rates of growth but
in the process meet with considerable difficulties, often
of a non-economic nature, which are reflected in above-
average tensions of costs and prices;

(b) regions which succeed in establishing and maintaining a
high rate of growth, and in doing so give rise to below-
average tensions in the general level of costs and prices;
and

(c) regions which systematically fail to utilise in full one or
more factors of production, and as a rule show an above-
average discrepancy between actual and potential rates of
growth.

I shall consider the problems of each of the three regional
groups in the reverse order of their listing.[1]

The Plight of the Low-Activity Regions

Under (c) are meant regions which are commonly described
as 'backward'. They have been left behind either because they
failed to industrialise (as in the case of most parts of southern
Italy), or because, having originally been in the forefront of the
Industrial Revolution, subsequently they did not partake in the
second wave of industrialisation and were left with a larger
share of declining industries (as in the case of some regions of

[1] It hardly needs to be pointed out that classifications are rarely satisfactory, either on conceptual grounds or because of the violence they do to
reality. In the case of regional problems, the distinction between advanced
and backward regions overlooks the existence of the so-called 'grey areas'.
On the other hand, classifications can only be appraised in view of the
argument for which they are to be used. Ultimately what matters, as
Campolongo points out [4], is the study of the essential features of the
development problems of each region.

the United Kingdom). Despite this and other diversities, the point common to them is a failure over a period of decades to adjust to demand shifts, to technological innovations, to cultural and social changes, in competition with the regions which happen to be more dynamic by their own deed and/or because favoured by design or accident.

Admittedly, changes in the structures are needed in order that these regions may overcome their condition of economic backwardness. To foster such changes, countries have created and use a vast armoury of instruments. The instruments of regional development policies range from incentives which influence the locational preferences of private businesses to the creation and operation of industrial plants by government-owned or controlled enterprises; from the building of industrial, commercial and social infrastructures to the sponsoring of programmes for general education, as well as professional training and re-training. Incentives take the form of subsidies for fixed costs: capital grants, interest-rate rebates and differential availability of long-term loans, accelerated depreciation on more favourable terms than applied nationally, leasing of industrial estates at low or nominal rates. In some cases they include subsidies of operating costs; these apply to new plants during the first few years of operation, when the productivity of a new labour force is, as a rule, lower.[1]

In some countries, regional policies also avail themselves of disincentives on the building of plants in congested areas. The

---

[1] In Britain, however, the regional employment premium, which was introduced in 1967 and is to be phased out completely by 1974, was originally intended to be a *permanent* subsidy of labour costs.

In the countries which have had recourse to labour subsidies, objections have been raised to the effect that such subsidies, unlike aids to fixed costs, represent a commitment to (perpetually) financing inefficiency. However, labour-cost subsidies can be regarded as a contribution towards the training of manpower, in regions where its employability has deteriorated owing to a history of high unemployment, or where agriculture is still predominant. How difficult a task it is to form an industrial labour force is described by Gerschenkron as follows: 'But the overriding fact to consider is that industrial labour, in the sense of a stable, reliable, and disciplined group that has cut the umbilical cord connecting it with the land and has become suitable for utilisation in factories, is not abundant but extremely scarce in a backward country. Creation of an industrial labour force that really deserves its name is a most difficult and protracted process.' ([11] p. 9)

desirability of offsetting the tendency of entrepreneurs to over-rate the external economies afforded by a central location and to underrate the social (and private) costs arising from excessive agglomeration might justify the introduction of a 'tax on congestion'. But disincentives have so far taken the form mainly of administrative controls; they have been accompanied by the shortcomings usually associated with such controls. Thus, when authorisation has not been granted for building new factories in the areas of high agglomeration, companies have at times installed new efficient equipment in old and inefficient buildings.

In addition to manpower and industrial policies, energy supply and transport policies are integral parts of the strategy of economic development. They are all long-term policies for gradually strengthening the industrial and general productive structures of the low-activity regions. However, the fact that in such regions unemployment is on average higher is due also to a greater cyclical sensitivity. Of course, this in turn is correlated to the industrial structure. Per capita output and earnings variations differ more systematically between industries than, within the same industry, between regions; but then, industrial specialisation by the regions means that some regions have more than their proportionate share of declining industries, others of dynamic ones. Thus structural differences make for a different cyclical performance.[1]

In view of this, national tax and budgetary systems nowadays allow for income transfers, and net injections of public funds at differential rates, that are meant to act as built-in stabilisers of levels of demand and employment in the weaker regions. We have within national states differential demand management, which is implemented mainly by wielding fiscal instruments; in some countries differentiated credit policies also play an important role. Since the Community will not for some time be in a position to make transfers on an adequate scale, it is often concluded that it cannot be expected to make an important contribution to regional problems. This sceptical view is reinforced

---

[1] Regional indices with cyclical sensitivity have been built for Italy by Tagliacarne [33], who has also attempted a synthesis of the same. They appear to show that in the 1971 recession the North was harder hit than the South.

by the observation of the results obtained by national policies of regional development, and of the difficulties which even bodies endowed with full fiscal sovereignty meet in making large scale transfers of public funds.

The fact that regional problems, which are often the result of the failure over many decades or centuries to find solutions for them, have not been satisfactorily tackled since regional policies first started to be thought of in an organic way in the inter-war period, points if anything to the need for reinforcing such policies. That need, it seems to me, is greatest in respect of stabilisation policies. This is so because regional problems have traditionally been regarded as falling in the realm of structural policies. The interaction between the structural and cyclical aspects having often been overlooked, the view has gained ground that stabilisation policies have little to contribute. Yet what is the rationale for pursuing the same demand policy for the low- and for the high-activity regions? Why should restrictive policies for fighting 'overheating' in the high-activity regions also hit regions which by definition are unable to generate or sustain demand-pull inflation? Why should the low-activity regions not be shielded from stop–go measures? As it is, the disinflationary impact of restrictive measures tends to concentrate in those regions where unemployment is already high: most casualties of a credit squeeze are usually to be found among the small firms, which in the weaker regions account for a higher share of the total.

What I am arguing for here, and throughout these essays, should not be construed as meaning that *the* solution for consolidated regional problems lies in the field of stabilisation policies. The point I am trying to make is that stabilisation policies which are appropriate for high-activity regions are not likely to suit the needs of the low-activity ones. While these latter will be further weakened by wrong stabilisation policies, appropriate policies can make a positive contribution, in parallel with structural policies. Hence the need for differentiated stabilisation policies.

In the attempt to upgrade the cyclical measures in favour of the low-activity regions to the level of a coherent policy, standing on an equal footing with 'general' stabilisation policies, it would be difficult to dispense with monetary and credit instruments. Contrary to the general expectation, during the post-war period the brunt of keeping their economies on an even keel has been borne in most countries principally by those instruments, and less by fiscal policies. It is hard to see this being reversed within the framework of a Community whose power to levy taxes will be very limited, so long as effective control by a truly representative European Parliament is lacking.

Yet the need for the Community to share economic responsibility for the regions with national governments is posited by the mechanics of the process of monetary and economic integration. As member countries' economies become more and more open regions of the Community, autonomous expansionary policies which the weaker regions in some countries may need will bring about a larger deterioration in the payments position vis-à-vis the rest of the area, if *financed locally*. Without injections of external funds, such policies would become almost impracticable.

Furthermore, monetary unification is bound to strengthen the tendency towards equalisation of money-wage rates, and to do so at a pace which might, on balance, be faster than that of the rapprochement of levels of productivity. The low-activity regions will be more vulnerable to cost-push inflation caused by demand-pull in high-activity regions. Other things being equal, their competitiveness will suffer.

Of course, other things will *not* be equal. The depressed peripheral regions of member countries, countries which themselves happen to be in a peripheral position within the larger Community area, will see the stimuli emanating from the national growth poles grow weaker, while finding themselves farther removed from over-expanding European centres.[1]

The notion of 'economic distance' is at the centre of the theory of industrial agglomeration, which was pioneered by

[1] It may seem surprising that in the age of multi-modal transport systems, distance or proximity, and changes in them, should bear significantly on the pattern of growth. But transportation, as with the production of all other goods and services, requires an input of factors, i.e. is an element of production cost. Once the analysis of transfer costs, which include costs assembling, insurance, interest on capital cost of goods transported, clerical costs, etc., is integrated with the analysis of weight- and bulk-to-value ratios, we get an indicator of production-cost differential arising from a peripheral location.

Weber [36] and Lösch [23]. Subsequently, regional economists have evolved such analytically and operationally useful concepts as the nodal regions, gravity models, and so on. Richardson has succinctly, but lucidly, outlined some of the tenets of that theory:

> Acceptance of the lack of uniformity in the space economy and recognition that it may have economic significance lead us to the concept of nodal, or polarised regions. Nodal regions are composed of heterogeneous units (e.g. the distribution of human population leads to cities, towns, villages and sparsely inhabited rural areas – in other words a hierarchy of settlements) but these are closely interrelated with each other functionally. As suggested above, these functional interconnexions are revealed in flow phenomena. These flows do not occur at even rates over space. The heaviest flows tend to polarise towards and from the dominant node (or nodes), usually large cities. Around each node there will be a zone of influence or spatial field in which interaction of many kinds takes place. However, *as the force of distance exerts itself the flow densities decline as we move away from the control centre.* Eventually, at a certain radius they will fall below a critical level and this sets the outer limits of the spatial field. *That these flows vary directly with the size (or attraction) of the node and inversely with distance from it forms the basis of gravity models,* the most operational technique for polarisation analysis. ([32] pp. 67-8; my italics)

These and other changes, which will affect both market conditions and policy choices as member countries become regions of the Community, would aggravate the difficulties of the low-activity regions, unless offset by purposeful Community policies of balanced growth. Economic development theorists make this point generally by stating that the polarisation, or 'backwash', effects are much weaker between nations than between regions.[1]

High-Activity Regions with Low Inflation Propensity

These regions can be said to possess a 'gift for growth'. If the problems of spactial balance did not receive the attention they

---

[1] See, for instance, Hirschman [17], esp. pp. 187-201.

deserve, they would act as an irresistible magnet on resources throughout the unified area.

In a context of unbreakable 100 per cent fixity of exchange rates, they would develop a competitive edge vis-à-vis the products of the regions with a high propensity to inflation. They would be at the centre of a process of growth led by exports, with positive feedback to perpetuate it. In an 'export-propelled' growth model, such as Beckerman applied some years ago to explain the patterns of growth in Western Europe ([3] pp. 912-925), a high rate of increase of exports generates productivity gains, lower costs and increasing returns to scale; it then elicits a higher rate of savings and investment, which in turn brings forth a higher rate of growth, higher productivity, a decline in costs and prices relative to those in competing countries or regions, higher exports, and so on in a circle.[1]

Mobility of productive factors helps to maintain this *differential growth spiral*. In addition to the capital resources becoming available through higher savings formation locally, these regions tend to attract outside capital, being able to offer a higher return out of the higher product they can extract from the capital they use. Free circulation of manpower also removes the obstacle which the process would otherwise meet as it hit against the full-employment ceiling. This has led to suggestions that a policy for manpower movements within the Community, and from outside, might be necessary in order to curb agglomeration in a more effective way than appreciation of diseconomies of congestion and, in general, of the net effect of externalities is likely to do in a system of decentralised decisions about location and profitability.

The tendency to economic concentration would be strengthened by an arrangement in which exchange rates were to be permanently frozen, ahead of the rapprochement of the propensities to inflation. To freeze exchange rates, while the ratio between price levels in different regions and countries cannot

---

[1] As in the present set-up national boundaries do not coincide with the homogeneous economic regions, but do define monetary areas, it is difficult to develop the argument solely by making reference to regions, without thereby overlooking an important aspect of reality. This is why I am using both terms throughout, sometimes together, though this may generate an impression of (unavoidable) ambiguity.

be kept constant, since with different inflation propensities prices will move at persistently different speeds, leads to increasingly undervalued and overvalued currencies.

Currency undervaluation amounts in fact to export subsidisation: from the conversion of each unit of foreign currencies, a higher amount in domestic currency accrues to exporters than it would if the rate was not undervalued. They are therefore able to undercut prices of goods made by foreign producers; to the extent that they do not cut prices, they benefit from higher profit rates on exports than on home sales, and so have an incentive to raise the fraction of output exported. Thus the first link in the chain of reactions, which leads to territorial over-concentration of resources and of the growth process, is due to the cumulative distortions in exchange rates arising from conditions of dynamic disequilibrium. If, while the causes of the latter are being gradually removed, a mechanism of exchange-rate adjustment could prevent currency undervaluations (and overvaluations), countries with a low inflation propensity would be able to curb the tendency for net exports of goods and services to, and imports of productive factors from, countries with a high inflation propensity and low-activity regions. They would find it more profitable to export capital and know-how in the process of shifting production to these areas, which would otherwise continue to be markets for their exports.

Exchange-rate adjustments would also help to curb the importation of inflation from countries with a high N.P.I. It is true that, against the pressure on resources caused by large and persistent trade surpluses, there would be the relief afforded by the inflow of capital and labour attracted from the rest of the Community. But as the experience of countries which have undergone fast growth concentrated in a few regions shows, the inflow of resources from outside is not a complete offset. In particular, immigration cuts both ways: it adds to the supply of labour but also to demand for overhead investment, housing, social and other services. Taking into account that even if the additional demand for labour can be met, the supply position will take time to adjust, it becomes a case of thin balance whether the inflow of productive factors will mitigate or aggravate inflationary pressures.

It is not difficult to understand why regions and countries in this group cannot be complacent with inflation, and the risk of forming a community of inflation. Lower inflation rates give them a competitive advantage which acts as a propellent of growth; indeed, the low propensity to inflation belongs to the properties which make their high and steady rate of growth self-warranting. But they cannot be content with relative monetary stability when elsewhere rates of inflation are as high as they have recently been in quite a number of countries.

Countries with a low N.P.I. aim at absolute monetary stability, which is a condition for their economic efficiency and social peace. They are in some important instances market-orientated economies, more responsive to the indications of the price mechanism. And sound money is needed to keep that mechanism working in its role as resource allocator. Their market orientation is to be found also in the field of industrial relations and wage bargaining. It is not surprising that they should value it so much and safeguard monetary stability, given the lasting difficulties which the search for an incomes policy in European countries with a higher inflation propensity is meeting. The attempt to secure cost and price stability through incomes policy, without resorting to outright governmental fixing of wages and prices, and throttling the forces of competition and economic change has not yet succeeded.

High-Activity Regions with High Propensity to Inflation

The regional grouping under (*a*) above comprises countries and regions, most of them industrialised, which are particularly vulnerable to inflationary processes. The fact that they have a high inflation propensity, as a property of the economies themselves, implies that a stabilisation policy aimed at cutting down the rate of price increases to that appropriate for low-inflation-propensity regions would be very costly in terms of output forgone. While in the latter regions the rate of inflation which will maximise economic growth may be nil, in the former this optimum rate is likely to have a high positive value, which can only be changed over the medium to long term.

Clearly, however, the inflationary pressures witnessed especially in some countries of the enlarged Community go far beyond what can be attributed to the economies' inflationary propensity. The sharp acceleration of price increases since 1969, which marked the second inflationary outburst in post-war years[1] following a prolonged period of creeping inflation, could hardly be explained without positing mismanagement of demand. The tendency for policies to err on the side of excess demand is, in a subtle sense, itself the consequence of the high propensity to inflation. All the same, it pertains to *policies*, not to the behaviour of the national universe of firms, institutions and people, and as such is already amendable to harmonisation in the short term.

Correction of demand policies which overshoot the mark, even after allowance is made for the economy's propensity to inflation, would not represent a 'sacrifice' of national or regional interests to the cause of European monetary unification. Correction in this case would be required in the interest of the economies inflating, or over-inflating; for there can be hardly any doubt as to the damage which can be wrought by the high rates of inflation experienced in the last few years.

It is also clear that the ability of some countries to make proper and effective use of the traditional instruments of stabilisation policy has very much deteriorated. This, coupled with the failure to date to find in incomes policy an acceptable new instrument, is putting those countries in a position rather similar to that of many developing countries. The latter, not having yet been able to evolve a diversified set of policy instruments, have a preponderant recourse to the foreign-exchange system.[2] So they use exchange controls, multiple exchange rates, outright devaluations, as means to achieve objectives such as the redistribution of income between broad classes, or between factors of production, after the changes arbitrarily brought about by inflations they are unable to master.

On the other hand, it cannot be assumed that European countries would adjust to high rates of inflation as they did with creeping inflation for nearly two decades, or as some South American countries, which have finally settled down to chronically high rates of money depreciation. The experience in Europe suggests rather that persistently high price rises would degenerate into the kind of hyper-inflation which in the early

---

[1] The first was started by the outbreak of the Korean war.
[2] Cooper has drawn attention to this point ([6] pp. 10-11).

1920s wrought havoc in several Central and Eastern European countries. At the end of the Second World War some European countries found themselves in a predicament which nearly inflicted upon them a repeat performance of the 1920s. But they were able to turn the tide in favour of stability by implementing with sufficient determination outright monetary reforms, or measures of stabilisation which had an equivalent end effect. It cannot be altogether ruled out that, in the absence of the obligations arising from E.E.C. membership, at a time when the Community is seeking from its members a stronger monetary cohesion, some countries would not succeed in stopping the money landslide: in a few cases, drastic action may be needed to secure the minimum-grade performance compatible with economic and monetary unification.

As currencies get irrevocably linked together and total freedom of circulation of productive factors and goods is attained, an inflationary excess by one government would risk spreading all round and starting a scramble for resources. This would eventually destroy the Community's overall internal and external equilibrium. Even before that stage was reached, excessive monetary expansion by some member countries would jeopardise allocative efficiency. It would also run counter to the principles of equity and fairness, in so far as it required more severe self-restraint by other members, who among other things would in fact be jointly responsible for the foreign liabilities others would incur.

Of course, the mechanics of monetary unification imply, in principle, that the freedom of national authorities in pursuing inflationary demand management would be curbed.[1] Since the support of national currencies at basically fixed intra-group rates would remain the responsibility primarily of the national authorities, in the case of a liquidity drain these would have to adjust policies as required by the need to stop it. Governments which could no longer finance a budget deficit through recourse to the central bank would have to cut it within the limits of their ability to raise funds on the Community-wide financial market. To the extent that the market might not be relied upon to enforce restraint on large borrowers, such as governments, there might follow abuses, allocative distortions and disorderly market

---

[1] For further notes on this point see pp. 131 and 132.

conditions; administrative intervention, hopefully on a Community basis, might become necessary.[1]

Finally, inflationary policy aberrations would also threaten the continued existence of the union in so far as the adjustments necessary to undo their effects would put too strong a strain on the common monetary frame.

Policy Harmonisation and Conditions for its Effectiveness

The prolonged recrudescence of inflation has reinforced the plea for harmonisation. For although there is a certain amount of ambiguity in the requests to harmonise policies coming from different quarters and countries, the prevalent motivation is that reciprocal free access to resources should be made conditional upon enforcement of monetary and budgetary discipline.

Harmonisation, however, has been an elusive goal so far. The Commission of the E.E.C. has itself on several occasions drawn attention to the lack of coherence in member countries' policies and to the threat which it represents for the Community's fragile monetary infrastructure.[2] In the Werner Report it was stated that:

The efforts made . . . have not in fact led to co-ordination or effective standardisation of economic policies in the Community. . . . In general, consultation procedures have not yielded the results expected, either because they have been of a purely formal character or because member States have taken refuge in escape clauses.

The extension of the liberation of movements of capital and the realisation of the right of establishment and of the free rendering of services by banking and financial undertaking have not progressed far enough. The delay has been caused by the absence of sufficient co-ordination of economic and monetary policies. . . .

To secure harmonisation, the Werner Group proposed the formation of a 'centre of decision for economic policy', which

[1] For a suggestion concerning this point, however, see p. 176.
[2] See, for instance, the introduction to the *Third General Report on the Activity of the Communities for 1969* [8].

being a political body would have to be liable to effective parliamentary control. It follows that the creation of what was to be the main engine of co-ordination was made contingent upon the election of a truly representative European Parliament. Otherwise, it was suggested in the Werner Report that harmonisation should be sought by reinforcing the procedures of consultation, which would have to be preliminary and compulsory, and by improving the exchange of information: 'The co-ordination of economic policies must be based on *at least three annual surveys* in depth of the economic situation in the Community, that will make it possible to decide on guidelines in common. . . . In order to facilitate the detection of dangerous situations, a system of Community indicators will be worked out.'[1] These devices are being resorted to by the institutions set up in the post-war years to promote international co-operation. The results are scant.

It seems to me that harmonisation cannot be expected to make much headway unless one is clear as to its limitations and the conditions for its acceptance.

In the first place, one should not ignore or underrate the importance of the fact that against the benefits of harmonisation, or the losses which may follow from failure to harmonise, governments are bound to set the opportunities for a fuller attainment of specific national objectives which non-harmonised policies can offer. In view of this, harmonisation should not be sought *per se*; attempts to push it beyond what is technically necessary for monetary unification is bound to generate increasing resistance. All-embracing or 'universal' harmonisation, towards which the Werner Report leans, is proposed out of concern for the fragility of the Community's monetary structures. It is felt that forces making for divergences should be nipped in the bud, by controlling the mechanisms which generate them. State budgets are, of course, one such mechanism; hence the request for harmonisation of budgetary policies.

While there is a good point in the argument that the common monetary frame should be spared, at least in the early stages, some of the strains generated by centrifugal forces, one should bear in mind that in principle budgetary autonomy is com-

---

[1] Italics as in the text of the Report.

patible with economic and monetary union, especially if there is an important federal budget and some *common* mechanism of regulation of capital markets. This is shown by the experience of countries such as Australia, Switzerland and the United States.[1]

Next, it would appear that harmonisation requires the Community itself to evolve and state a sort of basic philosophy concerning economic policy choices. As a rule, governments are wedded to some specific order of priorities among the many objectives which are expected of them. That order is liable to change in a different and unpredictable way, as different governments may at one time respond mainly to calculations of short run expediency, another time to indications of long-run economic efficiency, at other times still to social, political or prestige considerations.

This variability of orders of priority does not simplify the task of reaching a consensus on a mutually consistent set of objectives, but it does point to the need to avoid situations in which governments might make wrong assumptions as to the policies chosen by the Community as a whole. True, a prior ordering of priorities on a Community basis, even if it could be achieved, would risk becoming more or less quickly obsolete; one hardly needs to recall in this respect that, in the view at the time by far prevalent, stagnation of demand and production was going to be the main hurdle for economic policy-makers after the Second World War. By implication, this also weakens the case for reliance on once-for-all fixed presumptive criteria for judging incipient imbalances and specifically allocating the burden of adjustment between deficit and surplus countries.

The need for caution, especially as concerns the specific formulation of presumptive guidelines and criteria, does not, however, exclude that, as efforts are being made to build economic and monetary union, a consensus should be sought about the basic philosophy which is to inspire the Community's

[1] Corden, has argued, along similar lines, that full fiscal integration is not a necessary condition of monetary integration, but 'efficient short-term management may require some harmonisation or control of over-all budgetary policies' ([7] p. 41). In the Federal Trust Report (see Appendix) it was suggested that 'fiscal policies might well be left to the control of the individual nations'.

policy. Reaching that consensus may involve a difficult and long-drawn-out process; but while going through it, the reservations and misgivings which governments entertain about harmonisation would be brought into the open, and hopefully disposed of.

In my view, it would pay to lay down explicitly that it belongs to harmonisation (*a*) to define the Community's current paths to internal and external equilibrium, as well as the longer-term goals, and (*b*) to prevent situations in which some member countries could pursue inconsistent policies and drag the rest of the Community after them, whenever empowered to do so by manoeuvring market forces and their asymmetries.

The asymmetry which puts on surplus countries a lighter pressure than on deficit countries to correct a payments imbalance has not helped to fight inflation in either, or to foster payments equilibrium. An unambiguous acknowledgement of the responsibility in principle of both deficit and surplus countries is needed.

It should also be made clear that, while the present emphasis on 'harmonisation against inflation' is fully justified in view of the current high rates of price increases, and the persisting threat of their acceleration, harmonisation should not disregard the fact that the economies themselves possess different propensities to inflation and that the low-activity regions need a differentiated policy of demand management to promote their economic growth.

But before dwelling on the implications of this, I wish to point out that the consensus about the basic philosophy and the institutional changes needed to implement it should facilitate actual harmonisation of policies. Moreover, the growing interpenetration and attendant interdependence of the national economies *per se* will foster harmonisation. Already those economies *tend* to behave as regions of a wider area: divergences in national demand policies affect primarily the balance of payments. Excess demand is partly met by an increase in imports, so that it has a direct impact on the trade balance and a weaker impact on domestic price and production trends. Though not fully, adjustments in the supply–demand relationship already conform to the interregional pattern. As interdependence increases the disturbances and other costs of

mutually inconsistent policies, the automatic factors making
for harmonisation will grow stronger and stronger.

Finally, harmonisation would be strengthened by taking steps
now towards the 'Europeanisation' of the national groups of
policy-makers. If for political and constitutional reasons the
creation of the 'centre of decision' proposed by the Werner
Group is not feasible, a start in a lower key might be made by
having one member of the directorate or board of directors of
national central banks appointed by an organ of the Community.[1] At the beginning of the experiment, the Community
appointees would sit in the capacity of non-executive directors;
they would be chosen among those in the same or similar position in their respective central bank.[2] In short, European central banks would exchange staff at the general management
level.

This would be more than a political (and public relations)
gesture. Indeed, the tendency to consider institutions and markets as abstract entities, acting and moving with a will and
attitudes of their own, should not make us lose sight of the
fundamental fact that it is the people who make them up:
groups and individuals, with their different instincts and experiences, with the knowledge they have accumulated and the
facts to which they may or may not have access. Personal
interchange is already a prominent feature of the integration
of market institutions. An increasing number of banks, bank and
financial consortia, as well as industrial and commercial companies, have multinational management and interlocking board
membership. Something similar is now needed for the technical
institutions which help to mould national policies.

This step might be taken even before a European Parliament
is called into existence; for it would still be in the realm of
'technical' measures of integration. Arguably, this would not be

[1] I am hypothesising an equal number of directors, which is not the case
now. Eventually, one would have to allow for differences in membership as
regards, for instance, the weighing of the voting rights of the Community
appointee, as well as in procedures of decision-making.

[2] Furthermore, it might be established that if a country repeatedly failed
in the harmonisation exercise, an additional appointment to the board of its
central bank might be made by one of the political organs of the Community – possibly the Council of Ministers. The circle of those eligible for
this appointment would not be restricted to central bankers.

so if one attempted to extend the same arrangement to the national treasury or finance ministries. At any rate, the member countries' agreement to introduce a human catalyst of harmonisation is more likely to be given if a consensus is reached on the nature of harmonisation itself, its conditions and limitations.

Harmonisation and Exchange-Rate Flexibility

One should not expect of harmonisation more than it can, by its nature, do. Because *harmonisation is about policies*, it can take care of discrepancies in cost and price trends only to the extent that they are due to inconsistent policies. Inflationary mismanagement of demand in several European countries has no doubt been a factor in bringing about those discrepancies. But cost and price discrepancies cannot be regarded solely as the result of the authorities' perverse behaviour in the framework of an otherwise self-adjusting system: the hard core is due to the different behaviour of the economies themselves, as determined by their different propensities to inflations.

Since a long process of rapprochement at a disaggregated and even capillary level is needed to bring national and regional inflation propensities into line, as they are in fully integrated economies, correction of stabilisation policies cannot eliminate those discrepancies altogether. And indeed they *should not* as long as the economies are only semi-integrated. Different propensities to inflation imply that even if governments agreed on the same demand-management objective – say 97–98 per cent utilisation of productive factors, or 2–3 per cent unemployment – countries with a low N.P.I. would see prices increase by, say, 1·5–2 per cent, while in those with a high N.P.I. the increases might be 3–4 per cent or more. If the mechanism of monetary unification requires member countries to allow increases at a rate roughly equal for all of them – a constraint which would arise from irrevocably freezing exchange rates now – countries with a low N.P.I. will have to absorb extra doses of inflation and/or those with a high N.P.I. will have to depress levels of demand and unemployment further. As will be seen below, it is more likely that the adjustment would be made at the rate postulated by the low-N.P.I. countries. Thus countries with a high propensity to inflation would have to endure a (larger) deviation from the rate of cost and price increases consistent with their N.P.I. Because in the end their process of growth would be hindered, it is difficult to see how today's inflationary-growth countries could accept becoming the new low-activity regions of the Community.

It should be clear from the foregoing that, as long as propensities to inflation differ, *policy harmonisation and internal flexibility of exchange rates should not be regarded as substitutes*: they are both needed because each has a different role to play. Harmonisation should *eliminate* discrepancies in cost and price trends arising from inconsistent policies and from miscalculations in implementing them. In circumstances such as those now obtaining, it would no doubt have to curb inflationary mismanagement of demand, so as to eliminate altogether the component in cost and price rises which is basically due to wrong policies. This *must* and *can* be done through policy confrontation and harmonisation. But at rates of inflation lowered through harmonisation, there still would be differential cost and price increases caused by the economies' different inflation propensities. To suppress these discrepancies through a further correction of policies would be costly, in terms of disturbances to the growth process; therefore it will not be accepted. Because harmonisation cannot and should not be expected to work here, we need another instrument: we need intra-group exchange-rate flexibility to *offset* discrepancies due to differences in propensities to inflation, as long as the process of thorough economic integration will not have unified the values of those propensities. We need flexibility in exchange rates because cost and price discrepancies of up to 2 or $2\frac{1}{2}$ per cent per year, which harmonisation cannot prevent, should not be allowed to accumulate and finally render the structure of exchange rates hopelessly unrealistic.

The interpretation underlying this approach helps to solve the assignment problem for two essential tools of policy, which so often are thought of as alternative, whereas in fact they usefully complement each other, whenever N.P.I.s differ. We have a criterion for defining the task, and appraising the performance, of harmonisation on one side, exchange-rate flexibility on the other. That criterion also tells us when misuse of each of the two tools would start. If the measurement of cost and price discrepancies, ascribable to differences in N.P.I.s, showed them to lie within a range of 2–2½ percentage points, policy harmonisation, which aimed at reducing actual discrepancies to still lower values, would be misdirected. Conversely, resort to exchange-rate flexibility in excess of 2 or 2½ per cent per year would have to be deemed as abuse in the use of a policy instrument.

As is so often the case, the neatness of the theoretical construction is unlikely to be found in actual fact. There are, in the first place, important problems of measurement. My propositions about propensities to inflation, optimum rates of price increases, range of cost and price discrepancies in Europe *due to gaps in N.P.I.s* are in the nature of hypotheses which need to be tested. I have made and used them on the basis of their apparent plausibility; they are extremely helpful in explaining some disconcerting phenomena of the post-war experience in economic integration. I hope, therefore, that these propositions may beget the statistical research apt to validate them empirically.

Aside from problems of an empirical nature, however, a few qualifications need to be made here concerning the theoretical aspects of the argument. As far as propensities to inflation are concerned, it is assumed that they would undergo gradual, convergent changes until their values finally coincided, thus meeting the main requirement for the creation of an optimum currency area. In the specific case of European monetary unification, this implies the exclusion of drastic changes for a generation, roughly the period of time needed for the transition to full monetary union. In fact, the system would admit of member countries and regions switching from the low- to the high-inflation-propensity group, and vice versa, for the change would reflect itself in a switch of the respective currencies from upward- to downward-crawling, and vice versa.

Concerning flexibility, one should bear in mind the fact that the interpenetration of the economies is bound to reduce the ability to adjust relative price levels by exchange-rate changes, especially if and when a common European currency is put into circulation side by side with national currencies. 'Money illusion' will also suffer as a result of the increasing alertness to the erosion in the purchasing power of money rewards, and of the various mechanisms which individuals and organised groups build into contracts, wage agreements, and pension and social security schemes in order to cope with chronic inflation. The forces at work during the transitional period will on the whole tend to reduce the effectiveness of the contribution which flexibility can make to the adjustment process. This is as it should be; for the regions of an area which is finally to form a monetary union should eventually be able to dispense with internal exchange-rate flexibility. If its effectiveness fades away, there will be an added reason for locking exchange rates irrevocably together, and even adopting one common currency.[1] But despite the weaknesses likely to accompany it, flexibility belongs to the logic of integration during the intermediate stage.

Unsuitability of Freely Floating Exchange Rates

Freely floating exchange rates are rightly considered as the antithesis of a unified market, and not just because they imply the need to cover against exchange-rate losses. There is a social cost in this, which is represented by the amount of resources absorbed by such operations. Moreover, forward cover may not be forthcoming for longer-term operations, or for some currencies; and again, the terms on which currencies can be sold forward are likely to vary between the moment when a tender is made for a contract and the time when the latter is actually awarded. These and other inconveniences are apt to hinder trade, capital movements and, therefore, integration. They also recur, however, with a system of fixed exchange rates which undergo large changes at long and, at any rate,

[1] In this regard, however, it is in order to add a warning note. Many economists argue that, as 'money illusion' is on the way to evanescence, it should be easier to dispense with exchange-rate changes: why engage in this exercise when it is losing effectiveness? While I am in agreement with the premise, I draw a different conclusion. For, over a wide range of situations, the decline in effectiveness (vis-à-vis previous periods) may be made good by augmenting the doses. If exchange-rate changes come increasingly to represent the most convenient way of making needed adjustments within and between economies, the weaker effectiveness of each unit change is likely in fact to give rise to a need for more changes. The tendency towards increased reliance on exchange-rate changes seems already to have set in, in the world at large; it thus becomes even more necessary for countries which are moving towards monetary union to devise workable forms of regulation of limited flexibility.

irregular intervals. Indeed, it is open to doubt whether under present and prospective circumstances the inconveniences of that system are less severe than those of even free floating.

In addition, however, as exchange-rate changes become routine, tolerance builds up even in respect of their becoming large and only one-way; so that free floating in the end takes out of the system the ability to set any limits to the autonomy of national economic policies and potentially allows more room also for demand mismanagement. Whereas a system of stable rates, with an appropriately limited amount of international liquidity, tends to put pressure on countries generally to attain the standards of efficiency and monetary stability set by those with the hardest currencies, under freely floating rates it is likely that greater autonomy would lead over the longer term to a wide gulf between stronger and weaker national economies.

Finally, there are very serious doubts concerning the possibility of operating in a reasonably orderly fashion free floating of national currencies. This means that freely floating rates are to be deemed inappropriate generally, and not just when the formation of an economic and monetary union is sought.

Most of the post-war discussion of floating rates has been about their effectiveness in correcting disequilibria in the *trade balance*, and it has greatly improved our understanding of the many conditions which have to be satisfied for an exchange-rate change to succeed in bringing about an increase (decrease) of the foreign-exchange earnings of a deficit (surplus) country. On the whole, that discussion has revalued floating rates as an instrument for restoring equilibrium in the trade balance, by proving unjustified the 'elasticity pessimism' to which the analysis of inter-war statistical data had given rise.[1] In the absence of generalised quantitative controls and other hindrances to trade, the Marshall–Lerner condition, that for a devaluation to improve the trade balance the sum of import and export demand elasticities must be larger than unity, is easily met. In a recent contribution, Hinshaw [16] has also

[1] The term 'elasticity pessimism' was introduced by Machlup, who pointed to the downward bias in the early estimates of price elasticity of demand in international trade [24] and defended the merits of the elasticity approach relative to the absorption, or aggregate spending, approach proposed in 1952 by Alexander [25, 26, 1].

argued that low *import*-price elasticities do not imply low *export*-price elasticities;[1] that import-elasticity pessimism is consistent with optimism as to the absorption effect, or the ability to bring into line real expenditure by the domestic sector with the level of income in real terms; and finally, that absorption optimism is justified even at full employment in the devaluing country, if the latter succeeds in securing the stability of the general price level.

A conspicuous feature of the floating-rate debate has been the absence of money. On the whole one can agree with Tsiang that the conventional elasticities formulae of the effect of devaluation took no account of the monetary factors, since implicitly they generally assumed a constant money income ([35] p. 914). When the vistas opened by Alexander's absorption approach helped to rediscover the role of money, the latter was again analysed in terms mainly of its 'multiplier' effect on the trade balance. But the study of the effects, stabilising or destabilising, of capital movements has not been systematically incorporated into the mainstream of the floating-rate theory, one notable exception being Einzig's statement of the case against floating exchanges ([9] esp. chaps. 6 and 7).

Capital movements have in the main been studied separately,[2] which means that these studies have, in their turn, tended to ignore the conclusions reached by the theorists of the trade-balance effect.

The introduction of capital movements in the model leads to a shift of emphasis, from the oversimplifying assumption of the existence of two diametrically opposed exchange-rate systems to the consideration of the intermediate arrangements which lie between irrevocably fixed rates at one end, and freely floating rates at the other. The trade theory of exchange rates and the optimum currency area theory, which have failed to consider the many variants of unpegged exchange rates, and their different implications for the adjustment process, have seen their chances of being operationally relevant reduced.

[1] The latter is of primary interest in the use of floating rates for international adjustment and, according to Hinshaw, can be expected to be well in excess of unity, given certain export supply functions.

[2] A most interesting debate regarding the effects of exchange-rate flexibility on capital flows and the constraints of flexibility on interest-rate policy has recently taken place between Katz, Branson and Willett [20].

What seems to be needed is an integrated theory of the effects of exchange-rate changes on the trade balance and on capital movements; in other words, a synthesis should be attempted of how both the current and capital accounts are affected, and of the interaction between the two, once the process has been set off by an actual or expected exchange-rate change. This means, among other things, that the length and variability of lags in the adjustment of the trade balance should be studied in relation to the lags with which the propensity to hold monetary and financial assets and liabilities in one country changes, and these are actually exchanged against holdings in another country.

As concerns the trade balance, it has long been recognised that elasticities are higher in the long run, which allows for substitution of methods of production, for adjustments in consumer spending in response to changes in relative prices at home and abroad, and so on. But high long-run elasticities are not sufficient to secure stability under freely floating exchange rates. Fortunately, from more recent analyses the elasticity of export supply and price elasticities of demand (for export commodities which are produced by several countries) can be deduced to be quite high in the short run also.[1] But even the short run may in fact be too long when compared with the speed of reaction of monetary and financial capitals, which tend to make the adjustment instantaneous, and at times even anticipatory.

Moreover, if there is a cause of dynamic disequilibrium at work, such as differences in N.P.I.s, there is no guarantee that, under fully floating exchange rates, rate adjustments will take place to the extent and with the graduality implied by those differences. On the contrary, net changes in exchange ratios, sufficient to compensate over time for different N.P.I.s, might be arrived at through wide gyrations. Whereas different N.P.I.s mean that some currencies will be persistently but perhaps only slightly stronger relative to others, and conversely, exchange rates under free floating might cumulatively reflect, at any given point in time, their relative strength (weakness) over a period of a week, a month, a year, or longer. Exchange rates would fluctuate as the disequilibrium period relevant in the calculations and choices of the market changed from a shorter to a longer one, or vice versa, so that under unregulated flexibility

[1] This is the conclusion that Hinshaw [16] arrives at.

there would be an alternation of bouts of both appreciation and depreciation for basically strong as well as basically weak currencies. Departures from equilibrium rates would be more frequent and larger than needed.

Exchange-rate gyrations would only in an arithmetical sense largely cancel themselves out. They would hamper trade transactions, tend to have perverse effects and lead to competitive devaluations. This is what happened in the inter-war period; the exchange-rate instability which then obtained has influenced much of current thinking and explains the deep scepticism as to the contributions which orderly exchange-rate changes can make to restoration of equilibrium.

Methods to Regulate Exchange-Rate Floating

It is clear from the foregoing that these drawbacks apply to free floating; hence the need for some sort of regulated floating. In particular, step-by-step changes would reconcile long-term flexibility exchange of rates with the need for their stability. A scheme to this effect was elaborated in 1933 by Harrod ([15] p. 91).

Parities would be allowed to move more or less continuously, by reference to the average market valuations in the preceding two or five years; and there would be a maximum by which parties could be adjusted downwards (2 per cent per year). The scheme was again put forward a few years ago by Williamson ([37], p. 2), who named it the 'crawling peg',[1] and by Meade ([29] pp. 3–27). In Professor Meade's scheme, countries would be permitted at their own discretion to change the parity by not more than one-sixth of one per cent per month, so that if the right to change the parity was exercised every month, the total change over a year would be 2 per cent. The proposal was endorsed by a group of twenty-seven economists, who signed a statement advocating the right for countries 'unilaterally to

[1] By 'crawling peg' is meant a 'system under which such par changes as occur are implemented slowly, in such a large number of small steps as to make the process of exchange-rate adjustment continuous for all practical purposes'. Williamson suggests that 'those countries accepting the obligations of Article VIII (sections 2 to 4) of the Articles of Agreement of the International Monetary Fund (i.e. those with convertible currencies) should undertake that any changes in par value needed to correct a "fundamental disequilibrium" would be carried out gradually, at a maximum rate of 1/26 of 1 per cent per week, rather than in a sudden discrete jump'.

change the par value of their currencies by no more than 1 or 2 per cent of the previous year's par value'.[1]

Finally, in the I.M.F. report on the role of exchange-rate flexibility, it has been suggested that: 'in order to facilitate small and gradual changes in parity as disequilibria develop and to avoid unnecessary delays in adjustment that may occur for various reasons, the Articles of Agreement might be amended to allow members to make changes in their parities without the concurrence of the Fund as long as such changes did not exceed, say, 3 per cent in any twelve-month period nor a cumulative amount of, say, 10 per cent in any five-year period'. ([18] p. 73).

Thus a consensus has emerged in the past decade around a constructive compromise, which favours a more active role for exchange-rate changes in the adjustment of payments balances, but at the same time meets the need to play safe with the potentially destabilising effects of capital movements by setting definite limits to floating.[2]

While the old theoretical dilemma of fixed versus freely floating exchange rates threatened to cripple the latter as an instrument of adjustment, the compromise in favour of limited flexibility is likely also to attract the consensus of official bodies, both national and international, in so far as it succeeds in securing a realistic balance between official interventions and market factors. Limited exchange-rate flexibility implies, no doubt, that the impact of those factors should be allowed to make itself felt in a less haphazard and more orderly way than it has so far; but it does not mean that the determination of exchange rates should be remitted to market automatisms altogether. As Lawson has pointed out:

the most important question for a government in respect of exchange policy is not should the exchange rate be 'fixed' or

---

[1] The statement is reproduced in Fellner ([10] pp. 112-14). The initiative was sponsored by W. Fellner, G. Haberler, F. Machlup and T. Scitovsky. The list of signatories includes M. Friedman, A. Hahn, A. Hansen, B. de Jouvenel, H. Johnson, F. Lutz, J. Meade, I. Svennilson and J. Tinbergen.

[2] Exchange-rate flexibility would be achieved not only by allowing parity shifts, but also by increasing the width of the band for permissible exchange-rate variations around the par value. A survey and appraisal of the various proposals for widening the 'band' is to be found in Halm [14].

should it float, but what should the exchange rate be? I am aware that some people seem to believe that if the exchange rate is determined in a free market without direct official intervention it will inevitably be the right rate, but this view seems to me to be a considerable over-simplification. A floating rate may be influenced indirectly in a variety of ways to make it float freely at quite different levels. ([21] pp. 11-12)

Within a context of limited flexibility, while there would be a continued need for economic and financial policies consistent with the basic stability of exchange rates, it would not be feasible totally to dispense with interventions on exchange markets. I cannot envisage, as instead Professor Giersch does, the work-ability (anyway not for a long time) of an arrangement whereby member countries of the Common Market would undertake progressively to limit exchange-rate fluctuations *exclusively* by means of monetary and fiscal policies, which would be so harmonised as to transform 'mobile exchange rates into constant equilibrium rates' ([12] p. 49).

The doctrinaire view that authorities must not intervene presupposes that many conditions are satisfied, which is usually not the case. In fact, most proposals would have a *quantitative* limit set to flexibility by agreement; and this means that the authorities would have to intervene. What is more, a consensus seems to have crystallised around step-by-step shifts adding up to 2 per cent per year, which is the figure mentioned by Harrod, Meade and the group of twenty-seven economists. In view of this, it is somewhat surprising that official bodies, by nature and tradition made suspicious of exchange rate experiments, should be reluctant to commit themselves to quantitative limitations of flexibility, and are prevalently inclined to accept smaller but, if necessary, more frequent rate changes, under the presumptive guidance of some set of indicators. This amounts, in fact, to a *more permissive* criterion, for the direction and the size of changes in the indicators would in turn largely be caused by the policies being followed.

This attitude can best be explained with reference to countries not bound by a programme of economic and monetary union; for it might not be safe to predict for the countries of the world at large the extent of cost and price discrepancies

E

likely to develop, given different N.P.I.s, different priorities among, and abilities to pursue, the various objectives of economic policy, and so on. In fact, from this viewpoint one might even doubt the appropriateness of the solutions being evolved internationally for the problems likely to confront us in the future. It may well be that smaller and more timely changes now seem liable to be used with acceptable and workable restraint, and are regarded as an adequate remedy because one extrapolates the experience of the past twenty-five years to the next twenty-five, without allowing for changes in economic and financial trends which, although difficult to predict, can be expected in the light of the current drift towards more autonomy of national policies.[1]

A European Monetary Convention to Regulate Internal Exchange-Rate Flexibility

The solution to be worked out for the E.E.C. must be seen in an entirely different light. Here exchange-rate flexibility can be resorted to *only* if it promises to substitute dynamic stability of intra-group rates for past and present unstable rigidity.

To reach that aim, the following conditions should, in my view, be satisfied.

Internal exchange-rate flexibility should only be used to *offset* discrepancies in cost and price trends arising from the economies' different inflation propensities.

Policy harmonisation should be made effective, in *eliminating* cost and price discrepancies due to inconsistent policies, among other things by taking the steps suggested earlier in this essay.

Quantitative limits to rate flexibility should be agreed upon at the start. They should correspond to the size of cost and price discrepancies which can be attributed to differences in N.P.I.s (if the assumption of basically stable, slowly moving N.P.I.s is correct, it does make sense to predetermine quantitative limits).

[1] The I.M.F. report on exchange-rate flexibility after stating that in cases in which exchange rates should be adjusted, this should be done without delay, notes that: 'However it would not be consistent with the Articles to make changes in par values that were so small that they were judged to be incompatible with the concept of correction of a fundamental disequilibrium, or so frequent that they were judged to undermine the maintenance of exchange stability' ([18] p. 72). See also quotation on p. 110.

Exchange-rate flexibility would be allowed only during the *intermediate stage*, that is, while N.P.I.s have different values; a series of steps should be taken, as indicated elsewhere in this book, to make N.P.I.s converge.

The size of intra-group rate adjustments *should shrink* as N.P.I.s converge and, therefore, cost and price discrepancies attributable to them decrease. The transition from the intermediate stage to full monetary union would not imply a jump, but would be made by gradually phasing out internal flexibility.

Member countries would *renounce from the start the right to change parities other than in the form and within the limits agreed.* In particular, they would undertake to dispense with large and sudden parity 'jumps', typical of the adjustable-peg system. A *timetable* should be agreed upon at the start, defining the number and length of periods, during each of which progress would be made towards the reduction and final elimination of internal flexibility. While the speed should be chosen on the realistic assumption that full monetary unification in Europe is, broadly speaking, a one-generation-long task, the length of each period should not be rigidly fixed; it should be possible for it to vary between a maximum and a minimum number of years.

To be more specific, but only by way of illustration, it might be established that:

1. During the first five to eight years, parities should be allowed to move 1·25 per cent upwards and 1·25 per cent downwards (2·50 per cent in total) per annum; the change upwards (downwards) might be raised to 2 per cent, in the absence of other member currencies (of comparable weight) moving downwards (upwards).

2. During the following five to eight years, these percentages would be reduced respectively to 1 upwards and 1 downwards, and to 1·60, per annum.

3. At the end of this second period, i.e. after ten to sixteen years since the inception of the programme, it would be decided whether to switch to 100 per cent fixed parities, or to have a third period during which flexibility would be further reduced to 0·75 per cent both ways, or 1·20 per cent one way.

There are several reasons for having the essential features of the limited intra-group exchange-rate flexibility, which would be permitted during the intermediate stage, embodied in a formal agreement. Can member countries embark upon building a monetary union without such a procedure? Monetary union is a long stride past customs union; it affects sovereignty directly and it would bring economic union with it. It will be a veritable *tour de force* if substantial progress towards it is accomplished before political unification.

A European convention on monetary and economic union would not only lay down the rules of internal flexibility. It would also formalise the obligations of member countries, such as the renunciation of any other form of parity changes, as well as their undertakings concerning the basic philosophy and methods of policy harmonisation. Finally, it would create the instruments and institutions for gradually putting into circulation a European currency. A huge amount of work is needed by way of both study of the issues at stake and negotiation of the solutions; it should be done by several specialised committees, with whose contributions the European monetary convention would concomitantly be drafted.

Legislated flexibility would be more credible than a less formal undertaking, at a time when credibility will be lent only at a premium. But clearly, the credibility of this flexibility arrangement will rest on the measure of realism which it will be seen to possess. After the many parity changes which have been forced on authorities who had to all practical purposes exhausted the possibilities open to them for currency support, parities have lost the connotation of finality that may have attached to them at some point of time between the currency realignment of 1949 and the 1967 devaluation of the pound. Confidence has been further undermined by the fact that, increasingly in recent years, the equilibrating mechanism built into the fixed-rate system has been foiled by inconsistent policies. These have in actual fact disregarded the external constraint, which fixed rates of exchange are supposed to be, until it has become too late to choose any other course but changing the exchange rate. Thus, even in periods of 'normality', governments have behaved in some cases in a fashion not very dissimilar from that which in theory only can obtain under floating rates.

To talk about fixed parities now invariably elicits the question: fixed for how long? In the world at large there is a disposition, which is also psychological, to let parity changes play a greater role in the adjustment process. Even if there were no other reasons for allowing exchange-rate flexibility, it is likely that this step would have to be taken on psychological grounds – that is, because of the widespread conviction that it is needed. Disconcerting though this may be for some economists, it is a fact of life.

Thus a policy stance defensible under present and foreseeable circumstances would have to allow, even within a restricted group aiming at monetary union, the measure of rate flexibility postulated by differences in N.P.I.s, which as we have seen cannot be eliminated overnight. Moreover, in order to be credible it would need to appear workable; to this end, integrating steps in the fields of policy harmonisation, capital movements and their orientation, and so on, need to be taken. While I shall deal in the next essay with freedom of capital movements and the convertibility aspect of monetary union, I wish to comment here briefly on 'workability' as an intrinsic quality of the exchange-rate arrangement itself.

It is often said that, because it is very difficult in practice to judge whether the exchange rate is in disequilibrium by as little as 1 or 2 per cent, small rate adjustments are not a practical proposition. From the foregoing, however, it is clear that what needs to be measured is not an actual small disequilibrium, but rather the tendency for costs and prices to rise faster in some countries as a result of a higher inflation propensity. A 1 or 2 per cent disequilibrium would not require correction of the rate of exchange if it were not recurrent; but its cumulation over periods even as short as five to ten years would render untenable the initial structure of exchange rates. Correspondingly, rate adjustments of the same yearly size would amount, over the said period, to the large parity changes which could not be avoided under the adjustable-peg system. It is the unmeasurable uncertainty which those changes generate that has really disruptive effects on the Common Market; gives rise to those massive, uncontrollable waves of speculation that make the expectations of parity changes self-fulfilling; and thus prevents the full and irreversible liberalisation of capital movements.

In the light of this it is difficult to see how parity 'jumps' can be allowed at all. In the Werner Report they were not ruled out up to the expiry of the transitional period. On the face of it, this appears reasonable, but I submit that it is the wrong approach: the transitional period will not fulfil the task for which it is conceived, the openness and integration of the economies will not advance, if entrepreneurs are not in a position to make reasonably safe assumptions about movements in rates of exchange, if speculation about their 'jumps' threatens to dilate and distort capital movements. The transition to full monetary union will be delayed indefinitely, with the danger of backsliding into more restrictive fragmentation of national markets.

Parity 'jumps' are not ruled out in recent proposals either. Professor Triffin has argued that 'It must, however, be recognised that this stability (of exchange rates between the Community currencies themselves) cannot be prematurely declared irrevocable. It will certainly remain subject to revision in the light of present uncertainties, both outside and inside the Community. It can only be a question at this stage of establishing – in the language of the recent monetary agreement between the Benelux countries – provisional "pivot rates" rather than final parities But these "rates" should be modified only by common agreement, or by the application of commonly recognised objective criteria, such as, for example, losses or gains of reserves or recourse to the agreement for short-term monetary support or medium-term financial assistance for amounts deemed manifestly excessive either by the creditor countries or by the debtors.' ([34] p. 30).

It would thus appear that Triffin considers parity changes conducive to stability if they could be made contingent upon agreement or the indication of 'commonly recognised objective criteria'. Whereupon my query is: how much does it matter to industrialists, to bankers, to exporters and importers whether the jump is made with or without common agreement, with or without the indication of 'objective' criteria, so long as the size of the change may be indefinitely large?

In principle, common agreement implies that exchange-rate changes would be made less discretionary from the point of view of a single country; and this may lead, again in principle, to a more orderly and stable system. But if changes are made in a state of necessity, common agreement becomes little more than a rubber-stamping procedure. Assuming on the other hand the procedure to be a meaningful one, with the possibility of the agreement not being granted, there would be a danger of adding to disruptive uncertainty. Unless it is established that parity changes are only allowed *up to the narrow extent* implied by differences in N.P.I.s and formally agreed, it will be difficult to harmonise policies, or even to curb the forces which make for further divergences. Parity changes will in the end become more and more frequent and sizeable; and if they are not seen as an *extrema ratio*, this will be because they are already being assimilated in the public psychology as routine business.

Concerning the application of objective criteria, how much would the reference to reserve losses and gains, which in turn are largely a result of the policies being followed by member governments and of capital movements motivated at times by self-fulfilling expectations, help to circumscribe the exchange risk on ventures in another member country or currency?

As Governor Carli of the Banca d'Italia has recently pointed out, it cannot be denied

> that the introduction of flexible exchange rates creates uncertainty. . . . The uncertainty problem is, in turn, directly connected with the question of whether speculation can act as a stabilising force. . . . That the speculators' behaviour may have a destabilising influence, in that they have to foresee what the fiscal and monetary authorities' policies will be in the new circumstances, does not seem to be a risky assumption to make. Nor can the possibility be excluded that a self-perpetuating process might arise, whereby the perverse behaviour of speculators would, in turn, influence the decision of policy-makers. ([5] p. 141)

With or without common agreement, with or without reference to objective criteria, exchange-rate changes are likely to have a disruptive impact on the building of monetary union, *if they are large*. Instead of providing the stable framework on the basis of which Community-wide long-term planning could make profitability valuations with reference to fundamental economic criteria, such as the marginal productivity of capital, they create incentives for short-term speculation.

If exchange rates, as we have seen, cannot be dispensed with altogether as a policy instrument, that is, as a variable, during the intermediate stage, at least rate changes should *only* be made gradually and smoothly. Businesses would be able to take small, gradual changes in their stride because it would confront them with a manageable and definite amount of uncertainty. They know that decisions taken in a context of less uncertainty are likely to be more successful than decisions in a context of more uncertainty. There would be no market anarchy. Forward-exchange markets would not be in danger of collapse. They would be needed, of course, as long as intra-E.E.C. exchange rates were not irrevocably locked together by 100 per cent fixity. But I would expect their activity to be moderate and the spreads with spot exchange rates to be within the limits justified by the narrow amount of flexibility agreed upon. Small capital movements would promptly bring about the maximum permissible exchange-rate adjustments, thus cutting the ground under the feet of additional short-term speculation.

The parity adjustments postulated by this scheme could well be fitted into a 'band', such as is applied now. It is true that it is planned to reduce its width, but the size of permitted parity adjustments is also scheduled to shrink, as in the illustration given above.

To put in an enlightening perspective the impact of the regulated flexibility proposed here on the smooth working of markets, it helps to draw attention to the fact that no dramatic movements of the rates of exchange would be necessary in order to adjust parities. In fact, no change at all might be needed when the parity adjustment was announced; only the position of the rate within the band would shift. Furthermore, it should be borne in mind that the parity changes indicated would not be materially larger than the movements in exchange rates which can take place within the present width of the 'band'. The latter can do so quickly, and equally quickly reverse themselves, and so on and so forth in the course of a year or a quarter of a year, or less still. The fact that the parity changes needed to give long-term flexibility to exchange rates might cumulate year after year, during the intermediate stage, would not intensify the disturbances which an exchange dealer has to face in his daily routine for movements within the band, and would not magnify uncertainty to an extent that would cripple the development of Community-wide operations by entrepreneurs.

Finally, the complex of measures advocated here would also help to prevent situations in which hot-money waves from outside the Community have overwhelmed in turn the markets of individual member countries. If those measures make credible the pledge not to change parities otherwise than as agreed in the suggested European monetary convention, then there would no longer be any scope to consider E.E.C. currencies as *different* currencies for purposes of speculation. Such rate flexibility as would be permitted would not allow the large and quick profits which make speculation worthwhile in the case of a sequence of individual parity 'jumps'. From this viewpoint, the E.E.C. might approach the one-currency area pattern already in the intermediate stage.

If, as part and parcel of a deal for Europe's monetary unification, countries agreed to relinquish *now* the right to make large and abrupt parity changes, against an option to use the kind of regulated flexibility outlined here and which would eventually be consecrated through the signing of a convention, a big step forward would be made.

The New European Currency, Balanced Regional Growth and the Community's Overall Monetary Equilibrium

Internal limited flexibility of exchange rates would allow the economies of high-activity regions and countries with a high propensity to inflation time to adjust to the lower rates of cost and price increases which would be acceptable to the Community as a whole. While in principle income transfers may have an effect equivalent to depreciation of the exchange rate, it is difficult to see how such transfers could take its place on any large scale in the case of high-activity regions; for that would imply that some regions and countries would be making grants to their direct competitors in regions and countries which would continue to be prosperous if only they could allow cost and price rises in line with their propensity to inflation. Indeed, if fiscal unification went as far as to permit such transfers, it is more likely that the high-activity, high-inflation propensity regions and countries would pay more than they would receive; they would in other words have net negative transfers. The 'fiscal drag' which is a built-in feature of modern tax systems would affect especially the regions where the growth of money incomes was likely to be highest, since to the rise in real terms a large nominal increase would be added by rising costs and prices.

Internal flexibility might also help the low-activity regions to improve their competitive position. This, as we have seen, would probably deteriorate as a result of the tendency towards equalisation of salaries and wages, which economic and monetary union would strengthen. Yet the solution does not lie in the perpetuation of old disparities and the formation of new, irreversible ones, but in the narrowing of productivity differentials, which would make sense of wage equalisation. The greatest contribution to achieving this aim can be made by promoting accelerated capitalisation in the weaker regions. For reasons previously mentioned, it is unlikely that for a long time the Community as such will be in a position to integrate capital formation in those regions through fiscal transfers of income. Such transfers as take place to date are mainly sectoral in character and do not necessarily tend to close regional gaps.

None the less, it is unthinkable that member countries should irrevocably renounce the use of such instruments as autonomous exchange-rate changes, exchange and other controls on the movement of funds, and the use of savings, monetary and credit policy, without the Community itself sharing responsibility with national governments for 'problem regions'. The formation of a monetary union, especially if it is made to hinge upon early unification of intra-group exchange rates, is bound to affect the process of growth differently in the different regions and countries of the Community, as the preceding considerations hopefully have shown. Hence the need to build into the very machinery of monetary unification the instruments which the Community can wield to help finance a policy of territorially balanced growth.

This raises several difficulties. If it implies Community-wide co-ordination of investments, we know that similar attempts in early post-war years among the Western European countries (and in Eastern Europe) have mostly failed. Nationalism, ideology, inertia, all militate against a supranational approach in this field. None the less, the difficulty may not prove an insur-

mountable one within the E.E.C. today or in the immediate
future, given a degree of European political solidarity and of
local participation in the process, an inclination to look at the
more subtle experiences made by a number of member countries
as regards 'direction' of investment activity, and the awareness
that *not everything, everywhere, needs to be co-ordinated in order to
implement a European management of growth.*

The objection on which I wish to concentrate, however, is one
more central to my argument. I have proposed that a new,
additional currency should be put into circulation in the Community by a European bank of the universal type, which for
working purposes I have called the Multi-role European Bank.
The M.E.B. would, among other things, issue medium- and
long-term securities denominated in the new European currency.
It would also be enabled to use the issues of the new currency
by granting credit in a fashion that would make possible
regionally differentiated demand management and contribute
to balanced growth. The link that exists between the mechanism
of monetary unification and the process of growth would thereby be correspondingly reflected in an institutional and instrumental arrangement, which would use the European seigniorage
gains for closing regional disparities and preventing new ones.

Against this, it has been argued that greater Community
assistance to areas with unutilised resources should be sought
through the European Investment Bank and by means of fiscal
measures, while the creation of a common currency should be
motivated by 'the need to pursue stabilisation policies – especially regarding prices – designed to neutralise inflationary or
deflationary pressures originating outside the area' ([28] p. 5).

I have already stated my views concerning fiscal measures
and what can be expected of them in the near future. As to the
plea for an expanded role for the E.I.B., I am of course in full
agreement. One reason why I have suggested setting up a
wholly new institution is my wish to underline the jump that is
needed from the amount of resources now being channelled to
the weaker regions, to the size of those that ought to be forthcoming in order to implement a Community policy of balanced
growth. If, however, the E.I.B. could be made to grow into a
multiple of what it is, then so much the better. For the separation of the 'development' bank from the monetary institution

is also apt to allay the fears of those who see in a meaningful Community undertaking in favour of the weaker regions the seeds of the inflationary forest which would soon envelop the Community. . . .

I have proposed the merging of the development and monetary functions into one institution because I believe that, in spite of all aspirations and efforts, great hopes cannot be entertained that resources will be raised for the less favoured regions of Europe, other than on a scale which for years to come promises to be far below the increase in their needs, connected with the formation of the economic and monetary union. Hence the need not to disperse such resources as will be available among several institutions. This arrangement, while allowing for the separation into two departments of the operations pertaining to the two different functions, would secure the unity of direction which to me seems necessary if the Community, out of modest resources, is to make a breakthrough as a significant force on national money and capital markets.[1]

The idea central to my proposals is that monetary unifica-

---

[1] It should be noted in passing that Harold Lever, a British M.P. and former Financial Secretary to the Treasury, has recently proposed a development bank for the high-unemployment areas of the British Isles, which should be a department of the Bank of England:

'. . . The time has come to set up a vast development bank for the regions. We should think in terms of a very large sum of money. Initially, £1,000 million would not be too great a sum to put into the hands of a new vast development bank to enable it to finance development and employment in the regions and in the areas of high unemployment such as Lancashire and Yorkshire.

'Why do I want such an instrument? Briefly put, if we could think of the areas that I am referring to as if they could be aggregated into a country, probably they would want to have a currency with a different parity from our own to get their economies going. . . .

'. . . The advantage of this idea is that it would be more comprehensive than anything that has been done so far. It would leap over boundaries; that is, there would not be the problem of the grey areas, the near-grey areas, the black areas, and the super-black areas. There would be a flexibility in dealing with projects which would be far greater than anything which has been established so far. . . .

'. . . The right institution to operate such a development bank would be the Bank of England. The development bank should be a department of the Bank of England so that it would tie in with the country's general economic and financial management. . . .' ([22] cols 1526 pp.)

tion should proceed hand in hand with the assumption of direct, albeit partial, responsibility by the Community for promoting growth in the weaker regions. If we want monetary unification as soon as we appear to, to judge from the succession of attempts which are being made in the field of exchange-rate policy, then it seems to me that parallelism between a unified European management of money and a European policy of balanced growth can only be secured by harnessing for the needs of the latter the income and the opportunities which would arise from the issue of a European currency. Any issuer of money reaps a gain because it can issue it in exchange for earning assets; the gain would be made even under a commodity-money system because it arises from the restrictions generally applied to entry in this field. The creation of fiat money not only implies a social gain in so far as it releases the resources which would be absorbed by the production of commodity money, but it also transfers to governments the seigniorage gains which would otherwise go to producers of monetary metals.[1]

The point is whether the Community can be made to share in those gains, which it would use as leverage for raising the additional resources needed by the weaker regions and, possibly, for subsidising interest payments on loans to them. So far, of course, the seigniorage gains arising from international payments, including intra-Community payments, have mainly been reaped by the reserve-currency countries, which have financed their deficits by borrowing resources from the rest of the world, and have generally paid for them less than their 'opportunity cost'.

Moreover, admitting the Community to the money-issuing function would give the countries and regions concerned a better assurance, while national money and capital markets remain fragmented and largely sheltered by restrictive attitudes and by administrative controls of one sort or another, that the means needed for regionally differentiated demand management would be forthcoming. If Europe's economies are only semi-integrated, they need differentiated policies also for stabilisation purposes. Since monetary and credit instruments have been and are *magna*

[1] In addition to profit from monopoly power, seigniorage *lato sensu* may also imply gains which are more akin to a pure economic rent. For a discussion on the nature of seigniorage and the problem of its distribution, see Grubel ([13] pp. 269-82).

pars of stabilisation policies, the creation and management of a common currency must discriminate *sub specie regionis*. It must take into account regional differentiation in the pressure of demand and prevent restriction in the regions where it would be inappropriate. This would normally be done by the Multi-role European Bank extending rediscount facilities to banks financing economic activity in the regions eligible for such special assistance. In addition the M.E.B. would extend credit to firms and their plants, as well as to local authorities, in the said regions. To that end, it would also finance itself, subject to certain provisos, through the issue of the common currency.

The main proviso is that the Community would have to set the benefits of attaining a less uneven pattern of utilisation of resources, as between regional groupings, against the cost of upsetting overall equilibrium, whenever the specific constellation of circumstances made the trade-off necessary. Clearly, caution would commend itself in circumstances such as the present ones, when fighting inflation is the overriding need. If we instead had to face a situation in which there was a production gap even in the high-activity regions and inflation had been generally subdued, caution would have to make way for boldness.

What is required is the definition and implementation of a European money-supply policy. This is postulated by integration itself and cannot be avoided without having exchange-rate changes play too great a role in the adjustment process to be compatible with monetary integration. The issues of European currency on one side, the increases in national money supply on the other, would have to be regulated concomitantly, within the framework of a unified money-supply policy. This, as with any policy which aims at high levels of employment, makes tolerances smaller; it may therefore require more sharply defined targets and a more precise dosage, but it need not lead to inflation.

Old precepts of the technical orthodoxy, such as the separation of short- and long-term credit, which is in any case already blurred in the spectrum of assets held by some central banks and commercial banking systems, appear in the light of post-war experiences as no more than tactical foxholes in the fight against inflation. The consensus about the cost-push nature of inflation implies that money is no longer the chief igniter of inflationary processes and that the latter's roots stretch beyond monetary techniques and policies. If inflation is largely a by-product, as it were, of the fight between organised groups, some aiming at changing, others at retaining, the current pattern of distribution of wealth and income, of accumulation and consumption, of private goods' consumption as against that of public goods, of social concentration of power and of regional polarisation of economic activity, then inflation will in a meaningful sense be doomed to the extent that less disruptive means are found, and accepted, for settling these issues as they arise in the public conscience.

We should be aware of this when setting about to create Europe's money. And we should not shrink from the task even at the risk of being or appearing partisan. For even if partisan-ship will not always be accompanied by exciting theoretical advances, it is sometimes necessary to foster great causes.

Steps to Establish the New European Currency

In speculating about the impact which the issue of a European currency might have on the Community's overall equilibrium, it must be pointed out that the implementation of these pro-posals would simply mean that the principle of a link between monetary unification and the process of growth would be recognised, and a mechanism put in place to carry out policies consistent with that principle. But the actual issues of European currency, and the part of them which would be devoted to operations in favour of the weaker regions, would be decided periodically on the basis of criteria which are likely to be restric-tive. Not only on substantive grounds will there be reluctance to authorise the creation of claims on real resources, which cannot be presented for redemption by the countries accepting them as payment for their net exports, but also the technical difficulties connected with having a new currency accepted may make it necessary to lean towards restrictiveness.

To help a currency to come into its own, its supply must be regulated in direct ratio to its usefulness. There is a relation between availability and usefulness that, although not easily lending itself to quantification in each specific case, is a con-dition for money to fulfil its role efficiently. The issuing of a European currency therefore presupposes the creation of a demand for it, the latter depending in its turn on the uses for which it will be eligible. In principle, the European currency should be eligible for any use; the fewer the restrictions placed on it, the greater its 'moneyness', which essentially implies unimpaired power and convenience of disposal over an asset, in exchange for any other (physical and financial) asset.[1]

Thus the 'shiftability' from national currencies into the European currency, and from the latter back into the former, should be unimpaired. Because there are some restrictions on the use of the dollar by E.E.C. residents, which are likely to be reinforced as a result of the recent crisis, the European currency would on this score be better placed vis-à-vis what will be its most formidable competitor. If holdings of European currency can be used more freely than the dollar in intra-Community payments, and in payments with third countries, there will be a demand on the part of those involved in international transactions for building up such holdings.

Moreover, its use might be enhanced, as suggested in the report of the Federal Trust Study Group (see Appendix) in such ways as having member countries' governments accept it for payment of taxes, and issuing part of the national debt denominated in the European currency.

Its use by large industrial and commercial companies might be further encouraged through some financial inducement to invoice in European currency. One such inducement might be the availability of forward cover on more convenient terms than

[1] As Machlup has pointed out, no rule tends to reduce within countries the moneyness of national currencies; the legal-tender device has in fact been invented in order to foster it. Controls over money have been sought by restricting the discretionary power of central banks through provisos such as a minimum gold (and/or foreign exchange) holding ratio to bank-notes in circulation (and/or deposits). Minimum reserve ratios are also needed for *external* payments: 'For interbank payments in the same country, the assets (amounts, quality, composition, liquidity) of the national reserve bank are irrelevant; they become relevant only for payments to persons or banks in other countries, that is, for *international payments*' ([27] p. 343). Similarly, for the proposed European currency, the question of the backing would be relevant in respect of the Community's external payments position. But the fact that the M.E.B. would also have on the asset side of its balance sheet claims arising from the financing of approved projects in the weaker regions, would not make of the European currency a sort of 'funny money'. The absence of restrictions on its use and the regulation of its supply in relation to demand with a view to the Community's overall equilibrium, are much more important to its moneyness.

would be available for national currencies. In other words, an appropriate forward exchange-rate policy might be part of the process of getting the European currency established.

To start with, it might be expedient to select in an 'automatic' fashion companies and other users best equipped to deal in a new currency by issuing only large-denomination notes. The shift to smaller denominations would be regulated in correspondence with the ability and willingness of new classes of users to deal in it. Ultimately, the European currency, as already pointed out, should be available for any user and any use, including the payment of wages and salaries. As long as the E.E.C. remained a multi-currency area, workers would be entitled to hold the European currency so received, or freely to convert all or part of it, as they wished, into national currencies. The payment in European rather than in national money would be just another factor among the many which enter into their calculations when they decide to take up a job.

The European currency would be used in the tourist trade at a relatively early stage. An unpleasant phenomenon accompanying exchange-rate flexibility is the inconvenience generally caused to tourists, as recent experience has shown. This may subside as flexibility becomes a more routine state of affairs. But even in the case of the limited and regulated intra-group flexibility which has been proposed here, the possible inconvenience to tourists would represent a drawback. This drawback could be largely eliminated through use of the European currency. Tour operators and important tourist establishments would quote their prices in European currency and use the same when making contracts with their clients. The cost of exchange-rate changes would still have to be borne; but at least its allocation between the two parties to the contract would take place in conditions of better equality in bargaining strength than when an individual tourist in a foreign country has to defend himself against the tendency of firms involved in money exchange so often to overrate the actual exchange risk and increase excessively the margin between the buying and selling rates.[1]

---

[1] Mundell has suggested that the 'Bank of Europe could also issue a paper currency of one or two denominations, not to replace the national currencies (which can retain their position), but to compete with the U.S. dollar, as now used by tourists and travellers throughout Europe' ([30] p. 23).

It will be difficult for a new European money to be of any great use to industry and trade and to replace an external currency as the Community's currency, unless it becomes fully acceptable in the private money and capital markets. To achieve this, more positive steps will be needed than the permissive attitude taken vis-à-vis the development of the Euro-dollar market, which borrowed the dominant world currency as its monetary unit. The M.E.B. would have to stand by as lender of last resort for claims denominated in European currency; it would thus extend rediscount facilities to banks operating in that currency.

One should also envisage the possibility of a start being made by using the European currency for intra-Community official settlements. Monetary union cannot be achieved without creating internal sources of liquidity; *the provision of Community liquidity is an essential part of the process of monetary unification.* Here the approach must be two-pronged. On private money and capital markets, Community-wide negotiability of more and more categories of national monetary and financial claims should be sought in order to facilitate the market settlement of payments imbalances, which would otherwise result in increased 'official' deficits and surpluses. In fact, what we need is to carry further and put beyond any doubt as to reversibility a process which has been going on for years in the wider international context. As Baffi noted a few years ago:

> The international money market is thus acquiring the character of a market in reserve money, in the larger sense that money flows take over in part the function performed by official reserves and in the stricter sense that official foreign exchange is channelled to it in various ways. . . .
> . . . An international market for reserve money fulfils the function of collectively assessing the credit worthiness of individual banks and countries, and meeting their needs, with greater flexibility than institutions like the Monetary Fund where available facilities are somewhat rigidly linked to individual quotas. Accordingly, the market reduces more effectively the need for owned reserves. . . . ([2] p. 20)

For such official settlements as would still be necessary, one must envisage, as part of the formation of monetary union, the creation of union official liquidity. In the next essay we shall see what arrangements have been made for intra-Community settlements coincidentally with the narrowing of the margins of fluctuation of intra-group exchange rates. Those arrangements as such are not conducive to integration, and I have suggested some steps that might be taken to increase the role of European currencies in intra-European payments.

Here I wish to point out that a mechanism of official settlements, with a larger role for a truly European element in it, might be the first step towards establishing the common European currency in one of its functions.

A Case for European S.D.R.s?

The foregoing suggests that a European currency might emerge in the first instance as an asset somewhat similar in character and function to the Special Drawing Rights. Even in this primordial form it should be possible to link currency unification to a Community policy of balanced growth, just as for the S.D.R.s the proposal has been made that their issues should be 'linked' to the supply of additional external finance to developing countries.

I am not suggesting, however, that the Community should encourage the creation of European S.D.R.s as such. This would not commend itself; at least not on psychological grounds, as such initiative might be seen as rivalling a world-wide arrangement still too weak to resist competition by the offshoot of a more homogeneous regional grouping.[1]

On the other hand, it would also be wrong to view in that

[1] Ossola has suggested that a European reserve fund should issue European units of reserve, which would gradually evolve into an intervention currency. The latter 'would have an intermediate character between S.D.R.s held only by monetary authorities and the dollar (held by monetary authorities, commercial banks, and private holders). The new instrument would circulate, at least in the beginning, only among monetary authorities and commercial banks. . . . This process of formation of an intervention currency might be considered unnatural in so far as it does not follow the traditional route, namely, of being first used by commercial operators, and held by commercial banks before being included in the reserves of central banks. In this connection, however, one should not forget that the process of S.D.R. formation was at first also considered unnatural' . . . ([31] p. 14).

light a European initiative of the type I have hinted at – if it did eventuate. Not only because the new European settlement asset and the S.D.R.s would differ in many technical aspects, but also because the potentialities of the former, comprising as they would the functions of a market currency, would go far beyond what is envisaged for the S.D.R.s.[1] To object to a European initiative on the grounds that it would not be compatible with a world arrangement for man-made reserve assets would be as if the formation of a customs union, among countries having political unification as their ultimate objective, were to be barred because it implies discrimination vis-à-vis non-members.

Whatever the technical profile, there is a perhaps weightier negative attitude which has to be overcome in order to pave the way for a truly European mechanism of settlements. Para-doxically, that attitude is rooted in the successful experience which the Europeans made during the 1950s with a regional payments system. Though successful, the experience was forced upon them by a condition of weakness, since their output was not able to compete with dollar goods; there was a shortage of dollars, hence the need to economise them. But regional pay-ments arrangements are not necessarily a cure for weakness; they can be made from strength as well – and this would be the case with the E.E.C. today. E.E.C. countries cannot be said to suffer from a serious shortage of reserves; they do follow trade policies less than liberal by normal world standards; nor do they appear not to observe standards of monetary discipline distinctly lower than those prevailing in the main competing non-member countries (and the performance on this score would be bound to improve as a result of the measures of harmonisation suggested above). Therefore a regional payments mechanism, which made larger use of the European national currencies or, what is relevant here, implied yearly allocations of a common European currency *in nuce*, should not be equated with an option for softness.

---

[1] However, in the I.M.F. report on the reform of the international monetary system, which was published after I had completed the type-script and handed it in to the publishers, one reads: 'It is not suggested at this stage that the holdings of S.D.R.s should move beyond the official circle: private holdings of and private transactions in S.D.R.s are, however, seen as a possible development for the more distant future' ([19] p. 39).

Of course, there are differences in the overall performances of the various European countries; as a result, some currencies are weaker than others. But is that a reason for rejecting an 'internal' reserve asset, if then the alternatives imply for the time being the accumulation of the liabilities of a third country (in a still weaker payments position)?

The answer must be in the negative in so far as there is a well-founded perspective of the Community being in overall external surplus vis-à-vis third countries, while following a liberal trade policy externally. That being so, surplus member countries would not have to accumulate *de facto* inconvertible claims vis-à-vis other members and be prevented from buying in third countries the goods essential to their efficiency and well-being, as would happen if imports had to be curbed in order to balance the external payments of the Community as a whole. This should be borne clearly in mind when appraising the risks that the low-inflation propensity countries fear to take by joining forces and pooling resources with their high-inflation-propensity partners. A guarantee against those risks is represented, under normal circumstances, by the external constraint. And if circumstances are such that the balance of trade and payments with third countries tends in fact to add to inflationary pressures internally, this means that the Community would still offer countries with a low N.P.I. a better general monetary environment and more chances of protecting themselves from inflation.

Indeed, low-inflation-propensity countries would, as members of the Community, be far better placed to fight inflationary impulses originating from outside; for as such there would no longer be the disproportion with the United States economy, and the supply of goods, services and financial capital which it can generate. This presupposes that few member countries would 'technically' be in a position to impose an anti-inflationary stance all round in the Community – which is not a risky assumption to make. The level of interest rates in the Community as a whole would very likely follow the lead given by the countries with a low N.P.I., which are very often quick to raise interest-rates as a means to fight inflation. Of course, one would have to allow for policy harmonisation as it gained effectiveness; and it is possible that in the process of harmonisation *excesses* are avoided which would do substantial damage to the regions. But market forces will tend in the first instance to generalise an interest-rate rise initiated by banks and other financial intermediaries in the low-N.P.I. countries. Under full freedom of capital movements, it would be vain to attempt to resist upward pressures of interest rates coming from a few member countries (if at least one major one is among them). It would be wrong to extrapolate the experience made in the last few years by the European countries in respect of United States monetary policies. The frustrations which have accompanied that experience have been due to the disproportion with the size of the United States economy. They were also due to the institutionalised dominant position of the dollar which, as things stood, was accepted more or less automatically for international settlements, at least up to the summer of 1971, lest a major international crisis were precipitated. But within the E.E.C. no such disproportion would play; the issues of the common currency would be regulated collectively; the ability to make payments, both private and official, through transfers of claims in national currencies would find its counterpart in the limitation of the power to create those claims. As pointed out in the first essay, central banks would have to behave more like commercial banks.

The foregoing suggests two main points. First, while member countries are in a strong payments position and such strength is expected to last, it will be easier to set in motion the process of monetary unification. Governments may after all give up their resistance to commit themselves, if low-N.P.I. countries do not have reason to fear that unification would mainly mean creating a hand-out mechanism for countries in balance-of-payments difficulties, and countries with a high N.P.I. feel that the constraints of monetary union need not be too severe while they are in surplus.

Second, it would appear that competition would be strongest among existing currencies. The currency of a low-N.P.I. country, which also tended to have high interest rates, might exert attraction strong enough to react on the habits of traders, savers, institutional investors and others in high-N.P.I. countries. In other words, *Gresham's Law would apply in reverse, the more stable currencies tending to eliminate the depreciating ones.*

However, it is more likely, given the inertia of those habits, that no dramatic shift would take place. If such a shift did threaten, it would be resisted by national authorities; so that, were interest rates high in the more stable currencies, they would tend to be higher still in the high-N.P.I. countries. The argument in favour of this is that, where prices are rising faster, a higher nominal rate is necessary in order to equalise returns in real terms. On the other hand, the narrowness of parity changes permitted under the system previously outlined would not need large interest-rate differentials; these will shrink as the scope for exchange-rate movements is reduced in accordance with the agreed plan, and as integration of the national markets advances.

At any rate, the introduction of a common European currency would not add to the problems. Its parity would be on a median course in respect of the national currencies, so that the interest-rate level, which the depreciating countries would have to maintain, would not as a rule be higher than as postulated by the level of interest rates in appreciating countries. Moreover, as illustrated in the first essay, the existence of a common currency is likely to facilitate payment adjustments in other respects. If it is earnestly feared that a new currency might quickly dislodge some of the existing national currencies, then there would be even stronger reasons for fearing competition by the currencies of high-activity countries with a low inflation propensity – unless, of course, one is prepared to backslide as concerns freedom of intra-E.E.C. circulation of capital, which would come very close to giving up monetary union itself.

REFERENCES

[1] ALEXANDER, S. S., 'Effects of Devaluation on a Trade Balance', *International Monetary Fund Staff Papers*, vol. II (1952).

[2] BAFFI, P., 'Western European Inflation and the Reserve Currencies', *Banca Nazionale del Lavoro Quarterly Review*, no. 94 (Mar 1968).

[3] BECKERMAN, W., 'Projecting Europe's Growth', *Economic Journal* (Dec 1962).

134   EUROPEAN MONETARY UNIFICATION

[4] CAMPOLONGO, A., 'L'Indirizzo Economico Regionale e la Comunità Europea', *Rivista di Politica Economica* (Dec 1970).

[5] CARLI, G., 'Improving the International Adjustment Process: Some Proposals', in *Convertibility, Multilateralism and Freedom: Essays in Honour of Reinhard Kamitz* (Springer Verlag, Wien–New York 1972).

[6] COOPER, R. N., *Currency Devaluations in Developing Countries*, Essays in International Finance, no. 86 (International Finance Section, Princeton University, June 1971).

[7] CORDEN, W. M., *Monetary Integration*, Essays in International Finance, no. 93 (International Finance Section, Princeton University, Apr 1972).

[8] E.E.C., *Third General Report on the Activity of the Communities for 1969* (Brussels–Luxembourg, 1970).

[9] EINZIG, P., *The Case against Floating Exchanges* (London: Macmillan, 1970).

[10] FELLNER, W., 'On Limited Exchange-Rate Flexibility' in W. Fellner *et al.*, *Maintaining and Restoring Balance in International Payments* (Princeton U.P., 1966).

[11] GERSCHENKRON, A., *Economic Backwardness in Historical Perspective* (New York: Praeger, 1965).

[12] GIERSCH, H., *Marktintegration, Wechselkurs und Standortstruktur: Fundamentale Fragen künftiger Währungspolitik*, Frankfurter Gespräch der List Gesellschaft (Basle: Kyklos-Verlag; Tübingen: J. B. C. Mohr (Paul Siebeck), 1965).

[13] GRUBEL, H. E., 'The Distribution of Seigniorage from International Liquidity Creation', in R. A. Mundell and A. K. Swoboda (eds.), *Monetary Problems of the International Economy* (Chicago U.P., 1969).

[14] HALM, G. N., *The 'Band' Proposal: The Limits of Permissible Exchange Rate Variations*, Special Paper in International Economics, no. 6 (International Finance Section, Princeton University, Jan 1965).

[15] HARROD, R., *Money* (London: Macmillan, 1969).

[16] HINSHAW, R., 'Elasticity Pessimism, Absorption and Flexible Exchange Rates', in W. Sellekaerts (ed.), *International Trade and Finance; Essays in Honour of Jan Tinbergen* II, (London: Macmillan, 1973).

[17] Hirschman, A. O., *The Strategy of Economic Development* (New Haven: Yale U.P., 1959).

[18] International Monetary Fund, *The Role of Exchange Rates in the Adjustment of International Payments—A Report by the Executive Directors* (Washington, D.C., 1970).

[19] International Monetary Fund, *Reform of the International Monetary System—A Report by the Executive Directors to the Board of Governors* (Washington, D.C., 1972).

[20] Katz, S. I., Branson, W. H., and Willett, T. D., *Exchange Rate System, Interest Rates and Capital Flows*, Essays in International Finance, no. 78 (International Finance Section, Princeton University, Jan 1970).

[21] Lawson, R. W., 'World Currency Problems', remarks by R. W. Lawson, Deputy Governor of the Bank of Canada, to the Economic Society of Alberta, Calgary, 17 Feb 1972 (mimeographed text).

[22] Lever, H., in debate on public expenditure, *Hansard, House of Commons, Daily Parts*, 9 Dec 1971, cols, 1526 ff.

[23] Lösch, A., *Die raümliche Ordnung der Wirtschaft: Eine Untersuchung über Standort, Wirtschaftsgebiete und internationalen Handel* (Jena, Fischer, 1940).

[24] Machlup, F., 'Elasticity Pessimism in International Trade', *Economia Internazionale*, vol. III, no. 1 (Feb 1950).

[25] Machlup, F., 'Relative Prices and Aggregate Spending in the Analysis of Devaluation', *American Economic Review*, vol. XLV (1955).

[26] Machlup, F., 'The Terms of Trade Effects of Devaluation upon Real Income and the Balance of Trade', *Kyklos*, vol. IX, no. 4 (1956).

[27] Machlup, F., 'The Cloakroom Rule of International Reserves: Reserve Creation and Resources Transfer', *Quarterly Journal of Economics*, vol. LXXIX (Aug 1965).

[28] Masera, F., *Monetary and Exchange Rate Policy of E.E.C. Countries* (Tilburg: Société Universitaire Européenne de Recherches Financières, 1972).

[29] Meade, J. E., 'Exchange Rate Flexibility', *Three Banks Review*, no. 70 (June 1966).

[30] Mundell, R. A., 'World Inflation and the Eurodollar', *Note Economiche, Monte dei Paschi di Siena* (Mar-Apr, 1971).

[31] Ossola, R., *Towards New Monetary Relationships*, Essays in International Finance, no. 87 (International Finance Section, Princeton University, July 1971).

[32] Richardson, H. W., *Elements of Regional Economics* (Harmondsworth: Penguin Books, 1969).

[33] Tagliacarne, G., 'The Italian Regions and the Recession: Method and the Use of Regional Indicators of the Cyclical Trend', *Review of the Economic Conditions in Italy* (Banco di Roma, Mar 1972).

[34] Triffin, R., 'How to Arrest a Threatening Relapse into 1930's?', *Bulletin de la Banque Nationale de Belgique* (Nov 1971).

[35] Tsiang, S. C., 'The Role of Money in Trade-Balance Stability: Synthesis of the Elasticity and Absorption Approaches', *American Economic Review*, vol. LI (Dec 1961).

[36] Weber, A., *Über den Standort der Industrien* (Tübingen, J.C.B. Mohr, 1909).

[37] Williamson, J. H., *The Crawling Peg*, Essays in International Finance, no. 50 (International Finance Section, Princeton University, Dec 1965).

4 Towards a European Money and Capital Market

A FEATURE of the rehabilitation of Western Europe's currencies after the Second World War was that, nearly up to the end of the 1950s, monetary and financial integration trailed behind trade integration. The tendency was to liberalise payments only to the extent implied by the measures of trade liberalisation.

The two main steps taken to free payments were the establishment of the European Payments Union in 1950 and the declaration of external convertibility at the end of 1958; both aimed at eliminating controls, bilateralism and discrimination mainly in payments arising in connection with trade and service transactions.

But after 1958 quick progress was made to free payments not directly linked to trade. In fact, criticism is often voiced today to the effect that liberalisation of capital movements was pushed too far – farther than implied by the Bretton Woods construction. With the tight separation of money and capital markets nearly a quarter of a century behind us, the massive movements of capital which in the last few years have finally made untenable currency parities that had anyhow become unrealistic, have led many to the conclusion that the drawbacks of freedom of circulation outweigh the gains.

But how can one visualise the choice of a policy of capital retrenchment while Western European economies were growing at a pace which was faster, smoother and more sustained over time than ever before in our epoch? The fences surrounding national money and capital markets were originally built during, and because of, the Great Depression. After the Second World War, on what grounds could one have justified sticking to controls in a context of growth which has had one of its mainsprings in the process of economic integration? Foreign trade has increased at an annual rate which is about twice as high as the rate of growth of output in Western Europe. Could this growth of trade have been achieved if tighter controls had been applied to make sure that the allocations of foreign exchange would actually be spent on imports; that exports would not be under-invoiced and imports over-invoiced; that credit terms would not be varied so as to turn the leads and lags, between payments and shipments, against a weak or suspected currency? To be sure, controls have been resorted to by some countries; but they have remained isolated episodes. They have not invited similar retaliatory measures by other countries, given the understanding that they would be done away with as soon as adjustment policies showed results. The point here is whether a generalised, more comprehensive and stricter application of administrative controls would not have suffocated the expansion of international trade.

Furthermore, could output have continued for so long to grow at so fast a rate had there not been a constant effort to secure an efficient allocation of resources, which capital movements are, in principle, instrumental in achieving internationally? Since a number of companies with important international operations and commitments happen to have their headquarters in small countries, and a substantial part of the owned capital of their subsidiaries abroad has to be provided by the parent company, how would their growth not have been checked (and that of less efficient producers elsewhere not subsidised) if international long-term finance had not been available? How could the Netherlands have closed the gap between the possibilities offered by domestic savings formation and the capital requirements of Royal Dutch Shell, Unilever, Philips and other Dutch companies catering for the needs of world markets?

Europe and the Euro-dollar

A key element in the explanation of the birth of Euro-currency markets and their expansion over many years is the quest for efficiency: efficiency in channelling the funds, with which the banks are entrusted, to countries, sectors and firms able to obtain the highest return on capital; efficiency in tapping new sources of savings, in devising and testing new borrowing instruments and lending techniques, in tailoring financial facilities to the size and nature of the needs of giant multi-national enterprises.

The short-term business in Euro-currencies sprang mainly from the urge to give foreign lending and borrowing a new international dimension. Euro-currency operations, although involving the granting of credit, were originated and are still carried out by the foreign-exchange departments of banks.[1] Foreign-exchange markets are in essence international. In order to work smoothly and efficiently they need a common denominator. They therefore tend to reinforce the role of a currency that is free from restrictions, widely based, generally accepted and in plentiful (but possibly not inflated) supply. They found it in the United States dollar, which possessed these qualities of international moneyness to a degree higher than any other currency. Moreover, it promised to maintain them for a long time, being backed by the country with the largest production potential, a technological and managerial lead, a dominant position in the world economy. That position, due also to the fact that in many ways it had been institutionalised by post-war monetary arrangements, seemed likely to outlive a productive decline relative to other industrialised countries, at least in so far as it proved temporary.

The same reasons explain why the pursuit of competitive efficiency did not lead to a solution based on a wider use of European currencies. London's merchant banks turned to the dollar as a means for carrying on their traditional role in the international money and capital market, because in 1957 the use of sterling acceptance credits for the financing of trade between non-sterling area countries was restricted. Ironically, at that very time the Bank of England, in the memorandum of evidence it submitted to the Radcliffe Committee, commented on the international role of sterling as follows:

[1] As is well known, the ability, not typical of those departments, to appraise customers' creditworthiness is one of the causes for concern as to the soundness of the Euro-markets.

The banking connections, branch establishments, agencies and correspondents which spread outwards to all parts of the world with this development of British trade provided the most widespread and convenient machinery of international payments between third countries outside the immediate British connection. And, backing this installed equipment of banking facilities throughout the world, the unrivalled credit facilities of London combined with the international produce markets, ship chartering markets, insurance facilities and general merchanting resources of Great Britain to enable international business to be transacted in sterling with the minimum of delay and expense. This remains the essential basis of sterling's position as an international currency to this day. ([11] p. 16)

While the United Kingdom's repeated balance-of-payments crises have made a retreat from the international role of sterling practically unavoidable, the Continental European countries, whose growth has been for the most part of the post-war period export-led, had the resource surplus but lacked adequate infra-structure and experience. Those who might have been better placed to take on an important role did not show the inclination to do so; partly, at least, this was due to the justified awareness that no European country could, alone, take in its stride the role of banker to the world – or even just to Europe. As a result of the inability of Europe to offer a solution of its own for building an optimal-size money and capital market, which as far as industrial countries are concerned was and is primarily a Euro-pean problem, the group of countries that has been growing fastest and increasing its share of world trade has had to rely on the monetary and financial intermediation of a country whose competitiveness and whose weight in world trade and output have been declining.

Clearly, these divergent developments have been a factor in the tensions and jolts of the international monetary system in the last twelve years or so. But the outcome would have been worse still had not another currency – in the event the dollar – been available for taking over from sterling; world trade would very probably have been hit by the sources of finance becoming less easily accessible, scarcer and dearer.

As banks in London and elsewhere drifted into transacting business in dollars on a regular basis, they needed to replenish their stock of dollars. They did so by bidding for dollar deposits, in competition with American banks, which in the United States were restricted by Regulation Q as to the interest rates they can pay on deposits. Interest-rate rigidity gave a strong boost to dollar deposit trading outside the United States – just as the rigidity of interest rates on loans in Italian lire sent the Italian banks in the early 1950s bidding for deposits in foreign currencies, which they could re-lend to residents at more competitive rates than those laid down in the inter-bank cartel. By switching to the dollar at a critical juncture, European banks were able to continue to play their traditional role in international banking. If the dollar was in actual fact the only practical proposition left for international lending in connection with trade and investment, *then to 'adopt' the dollar was the only way for non-American banks to get a share of the business and thereby prevent a monopoly by the banks of the country issuing the vehicle currency.*

Indeed, the permissive attitude which monetary authorities have maintained for a good many years vis-à-vis the Euro-dollar is explained, among other things, by their interest in letting their banking systems break out of the relegation into which the fragmentation of national markets, through a multiplicity of currencies and regulations, tended to push them. To reach that aim, individually they had to allow communication *at some specific points* between the national and the international market (thereby establishing contact with other national markets too); collectively, they abstained from encroaching on banks' Euro-operations, which came to be considered as a sort of no-man's-land.

Since market rigidities and official controls have not permeated the Euro-market's precinct, the competitiveness of that market and the flexibility of the facilities offered have attained an unparalleled strength. This in turn has strengthened its attraction, especially since the adoption of exchange-control measures has restricted the use of resources raised in the United States and downgraded the American market, large though it is, to the position of a local pool of finance. Thus the Euro-dollar has become during the 1960s freer than the dollar itself and has been able to fulfil a function for which the United States dollar was no longer fit. The Euro-dollar has become the only real global source of finance for the large national and multi-national companies.

Attractions of the Euro-dollar compromise

Moreover, the Euro-market created new opportunities for adding to the flexibility of national monetary and credit policies. Italy is an outstanding example in this respect. The regulation of the size and direction of the flow of funds has been used virtually in lieu of typical instruments of monetary policy. When the balance of payments has been in deficit, banks have been allowed to build up an external net debtor position, which they have been helped to reverse through the provision of dollars by the Italian exchange office, on a swap basis, when payments have swung into surplus. In the words of Governor Carli: 'The flow of funds between the national and foreign markets has been regulated by granting or denying banks the option to take up a net debtor or creditor position with foreign countries. The relative authorisations have had effects resembling variations in the refinancing margins granted by the central bank, and changes in the compulsory reserves' [6]. Thus communications between the national banking system and the Euro-market have been an instrument of monetary policy, rather than leading to loss of control over domestic money and credit conditions. It has demanded a remarkable amount of skill to operate a system 'open in terms of competition, and closed in terms of monetary policy'. Again, in the Governor's words: 'The many instances of intervention have always been dominated by the need to maintain the spur of competition and of integration with foreign countries in the matter of bank financing, while ensuring that the autonomy of the internal monetary policy is not impaired by movements of bank funds to and from foreign countries' [6].

The German monetary authorities have also pursued a very active policy, whose main aims were to undo the undesired consequences of a stabilisation policy which in the last few years has been more than any other at variance with the inflationary trend in the dominating economy – and to keep the domestic markets free from administrative controls. They have encouraged the outflow of funds generated by the balance-of-payments surplus in order to ease the inflationary pressures arising, on the monetary side, from that surplus. Throughout the period, the German central bank has made extensive resort to swap transactions with commercial banks which have had the effect of affording exporters of funds forward exchange cover at a cheaper cost than current market rates. (The condition that swap dollars should be invested in U.S. Treasury bills was dropped in November 1967, so that thereafter they were mostly channelled to the Euro-market.)

Eventually central banks undertook themselves and/or through the Bank for International Settlements operations on the Euro-dollar market. They were motivated on occasions such as end-of-year window-dressing by the need to maintain orderly conditions in a market which in the meantime had become too important to be left to itself. But along with the operations carried out through the national commercial banks, direct interventions were also made for reserve-management purposes. Given the increasing size of the dollar component in the reserves, the weakening of the United States exchange and payments position, and American policies biased against high rates of interest even in a context of rapidly rising prices, reserves have had to be managed in large surplus countries more and more with a touch of window-dressing skill in order to minimise adverse economic (and political) reactions internally.

Moreover, countries which kept their dollar holdings in the United States market, where interest rates were not high enough to secure a fair return on capital, plus an extra margin for recouping losses in purchasing power, in actual fact were having their national communities short-changed. Thus aside from the exchange risk, which eventually became the dominant pre-occupation, exchange-reserve policy could not ignore the need for making good, through a higher yield, the loss in real terms due to price rises.

The ready alternative to the unremunerative national market of the reserve currency was afforded by the Euro-dollar market, with its broad range of opportunities and with an interest-sensitiveness tending to mirror more closely the inflationary expansion of demand for loan funds. Had there been no such alternative, the absorption by the rest of the world of the United States balance-of-payments deficits would perhaps have been

F

accompanied by still stronger tensions than those actually witnessed.

The Euro-dollar system has developed and worked for a number of years to the reasonable satisfaction of the parties concerned. The size of the market was only $1 billion in 1959 (the first year for which an estimate is available), but only a few years later it had grown to represent a sizeable fraction of the money supply of the major Western European countries. Up to 1967 growth, however vigorous, meant adding to the Euro-currency pool the equivalent of a few billion dollars. But from about $17 billion at the end of that year, the market's size jumped to $71 billion at the end of 1971, according to estimates published in the Annual Reports of the B.I.S.

The growth of the Euro-currency market by leaps and bounds since 1968 has been partly due to the working of the deposit multiplier mechanism, which central banks have in fact been feeding by redepositing with the Euro-banks the dollars entering their countries, largely as a result of Euro-dollar borrowing.[1]

It should be clear, however, that European dollar multiplication follows from the adoption of the dollar as the international and European money. As no existing European currency was in a position to discharge that duty, and Europe was unable to give itself a new common currency, the adoption of the dollar represented a compromise solution (which for several years has also been found acceptable in terms of power politics, at a time when international monetary policy has frequently been used for political aims). If, in order to overcome its monetary fragmentation, Europe had to import the monetary standard, it at least succeeded in retaining on its territory the centre of short-term international lending. Eventually, it also succeeded in recapturing international medium- and long-term financing business, where the strong dependence on the United States capital market up to the introduction of the interest equalisation tax

[1] Friedman contributed a few years ago a clear analysis of the process of deposit creation on the Euro-dollar market [24]. Earlier, Klopstock had pointed out that 'the Euro-dollar expansion process is in theory similar to the one that is familiar in the creation of credit in the United States'. But he thought multiple expansion to be quite limited because of the leakages from the system being (still) very large [29]. More recently, Machlup has forcefully drawn attention to what he calls 'artificial creation of dollar reserves' by central banks ([33] p. 163).

in 1963 meant that the European markets were joined to one another through New York, rather than directly. In fact, there was a drift towards the transmigration of financial operations to New York, where an increasing number of European suppliers and demanders of capital would be matched.[1]

The attraction of this compromise solution was that the Euro-dollar is 'detached from the dollar in space and from Europe in currency' ([28], p. 177). It implied, in fact if not in form, that Europe would share in the power of dollar creation; Europe's holdings of dollars, arising out of the United States balance-of-payments deficits which it ultimately had to absorb, were fraught with problems but, by having grown so large, finally presented European banks with the opportunity to create dollar deposits roughly in the same way as American banks do. Of course, the Euro-system has not been as closed as it is normal for a national commercial banking system to be. But as the Euro-markets expanded, diversified, networked across national frontiers and successfully competed against traditional international money business, more and more leakages were plugged. Furthermore, while the potential of deposit multiplication out of a given monetary base is limited in national banking systems by reserve requirements, no such curb applies to Euro-dollar creation.

True, Euro-banks did not and do not have access to the rediscount facilities of the Federal Reserve System. But the foreign branches of United States banks have (more or less) automatic access to the facilities of their American head offices; and as to non-American Euro-banks, there are enough central banks of countries participating in the Euro-dollar system which were and are bursting with dollars. Once the Euro-market had become the channel of international banking business, including the financing of international trade, would not national dollar reserves be held also in order to back that market?

[1] In a United States report on the subject, it was noted *inter alia* that 'The failure of most European markets to absorb new foreign security issues in significant amounts stands in marked contrast to the extensive participation by Europeans in foreign lending through the New York market. Information on such participation is incomplete, but in some past years as much as one half, or even more, of European bonds publicly issued in the United States (as distinct from private placements) were purchased by Europeans themselves' ([39] p. 32).

I have throughout felt that the dangers attributable to the absence of a 'lender of last resort' have been over-emphasised. And not just because such a lender has not been absent after all, but mainly because it was unrealistic to visualise a situation in which such massive dollar injections from outside would be needed to prevent the Euro-markets from drying up, that the reserves of the Euro-system (including those held by participating central banks) would not suffice. This view was based on the awareness that there could be no American interest in starving the Euro-market of dollars (except perhaps as was needed to prevent undermining confidence in the dollar itself). In a situation in which there was an overall excess demand of dollars, such as would require the intervention of a lender of last resort, the United States by supplying dollars would merely be performing a technical function. Given the role attained by the dollar in the 1960's, there is a world demand for dollars, which is generated by transfers of real resources and financial assets among countries other than the United States. Therefore, increasing the supply of dollars does not automatically increase foreign claims on United States resources, as it practically did in the years of the huge American surpluses on trade and services account, when the supply of dollars had to be rationed in order to check the drain abroad of United States resources. Nowadays, by meeting a demand for dollars, the United States would instead be playing the role of dominant bankers to the rest of the world: not supplying real resources themselves, but the monetary and financial intermediation services needed to make resources move around the globe. It was therefore more plausible to expect, as in the case of an ordinary bank, disturbances arising not from a refusal of the bank to ensure continuance and expansion of its services to worthy customers, but if anything from the latter who would grow restive at the bank getting overstretched and thereby debasing the standard of value – its own and its customers.[1]

[1] At any rate, for years the market has functioned quite smoothly, with only a relatively modest amount of official assistance coming from the Bank for International Settlements, assisted by the Federal Reserve Bank of New York and the Swiss National Bank. Also, the operations which the German and Italian central banks have engaged upon mainly for reasons of domestic policy have on the whole had a stabilising effect on the market. Thus a recent study by the Bank of England could conclude that 'Although

Europe's Monetary Sovereignty and the Euro-dollar

The resilience of the market has proved stronger than expected; in 1971 it was able to overcome the most crucial monetary crisis since the end of the war. Far from shrinking, the Euro-currency market showed overall a new remarkable increase: from $57 billion to $71 billion. The dollar component declined relative to the Deutsche Mark and the Swiss franc. But clearly, there was no run on the Euro-dollar, so that the more plausible hypothesis of disturbances arising from customers' restiveness did not materialise even in the crisis year of 1971.[1]

To paraphrase the trio of United States economists who in 1966 put forward a 'minority view' about the problems of the dollar and world liquidity, in order to prevent the country that plays bank to the rest of the world from pursuing unsuitable policies, there is no need to mount a run on it; and perhaps a run would not even be feasible, except as a short-lived phenomenon. 'The depositors can have their say in less destructive ways, e.g. through participating in the management of the bank

---

periodic disturbances on the foreign exchanges have brought inevitable strains, the Euro-currency market has weathered these pressures with remarkably little disturbance. The only really noticeable impact has been the adjustment of interest rates, sometimes swift, to match the sudden changes in the supply of and demand for funds. The smoothness with which the market has lived through such times is largely due to its breadth and size' ([3] p. 18).

[1] These are some of the comments made in the B.I.S. Annual Report [2] concerning the evolution of the Euro-markets in 1971: 'On the other hand, shaken confidence in the dollar led at times to a demand for Euro-dollar funds for conversion into other currencies, although, on the whole, less evidence of this kind of activity is to be found in the Euro-currency statistics than perhaps might have been expected (p. 149) . . . although it had at times been feared that a dollar crisis such as occurred in 1971 might lead to a run on the Euro-dollar market, in fact nothing of the sort happened. Even during the crisis months there was some flow of dollars to the European banks, and the only lasting trace the developments in the exchange markets seem to have left is an increase in the importance of the non-dollar currencies. Similarly, the quarterly statistics do not lend much support to assertions that the Euro-currency market played a leading role in the exchange market turmoils in 1971 (p. 153). . . . It is worth noting that, in comparison with the potential gains and losses from exchange rate changes, the movement of Euro-dollar rates in 1971 was actually quite modest; this is an indication of the inherent stability of the market' (p. 164).

of last resort or through agreement on the scale of the financial intermediation.'[15]

Professor Kindleberger has been more explicit about this. He has suggested giving the Group of Ten 49 or 51 per cent representation on the Open-Market Committee of the Federal Reserve System. He has also proposed that the Bank for International Settlements, together with the central banks concerned, be put in charge of open-market operations in the Euro-dollar market to determine monetary policy for the West ([28] p. 225).

These proposals would not grant Europe participation in the management of the world's dollar supply. That participation already exists; as pointed out above, it is based on Europe's payments strength and on the market power of the Euro-banks. They would grant a measure of formal recognition to that participation, but it is open to question whether doing it in the way suggested by Kindleberger would help to second or frustrate Europe's present assertiveness in international monetary affairs.

Moreover, the problem is not so much one of giving Europe a sort of double monetary citizenship, as one of policies. Is a unified money-supply policy, which in the end means one common interest rate and credit policy, appropriate on both sides of the Atlantic? The question could be answered in the affirmative only if they comprised an optimum currency area. This does not appear to be the case when one looks at economic trends in the United States and Europe.[1]

The lack of synchronism in the cycle and the varying degree of success in mastering the adjustment process are not the result

---

[1] Up to the mid-1950s there were no appreciable discrepancies in the cycle between the two sides of the Atlantic, mainly because the economic cycle was dominated by the United States. The European economies were not strong enough to develop a cycle of their own; they behaved rather as the vulnerable outer appendix of the dominant economy. But the passive synchronisation with U.S. cyclical trends was broken in the second half of the 1950s. In 1957 the United States economy went into recession, while Europe continued prevalently to experience boom conditions. The following year the cyclical positions of both the United States and Europe were reversed. Again, in the first half of the 1960s Europe enjoyed mostly boom conditions, while the United States had a problem of unused capacity. The discrepancies grew larger in the second half of the 1960s.

of defective policy harmonisation. They point to the fact that the economies themselves possess a different vulnerability to inflationary or deflationary processes and a different capacity to create them; they have a different inflation–unemployment trade-off and a different ability to reconcile stability with growth. If the United States and Europe do not comprise one optimum currency area, a unified money supply and interest-rate policy would be inappropriate; therefore, suggestions and proposals hingeing upon co-ordination of such policies do not have much chance of succeeding.[1]

Frustration in Europe has been generated by the fact that while already in the second half of the 1950s Europe has achieved autonomy vis-à-vis the United States in the trade cycle, monetary and financial autonomy has not yet been recovered.

True, the Euro-dollar has given Europe the power to partici-pate in the process of creation of dollars, but at the same time it has strengthened United States dominance in European monetary affairs. The Euro-dollar has added a new dimension to international banking. It has completely eliminated the exchange risk for United States participants, when they shift from the domestic to the international market. Furthermore, the Euro-dollar segments of national money and capital markets

---

[1] Of course disequilibrating factors are also at work within the (enlarged) E.E.C. I have pointed out in the first essay that past disequilibria between E.E.C. countries appear larger than those with the United States, but that allowance should be made for Europe's different ability to sustain payments deficits. Given their institutionalised monetary dominance, the United States, in order to stop the deficit, did not have to devalue vis-à-vis the Europeans, who 'had' to accept the dollar. But European countries had to devalue if they were running a deficit, since their currencies were not eligible for international or intra-European settlements. In other words European countries, individually, have been in a currency area relationship to the United States to a larger extent than the same could be said to exist among themselves. Only it was not an *optimum* currency area relationship: the Europeans tried to keep their parities pegged to the dollar, but had to accept extra doses of inflation.

This has to be borne in mind when appraising such statements as the following: 'It is an inconvenient fact that the *most severe* trading and financial maladjustments between economies today occur *within* these designated blocks, and not between them. Thus for Britain – and for that matter for France – the biggest payments maladjustment in recent years has been vis-à-vis Germany; in the past five years, the mark has appreciated against the pound by almost 50 per cent' [26].

are linked to one another and to the United States market to an extent not previously experienced.

When a single monetary standard is used, interest-rate differentials quickly bring about arbitrage operations which eliminate them. Large and persistent differentials cannot be maintained without being swamped with funds from outside. The tendency to equalise interest-rate levels throughout the area is much stronger than when the multiplicity of currencies brings into play forward exchange rates. Of course, the adjustment of forward rates as interest-rate differentials change is not instantaneous and automatic. If that were the case, 'in the absence of official intervention to influence forward margins, bank rate changes would be quite incapable of ever influencing movements of funds or of gold resulting from interest arbitrage' ([19] p. 105); so that movements of funds are needed to reach the new equilibrium position, their size depending on a number of factors, including the breadth and size of the forward market. But an adjustment which also takes place through changes in forward exchange rates will as a rule bring about smaller capital movements than if full interest-rate equalisation must be achieved for reaching an equilibrium position. Finally, the intervention of monetary authorities on forward markets, offering cover at par or at preferential rates, has the effect of eliminating or reducing the cushioning normally provided by forward exchange rates at the points where the Euro-market communicates with markets for assets in national currencies.

All this has combined to accentuate monetary interdependence. But given the large disproportion between the United States and Europe, whose weight has been dwarfed by its fragmentation into separate national markets, the interdependence has been lop-sided. Although a multiplicity of factors emanating from the various national markets make themselves felt on the Euro-market, the basic trend of interest rates on Euro-dollars has been dominated by trends in the United States. Europe's national markets have often felt in a magnified fashion the impact of the sharp changes which American monetary policy has undergone since rigidities in the United States have tended to offload domestic tensions, and concentrate adjustment, on the free and competitive Euro-market.

As in the process its size has outgrown that of even the major national markets in Europe, the ability of European countries *for other than the short term* to pursue monetary policies at variance with those of the country that dominates because of the sheer size of the resources which it produces or can mobilise, has been substantially curtailed. This increased monetary dependence, having coincided with Europe's regained strength in the business cycle, has had destabilising effects. This was most dramatically illustrated in the last four years when United States stabilisation policy centred on monetary instruments, causing huge and sudden fluctuations in the supply and demand for funds. The drastically restrictive stance of American policy in 1969 and most of 1970, and the sharp change towards re-expansion thereafter have tended to raise interest rates in Europe when economic activity needed to be stimulated, and exerted a pressure to lower them when 'overheating' had set in. On the whole they have accentuated cyclical swings and weakened the effectiveness of policies pursued in the hope of curbing them.[1]

Europe's Attempts to Recover Monetary Control

Given these mutilations to its monetary sovereignty, it is natural to wonder at Europe's acquiescence. The question has partly been answered in the previous pages. Here it should be noted that the main features of the post-war monetary order were drawn up when Europe's economic and political weight, which

---

[1] Some authors go as far as to regard the Euro-markets as an outgrowth of United States markets, a part of these which, following the internationalisation of the dollar and of the bank infrastructure supporting it, has developed outside American territory. Thus de Lattre has argued that 'because of the outstanding part now played in the Euro-money market by the European branches of United States banks, the market has tended to become a new extension of the American money market, consequently losing some of its originality and independence' [14]. It should be noted, however, that more recently the role of the United States banks' foreign branches in London has tended to decline. Their share in the total of advances to non-residents has dropped from 65 per cent in 1969 to 57 per cent in 1970 and to 51 per cent in 1971. Also, the circle of borrowers tends to enlarge, as new ones are attracted to the market. The B.I.S. has reported that in 1971 there was a net outflow from the United States: about $4 billion were absorbed by the European area; $2·5 billion were rechannelled to the rest of the world. Gross claims on the latter had the most rapid growth, having gone up by $10 billion [2].

had already declined in the inter-war period relative to the extra-European industrial powers, was at its lowest as a result of the ravages wrought by the Second World War. In the last quarter of a century there has been a tendency for the balance to swing back in favour of Europe; but monetary sovereignty has proved slower to recover not only because of the natural inertia which any given *status quo* tends to develop, but also because of Europe's inability to act as one and so provide a viable alternative.

It is comparatively easy to point to the inconsistency of objecting to the limitations to national sovereignty likely to arise from European monetary unification, while accepting those arising from the Euro-dollar system. If the expedient to overcome the separation of national markets by borrowing a common monetary standard from outside has led to the importation of foreign monetary management, why should Europeans be unwilling to create a currency which would be tailored to suit their needs in the first place, and which they would collectively manage for themselves?

Perhaps the answer is that between the Euro-dollar becoming a significant and useful factor in the international monetary system and its rising to so strong a dominance that it can foil autonomous national monetary policies, over ten years have elapsed – and that is a lengthy enough period from the viewpoint of legislatures and parliamentary governments. During more than a decade, European countries have found the Euro-dollar useful as a tool for reconciling autonomy in national monetary policies with maximum integration as far as economies of scale and spurs to competition are concerned. They enjoyed these benefits without having their hands tied by intergovernmental decisions, or by a treaty. Of course, the unparalleled ability of the Euro-dollar as a market creation to produce a wide range of large-scale services itself represents a guarantee for its continued existence in some form. But in principle countries could withdraw from it altogether; and in actual fact they can regulate their participation as it best suits their needs. Lately, the tendency has been to reduce support of the market. The Group of Ten central banks agreed in the spring of 1971 not to increase their reserve holdings placed on the Euro-market. Moreover, attention has been called to the distortions produced, now that the privileged treatment originally granted to what was a small and frail market is no longer justified, by the fact that banks' liabilities in the respective national currency are subject to reserve requirements, while those in Euro-currencies are not. In the words of G. Carli:

'The purpose is to harmonise – above all in the general framework of integration of monetary policies and of Community intervention instruments – the forms of regulation of banking activities conducted in local currency and in foreign currencies. It is precisely the interdependence of these forms of monetary management and the ease with which basic liquidity is transferred from one sector to another, in a system based on the convertibility of the various currencies, that require the elimination of the currently existing privileges enjoyed in Euro-banking activity. For example, the imposition of reserve ratios similar to those applied to domestic banking operations – leaving the national authorities free to adopt the most favourable measures, but at the same time accepting the consequences on the domestic market – should be seen precisely as a step towards such harmonisation.[1]

These and the other suggestions which have been made aim at solving the problem of how to curb the hydra of Euro-deposit expansion, without disintermediating European banks from a business which has done so much to integrate Europe's money and capital markets. The problem is difficult of solution; not least because it is hard to envisage the Europeans recovering full control over money supply, *unless the United States dollar tap is properly regulated.*

Are the United States going to do this, and how? They could manage the growth of the dollar supply, giving a higher priority to the needs of the rest of the world than allowed for by the 'benign neglect' attitude. This would perhaps be the most suitable way to bring the rest of the world finally to accept a pure dollar standard, after a decisive step towards reducing the role of gold in the international monetary system was taken in August 1971. Through the Euro-dollar, Europe would at

---

[1] G. Carli has also suggested that 'certain quotas of Euro-bank funds should be invested in public securities or deposited, earning interest, with central banks or with specially appointed institutions' [5].

least share in 'market management' of the dollar.[1] But because the world is not an optimum currency area, conflicts would be bound to arise. It cannot be expected that the United States will bend the management of money supply to suit the needs of other countries' economies, in conflict with the requirements of their own; nor would it be in the interest of the rest of the world to have them pursue policies which would damage the dynamism of their economy.

Alternatively, the regulation of the dollar supply from the United States to the rest of the world could be done by letting exchange rates float, by introducing new exchange controls – or through a mixture of both, i.e. by breaking the direct link between the state of (dollar) liquidity in the United States and in the rest of the world.

Floating the currency which still performs the functions of international money raises several difficult points of technique and principle.[2] It is not clear to what extent agreement on the problem of the numéraire in the international monetary system would help to overcome them; it may not be that important to establish what is floating in terms of what. In the end, what matters from the viewpoint of competitiveness are the rates of exchange which, through their relationship to the numéraire, obtain between the major trading partners. Here the problem arises from the fact that E.E.C. countries find it difficult individually to vary the exchange rate to the extent which would be needed to curb the dollar inflow, without upsetting their trade balance too much, now that intra-E.E.C. trade exceeds for the average of member countries one half of their total foreign trade.[3] Furthermore, rates of exchange with the dollar which

[1] Haberler has recently argued that 'the dollar standard is not a bad or highly inequitable system, *provided U.S. inflation does not get out of hand*' ([25] p. 15; the italics are mine).

[2] In this respect it is worth noting the following remark by Emminger: 'It is simply not true – as has often been said in the financial press – that with the Nixon measures of 15 August the dollar has been floated. The dollar itself is not really floating vis-à-vis all the other currencies; it is rather the other currencies that determine whether and how they are floating in relation to the dollar. The U.S. has had to rely on indirect measures (and pressures) such as the import surtax and the cutting of the gold link, to induce other countries to let their own currencies float against the dollar' [21].

[3] Trade with the United States averages less than one-tenth.

are deemed by the authorities apt to assure equilibrium on trade and services account are not capable of checking the inflow of dollar funds in a fashion that would leave a reasonable amount of autonomy for domestic money management. Or, to put it another way, it is not accepted that the dollar glut, depending as it does on capital movements, can be eliminated by means that would worsen the current-account balance.

The difficulty is largely due to the fact that European countries are at the crossroads, half-way to full integration. They are at the crossroads in the sense of being *monetarily* integrated mainly with the dollar and *commercially* integrated with one another. Trade integration would militate in favour of joint floating vis-à-vis the dollar. But joint floating in a form which would imply immediate 100 per cent fixity of intra-E.E.C. parities and probably lead to E.E.C. currencies being pegged to one of them has proved unfeasible owing to the fact that economic integration, as measured by the different values of the N.P.I.s, has only progressed halfway.[1] In view of this, joint floating might be found acceptable in combination with the cushioning which would be provided by a new European currency and during the intermediate stage, by regulated intragroup exchange-rate flexibility, as illustrated in the previous essays.[2]

In order to isolate most current-account transactions from the impact of fluctuations in the supply of and demand for, currencies caused by capital movements, Belgium and France let the rate of exchange for capital transactions fluctuate. Whatever the tactical merits of this arrangement, there remains the fact that splitting the two rates amounts ultimately to a

[1] In the view of Emminger, 'joint floating vis-à-vis the dollar would only make sense if the participating European currencies had reached an approximately equal degree of strength and therefore had convergent interests as far as exchange-rate policy is concerned' ([22] pp. 1-2).

[2] Mercantilist sentiment is part of the difficulty. Countries are not interested just in *overall* payments equilibrium; they wish to make sure that the trade and service balance will stay in good shape. If outright devaluations are not resorted to, because it is thought that a technique so apparently identical with the one used in the inter-war years for beggar-my-neighbour policies would not be tolerated in the present climate of opinion, *competitive undervaluations* are often aimed at. Strong reliance on the foreign trade multiplier may owe something to instinct: all the same it is not easy to justify, after all that has been learnt about demand management (and in a context in which for most countries inflation is *the* problem).

revaluation, disguised in a way which hinders normal banking operations with burdensome controls, is open to abuse and would become increasingly difficult to stick to in the face of wide and prolonged spreads between the two exchange rates. Moreover, its generalised application in the E.E.C. would not be possible without discrepancies (and conflicts), given the different structure of member countries' balance of payments and, in particular, the different importance of the current account items lying in the proximity of the borderline, which would have to be agreed upon for the application of the commercial or the financial exchange rate.[1] Finally, a dual rate system would not help to check capital movements which take the form of 'leads and lags' in respect of payments for current-account transactions. As many countries know only too well, 'leads and lags' can feed massive assaults on currencies by residents themselves.

As to controls, the Americans have applied them with little success. The interest equalisation tax was introduced in 1963; there followed in 1965 a voluntary restraint programme for bank lending abroad and for direct investments by the big corporations. In 1968 voluntary controls were made mandatory: a moratorium was placed on direct investment in Western Europe; corporations were to restrict reinvestment of earnings severely; banks were not to grant or renew term loans (and were directed to cut short term credits to Western Europe by 40 per cent); other financial intermediaries were also similarly restricted. For years the American experience has seemed to confirm that controls tend to beget controls. The escalation of controls has not made an essential contribution to improving the United States foreign payments position, both because not all holes can be plugged and because the prevented outflows of capital are partly offset by inflows from abroad, which do not materialise. A distortion in the circuit of capital movements produced by exchange control is that they tend to meet abroad the foreign exchange demand of resident capital exporters, which is only apparently repressed.

[1] Fleming, after a thorough theoretical analysis, comes to the conclusion that 'the best that can be said in favour of the [regional] arrangement is that it might be less unfavourable to fundamental adjustment than purely national dual rate systems' ([23] p. 316).

Disillusionment with results, plus awareness that controls do not benefit United States business nor the status of the dollar as an international currency, were responsible for the decision in 1969 to start dismantling those which had been built in the previous six years. And of course, the measures of August 1971, which aimed at reducing the monetary role of gold (still perhaps the main competitor of the dollar for the function of official reserve asset) and at enlarging the importance of exchange-rate changes in the adjustment process, have reduced the need for administrative controls.

As to the measures taken by the Europeans, most monetary authorities have discouraged borrowing abroad – at least in so far as it would add to the dollar inflow. The European lack of interest in borrowing on the Euro-dollar market and the repayments made by United States banks to their foreign branches have meant that the problem that market has actually had to face for its survival is the lack not of a lender, but of a borrower of last resort. To be sure, new borrowers are not taking too long to appear – from countries outside Western Europe. While this change in the national groups of borrowers may be expected to heighten anxiety about the soundness of the Euro-dollar pyramid, what I wish to stress here is that as long as Western Europe remains (with Japan) the most competitive supplier of goods in international demand, the dollars which it is attempting to shut out when they appear in the form of capital movements will eventually work their way in as a trade surplus. The over-stimulation of new exports of goods is apt to jeopardise internal monetary stability more than capital imports. At this juncture, the threat to the international role of the dollar would be at its most serious. Controls on capital transactions would appear patently inadequate; the market convertibility or 'usability' of the dollar even for current account transactions might be impaired.

If the supply of dollars (including Euro-dollars) should get completely out of hand, so that the dollar could no longer fulfil the international monetary function of regulating the claims on the real resources of exporting countries by those in trade deficit, that currency would no longer qualify as a means of international payment. But because of the dire effects this would have on world trade and economic activity, it is more likely that the Europeans would float up their currencies. On the other hand, countries outside Europe which did not have an interest (being in structural deficit) or the ability (having close ties with the United States) to refuse the dollar as a means of settlement, would let any reservations they may have entertained vis-à-vis the dollar fall, would peg their currencies to it and contribute to form a dollar area. Concerted inter-bloc floating would prevent a collapse of world trade.

The Quest for Competitive Alternatives to the Euro-dollar

The defensive measures to which in the meantime Europe is resorting are already doing damage. Official policies dictated by the need to avoid a swelling of dollar reserves are turning residents, would-be borrowers on market considerations, away from the Euro-markets – a step towards the disintegration of money and capital markets.

It may indeed be difficult to cut down the role of the dollar through negative measures, such as exchange controls, whether adopted by the Americans, the Europeans or both. The fact that after a long series of balance of payments deficits, which during the last fifteen years or so were no longer regarded by the rest of the world as a constructive contribution to world monetary order, and despite the controls introduced since 1963, the dollar has continued to be so widely used internationally and to be the main standard of value for the Euro-currency market is an indication of the strength of the economic potential and technical infrastructure supporting it. Short of a disintegration of the European and world economy, *the dollar and its Euro-variant can hardly be dislodged without creating an alternative asset capable of competing with them.*[1]

In the previous essays I have outlined a programme that

---

[1] The standard reaction of those who daily engage in business on Euro-markets runs along such lines. It has been echoed in this year's report of the Deutsche Bundesbank, where one reads among other things: 'Also, after the suspension of convertibility and the crises of last year, it [the dollar] will continue to be used for those [intervention and reserve] roles in the absence of a suitable alternative. Thus, the gold–dollar standard has been replaced for the time being by a dollar standard. . . . This also leads to the conclusion that the dollar has throughout the chance again to strengthen its position as key currency provided the United States succeeds in restoring sufficient internal stability' ([16] p. 41).

would gradually give rise to such an alternative. I have centred the presentation on a different class of considerations: namely, on considerations pertaining mainly to a policy of regionally balanced growth. I believe that in building Europe's monetary unity it is the internal questions that will matter most, both because member countries and their regions will be affected most by it, and because the balanced expansion of Europe's economy will enable it to play a more effective role as a factor of stability and progress in the world economy.

But of course external monetary problems can spur the process of unification. Several proposals, concerning the path to follow for creating a common European currency, link it directly to the solution of the Euro-dollar problem. In particular, Mundell has proposed that banks operating in the Euro-dollar market should be required to hold a fraction of their deposits in the form of reserves with a Euro-dollar Bank controlled by the European central banks. He has further suggested that:

> the Euro-dollar Bank could receive the dollar deposits in New York in exchange for its own liabilities which could be either deposits or notes. In this way the liabilities of the Euro-dollar Bank would evolve into a European super currency, on the same level as the dollar. . . . The use of the Euro-dollar as a European currency does not imply dependence on the U.S. dollar. Once Euro-dollar deposits in London banks become convertible into a new intervention currency of settlement issued by the Bank of Europe, backed not just by balances in New York, but gold deposits earmarked by the European central banks to the account of the Euro-dollar bank, a Euro-dollar would be as good or better than a U.S. dollar. . . . ([34], pp. 22-4)

The attraction of this and similar proposals[1] is that they would afford a solution for the Euro-dollar problem which would unite Europe rather than divide it as alternative courses threaten to do. Also, they would lead to the creation of a European payments instrument on a scale postulated *grosso modo* by

[1] Elsassr has also suggested that Euro-dollars should be converted into a new European currency which would circulate alongside the national currencies. The European currency would first be used for private transactions, later as settlement and intervention currency for central banks [20].

the size of the Euro-dollar market, whose banking and financial infrastructures would be harnessed to support the new currency.

Furthermore, as one author points out ([20] p. 67), the functions of a European currency that came into being as a successor to the Euro-dollar might well include the financing of regionally differentiated policies. I, however, rather envisage the European currency entering into circulation by relatively small amounts, i.e. with a graduality which is typical of market processes, initially at least. A high degree of 'feel and flair' would be required of the M.E.B. and of the bodies to which it would be responsible, in order to find the currently right dosage. I do not think that, after the crises and setbacks of recent years, one can expect in the near future the authorities to take a strong lead over the markets. The conversion *en bloc* of Euro-dollars into a new currency presupposes instead that the authorities are in the mood for large-scale initiatives. The Euro-dollar and accompanying disturbances are already there; but governments believe, rightly or wrongly, that they possess the power to curb the Euro-dollar market and even to opt out of it if necessary. Clearly, these options could no longer be contemplated if the mass of Euro-dollars was replaced by an equivalent mass of European currency.

What appears more likely in the near future is a larger role for existing national currencies. In fact, however good was the show put up by the dollar on the face of last year's monetary upheavals, the fact remains that, as a result of them, assets and liabilities of the Euro-banks in European currencies increased in 1972 by about 60 per cent, raising their share of the total from 22 per cent in 1970 to 28. Deutsche Marks accounted for nearly two-thirds of the increase; the second largest increase, in absolute terms, was in Swiss francs; sterling had the largest increase in relative terms, but a modest one in absolute amount. Was this the prelude to the ascent of the Euro-currency market by the European currencies?

It may be that the unifying role of a common currency has been exaggerated. Correspondingly, the importance of the formation of a closely knit web of monetary and financial relations, of technical know-how and habits of working in common among institutions belonging to different countries, of the machinery for broad multinational participation in short-, medium- and long-term lending, may have been underrated. The vested interest represented by the bankers, the institutions, the people for whose needs the market has catered, may now after all prove an integrating force in its own right and facilitate the switch from the Euro-dollar back to Europe's national currencies, without this having to spell disintegration. The latest international monetary episodes, including the inclination promptly to change parities, or to let currencies float, point to the rising influence of the markets as well as to the disposition of the authorities to go a long way in accepting it. Indicative in a sense, of the present mood is the fact that *The Economist* has suggested a market solution for the problem of the numéraire:

It would be quite easy to draw up such a numéraire by creating an entirely new unit . . .; by stating its value in all the main currencies on the day of its establishment; and then announcing its varying value daily in terms of the weighted average movement of those main international currencies on the exchanges. There is no need to wait for an international conference to agree on this. If a number of big private organisations in the City, with a lot of international contracts to fix up, were to announce the option for their clients to state prices in terms of such a new numéraire, announced daily by themselves, that would do. ([17] p. 17)

Concerning this suggestion, it is interesting to note that it comes very close to envisaging a state of affairs which obtained for centuries in Italy (and elsewhere in Europe). As the late Professor Luigi Einaudi pointed out in a study about Ferdinando Galiani's eighteenth-century contribution to the theory of 'imaginary money', in the centuries from 800 to 1800 protection against currency depreciation was secured through the generalised use of a money of account. Currencies which actually circulated in Italy were the *fiorino, zecchino, scudo, ducato,* and so on. They were used to pay salaries, rents and interests; but these were all fixed in lire when contracts were made, although the lira did not exist either as a coin or a bank-note. The lira was 'a mere abstract number' playing the numéraire function, whose need is more strongly felt at times of monetary disorder, when currencies actually in circulation cannot be relied upon for stability ([18] p. 149).

Nowadays, monetary regulations are generally biased against the use in the private sector of value-safeguard clauses and especially of monetary clauses, such as the gold or gold-value clause. In the case of an initiative which the markets first took in 1961, when the first bonded loan was issued in European units of account (U.A.), it would appear that equivalence to a gold-value clause can be excluded, since for the U.A. it is possible after all to undergo an increase or decrease in the gold weight.[1] If all reference currencies change their par value in respect of the issue date, and two-thirds of them change in one direction, the gold value of the U.A. is adjusted by the same percentage of the currency of currencies which have moved least in the two-thirds group. Thus the revaluation or devaluation of single currencies does not affect the U.A.'s gold value, but only the exchange ratio between these currencies and the U.A. In fact, the gold value of the U.A. has remained unchanged at 0·88867088 grams of fine gold, even after the revision of the original formula which was made necessary by the currency realignment of December 1971 [30].

The U.A. has its closest precedent in the 'epunit', i.e. the unit of account of the European Payments Union, whose gold value was equal to that of the U.S. dollar and could be changed only by a unanimous decision of the Council of Ministers of the seventeen countries which belonged to the Union. In the revised formula, however, the U.A. is linked to the currencies of the countries of the enlarged Community.

Notwithstanding the many obstacles to overcome, including the complexity of the formula, U.A. loans have enjoyed a remarkable success. Over forty U.A. loans have been publicly issued so far, for a total amount of U.A. 500 million. What is more interesting, during the troubled months which in 1971

[1] Professor Collin, chairman of the Kredietbank N.V., has stated in this regard: 'But those who took the initiative to use a currency of account had to overcome some legal hurdles. Indeed in many countries the use of a gold clause is illegal. Therefore any clause that referred to a fixed gold parity had to be avoided. . . . It might indeed be construed as a gold clause and be declared null and void in some countries' ([9] p. 21).

preceded the floating of many of the reference currencies U.A. bonds were in strong demand. Between January and August 1971 as much was raised in U.A. as the total for the previous three years.

The original U.A. formula has had to be revised in order to adapt it to the changes arising from the Smithsonian agreement. Among other things, the meaning of 'par value' has been widened so as to include central rates. In fact, for the determination of the gold value of the U.A. in place of the parities declared with the I.M.F., central rates will be used, provided it is they that are actually supported by the monetary authorities' interventions [31].[1]

Units of account do not circumscribe the exchange risk altogether. In the case of U.A., there remains the risk to the borrower of a devaluation of his own currency, to the bondholder of a revaluation of his national currency, in terms of the U.A. This in turn means that the bondholder is protected against a devaluation of the borrower's currency, while the latter escapes the risk of a revaluation of the lender's currency.

It seems to me that the unit of account should afford those who assume obligations, or acquire claims in currencies other than the national one, reasonable protection against the possible exchange-rate gyrations of individual foreign currencies. In so doing, it should aim at a balanced spread of risks between borrowers and lenders. Experience has shown that formulae which put too heavy a burden on either of the parties to contracts tend to fall into oblivion or, at any rate, to be 'corrected' in every instance in which they come into play.

The same can be said of formulae that are too rigid, because they define the unit of account in terms of a given gold weight, or link it to some price index, with the intent of securing constant purchasing power for the unit. Making the latter as inflexible as a numéraire defined in real terms, however, would

[1] Other units-of-account formulas offering an exchange option, have not been able to weather the storm as well, mainly because they put too large a risk on borrowers when parities are no longer fixed, and create room for unjustified arbitrage profits. This is the case of the European Currency Unit, which was introduced in December 1970 when a loan denominated in such units was issued by the European Coal and Steel Community.

give contracts a stability which the long-standing conditions of monetary instability have made difficult to honour, especially when two different countries, and two different currencies, are involved. The use of a unit of account stable in terms of purchasing power would – one might argue – help to overcome monetary instability. However, the contribution such a unit could make to stability would be small, in my view. As already hinted, its rigidity would militate against its being widely used. And if a wide use of it were achieved, it would be difficult to maintain its constant purchasing power.

Such a thing does not exist in the world of real money, and is only possible by convention. Once the unit of account were so widely used and unconditionally accepted for contractual terms that people would no longer feel the need to convert unit-of-account obligations and claims into existing national currencies, but accepted the units themselves in final discharge of debts, then those units would be performing the function of money. At that stage, to secure their purchasing power stability would be as problematic as we know it is for existing currencies.

When it finally comes to the definition of a 'general' unit of account in the E.E.C., I think there would be considerable merit in devising a formula which keeps it separate from the purely numéraire function – a formula fit for both official and private use. The potentialities of the unit of account would be enhanced. And we shall need its services, especially if it does not prove possible to agree on, and stick to, the limitation and regulation of intra-E.E.C. exchange-rate flexibility, as suggested above for the intermediate stage.

In the meantime, units of account will have to face strong competition by those currencies which qualify for most monetary functions. The dollar has been – and still is – one such currency. In the Euro-currency market it has been the standard of value, or unit of account, accepted by lenders originally holding their funds, as well as by borrowers ultimately using them often, in currencies other than the dollar itself.

The most lively competition to the dollar comes from the Deutsche Mark. During the last two critical years among E.E.C. currencies the Deutsche Mark has exerted by far the strongest attraction, as an alternative to the dollar, on investors in the

Euro-deposit and Euro-bond markets, as well as on monetary authorities.[1] So that it would appear that the European currencies' ascent in the Euro-market is not going to be equally successful for all. The conditions which may allow the ascent to secure for Europe a better equilibrium with the dollar would also make a selection and establish a hierarchy between the European currencies. Gradually, one of the existing national currencies might emerge as the Community's currency.

I do not regard that as the most suitable approach to European monetary unification. The reasons have been briefly set out in the Federal Trust Report (see Appendix). I wish only to add a few remarks in the light of the fact that in the meantime proposals have been put forward that the European currency should be built around the nucleus of a member currency, and that sterling would be 'a natural choice'.[2]

The view that a national currency can discharge the function of European currency just as well as, and under certain aspects better than, a currency not linked to a national economy, implicitly presupposes that, once the process of unification is set in motion, there will be no room whatsoever for national autonomy in monetary policies. But unification will not be accomplished overnight; it will have to go through an intermediate stage during which the automatic and voluntary mechanisms of harmonisation, however successful they may be, will still not lead to the *complete* merger of monetary policies; within the context of stricter constraints, national monetary authorities will naturally enough still try to pursue policies tuned in the first place to the needs of their respective countries – and, whenever possible, to have them adopted by the Community as a whole.

If the (unrealistic) assumption implicitly made is dropped, it

[1] Throughout 1971, D.M. bonds have been in strong demand, their attraction being due both to the yield and to the prospect of appreciation of the D.M. International D.M. loan issues exceeded the 1970 amount; nevertheless, they did not regain the level attained in 1969, apparently because of less interest on the part of borrowers, who had to pay high interest rates on an appreciating currency, but also because of the regulation of issues exercised by the market control authorities.

[2] The proposal has been made, among others, by Cooper ([13] pp. 22-6). Cassell also deems it 'possible that sterling could become the common currency of the Community . . .' ([7] p. 226).

can be argued that choosing a national currency for the role of common European currency might confer an unfair advantage to the issuing country which would thereby find itself in a stronger position to decide upon a policy stance and impose it on the rest of the Community.

Moreover, the question would arise of the use and distribution of seigniorage gains. Even during the period when one given national currency was only to be used for interventions on exchange markets, substantial working balances would have to be built up in view of the expanding amount of trade and financial transactions taking place across national borders. Those balances would grow much larger once the 'Europeanised' national currency made a breakthrough in the private sectors of member countries. They would have to be periodically adjusted upwards to keep in line with inflated values at a time of high price rises, while their purchasing power in real terms would dwindle.

The allocation of the seigniorage gains would indeed require Community control also over the composition of the asset side of the balance sheet, as well as over the profit-and-loss account, of the central bank issuing the adopted currency. This and the need to regulate the creation of that currency for the purposes of a European money-supply policy, would make it necessary to give that central bank a European general management. At that stage, however, the national currency would be such only in name; in actual fact it would be a true Community currency.

It is difficult to see how the country concerned could give its agreement to this sort of arrangement. On purely economic grounds, it might object that the arrangement, far from conferring on it a differential advantage, would in fact totally deprive it of autonomy in monetary policy, an autonomy its partners would continue to enjoy, if only in a shrinking measure, for a number of years to come. Indeed, it is difficult to envisage the United Kingdom today in a position of dominance within a 'European sterling area' context, such as it enjoyed for a good many years vis-à-vis the rest of the sterling area, as we have known it. Even within a group of largely complementary economies, there used to arise conflicts of interests, which led to the establishment of autonomous monetary authorities in most parts of the area, for carrying out policies better suited to their own needs.[1]

Within the Community, it is unlikely that conflicts would be solved in such a way as to assure the United Kingdom a net balance of benefits, after allowing for the earlier loss of partial monetary autonomy such as would be enjoyed by other members.

Finally, as to the argument that the establishment of a common currency would be facilitated by 'adopting' a currency with the most widely based banking infrastructure and sophisticated know-how, it should be noted that the success of the City of London in rising to the role of world Euro-dollar centre proves that the infrastructure and know-how it possesses could be precious in nursing a new European currency. What that argument really implies is that London has a formidable trump card in the competition among the Community monetary and financial centres, about which more will be said in the last section of this essay.

[1] Conan speaks of the 'tendency of individual countries, as they became conscious of their needs and felt their way towards an autonomous monetary policy, to become increasingly disinclined to conform to a policy which was merely traditional, or imposed on them from abroad' ([12] pp. 150-1). He also quotes the following passage from a 1934 Report of the Monetary Committee in New Zealand:

'In the past the fundamental weakness of our banking organisation lay in the fact that its control rested in the hands of six independent boards of directors, only one of which possessed a head office in New Zealand. New Zealand monetary affairs were thus largely controlled from Great Britain and Australia, where the remaining five boards are situated. . . . In such circumstances it is clear that the trading banks could not have any definite or conscious monetary policy designed particularly to promote economic stability and the general welfare of the people of this Dominion.'

According to Viner, '. . . it may even be possible that London typically reduced her credits to abroad when it was most urgent that she should expand them and expanded them when contraction would have been more beneficial. It seems clear that as far as long-term loans were concerned England accentuated the cyclical fluctuations in the level of world activity rather than damped them down, and this for all we know may have been true also of her short-term transactions' ([40] p. 64).

Finally, Bell has argued that in respect of long-run economic growth '. . . overseas members would seem to be at a very clear disadvantage relative to the position of the United Kingdom' ([4] p. 271).

*The Narrowing of the Intra-E.E.C. Margins of Fluctuation and
the Need for Community Liquidity*

The ascent of a single E.E.C. currency to the role of European
money would have to overcome the opposition of the national
authorities, including perhaps those of the country issuing it.
The technical arrangements adopted in connection with the
most significant initiative taken so far in the field of monetary
unification would appear to show that E.E.C. governments do
not intend to see their currencies downgraded to a local role –
at any rate, not in order to promote one of them to the role of
European currency.

That initiative is the renewed attempt to narrow the margins
of fluctuation, after the plan to reduce the 'band' from 1·5 to
1·2 per cent starting from June 1971 had to be abandoned, as a
result of the crisis which broke out one month earlier when the
intervention limits were suspended for both the Deutsche Mark
and the Dutch florin. In December 1971, I.M.F. member
countries were allowed to widen the margins to 2·25 per cent on
either side of the parity, or of the newly agreed central rates.
This implied that between a pair of E.E.C. currencies there
could form a spread of 4·50 per cent and that exchange rates
could over time fluctuate by up to 9 per cent against one
another, while vis-à-vis the dollar those percentages were
respectively 2·25 and 4·50.

To eliminate the 'anomaly' of member countries being able
to fluctuate in terms of one another twice as widely as permitted
vis-à-vis a third currency, the programme which had been
awaiting application since the spring of 1971 was resumed last
March. The Council of Ministers of the Community then
decided that intra-E.E.C. currency margins should be narrowed
to 1·25 per cent on each side of the parity, to begin with; so that
the spread at a given point in time, as well as the fluctuations
over time, would not exceed those allowed in respect of the
dollar.

The exchange-rate provisions of the scheme might have been
implemented by means of several alternative technical arrangements. Perhaps, next to a continued use of the dollar for
intervention purposes, the simplest would have been to have
the monetary authorities of all member countries but one steer

the exchange rate of their respective currencies by intervening in one E.E.C. currency, while entrusting the latter's monetary authorities with the task of carrying out dollar interventions. Perhaps one reason why such a solution was not chosen is that by substituting an E.E.C. currency for the dollar it would have led to the establishment of a hierarchy among Community currencies, which governments seem to disapprove of in principle.

Instead, it was decided that interventions would be made in *all* E.E.C. currencies,[1] with the central banks of strong currencies themselves purchasing weak currencies and (or) those of weak currencies selling strong currencies, with which they would be supplied through a mechanism of reciprocal very short-term credits. As to the liabilities arising out of such interventions, it was decided that they should be settled by debtor countries using holdings of the creditor countries' currencies, if any, gold or other assets assimilated to it (Special Drawing Rights, credits with the I.M.F.) and dollars, plus other currencies, each *pro rata* to their share in the debtors' total reserves. The scheme has been in operation since 24 April 1972. On 1 May, the United Kingdom, Denmark and Ireland joined it; Norway followed suit in June. However, in the second half of that month a new exchange crisis broke out, precipitated by a 'flight' from the pound sterling. Having lost $2·5 billion in one week, the United Kingdom authorities decided, as a temporary measure, to put the pound on a floating basis as from 23 June. In the process the Italian lira was hit by speculation. At the Council of Ministers meeting which took place in Luxembourg a few days later, Italy was granted a temporary waiver from the E.E.C. intervention (and settlement) rules, which she had asked for as a condition for remaining within the narrower margin agreement.[2]

The narrowing of the margins, after they had been enlarged

[1] According to the original rules of the agreement on the narrowing of the margins, interventions in dollars are to be made when a currency is at the upper or lower limit vis-à-vis the dollar. Within the intra-E.E.C. and dollar bands, interventions are allowed only in 'concertation' between E.E.C. central banks.

[2] The Irish pound, which is pegged to the pound sterling, was also floated with the latter. Denmark instead withdrew from the E.E.C. margin agreement, but has kept the crown on a fixed basis and within the fluctuation margins allowed by the Smithsonian agreement.

in accordance with the Smithsonian agreement of December 1971, represents in principle a step in the right direction. They are now no larger than those applying to the dollar; they will have to be cut further and eventually disappear altogether. Moreover, the width of the 'band' (or the sum of the margins, above and below parity) is sufficient to allow for that degree of autonomy in interest-rate policies which member countries cannot dispense with, so long as divergences in cyclical fluctuations remain important. The new margins can also accommodate the parity changes needed to take care of cumulative maladjustments, assuming that the order of magnitude of those changes, such as are postulated by differences in N.P.I.s, corresponds roughly to that suggested on p. 113 above. At any rate, what may prove important on a longer view is that an experiment is being made in reducing the dependence on the dollar as intervention and settlement currency. The replacement is provided for the time being by all member currencies; eventually, the step might be taken to use a common European currency.

The initiative taken in April 1972 has more far-reaching implications than a *narrowing* of the margins of fluctuation at first suggests. This explains at least partly why it has had such a troubled start; the other part of the explanation is that the international monetary system itself is in a shambles.

It is not clear how it makes sense to defend the margins of fluctuation of exchange rates around a parity when there are no consistently applied sets of rules and limits as to changes of the *parity* itself, nor has there emerged as yet an undisputed pattern of behaviour by the authorities in the matter. The band and its delimitation have meaning in so far as they are applied to parities which are either fixed in some sense, or flexible according to rules and within defined limits. But the narrowing of the margins and the harder intervention and settlement terms, that for the time being accompany it in the E.E.C. agreement, put a burden on member countries, which these may try to elude under present circumstances by changing parities more frequently and more freely.[1] While parity changes may have to be made in

---

[1] Ossola, after examination of the technical and economic problems connected with the narrowing of the margins, concluded that, in the absence of effective alignment of economic policies, 'the likelihood of changes in parities would be increased under the new system' ([37] p. 119).

order to comply with the terms of the agreement, even in cases in which they would not be appropriate in the light of more fundamental economic considerations, it is clear that the more parities change the more they tend to identify themselves with actual exchange rates, and less relevant becomes the distinction between changes in the former and in the latter. The conceptual distinction between parities and exchange rates has in fact tended to lose significance; a sign of this is the introduction of 'central rates' as an intermediate, operationally more relevant, concept.

Furthermore, as long as there is no final decision about the role of gold in the international monetary system, the fact that the market price has reached a level nearly twice as high as the official price is an added factor of disturbance. In the circumstances, it has brought more quickly and more sharply to light the fact that the narrowing of intra-Community margins has been combined with settlement rules harder than those applied outside the group – an outcome which is not likely to foster the process of integration.

Intra-E.E.C. rules are harder because they reduce the 'usability' of the international monetary asset which is in plentiful supply, the dollar, while prescribing the use of harder (and more valuable) assets without so far adequately increasing their availability. To illustrate, whenever 'the snake' of linked E.E.C. currencies creeps away from the floor of the 'tunnel (i.e. towards their ceiling vis-à-vis the dollar), the authorities of member countries with relatively weak currencies have to spend foreign-exchange reserves in order to support their currencies vis-à-vis other E.E.C. currencies *in the first place*. The use of Community currencies for intervention on exchange markets and for settlement of balances leads to an increase in the demand for them. Demand may be further swollen by the preference to hold currencies whose margins of fluctuation are expected to be narrower – especially if, on top of that, there are expectations that their parities will make upward jumps. If increased demand is not matched (for some of them) by an expansion of supply, those currencies are bound to become harder still. As a result, there would be a tendency to economise in their use; in the extreme case also through more or less disguised attempts to reorientate trade flows which would run counter to the spirit, if not the written rules, of the Treaty of

172   EUROPEAN MONETARY UNIFICATION

Rome. The volume of intra-Community trade might be cut down to a level determined by the ability of the less competitive member countries to export to the more competitive ones in the group. It is more likely, however, that before getting to that sort of 'crunch', the application of the narrower margin agreement would be suspended (in part or in total).

The European Payments Union, and the monetary agreements which preceded it in the second half of the 1940s, encouraged intra-European trade because they made settlements between European countries softer than with the United States. It paid to import from other E.P.U. countries in order to economise gold and dollars, i.e. *external* means of payment. The contractionary effect on European–American trade was, however, tempered by the necessity to export to the United States in order to pay for imports from the dollar area, which the European partners could not supply. Intra-European trade today could not count on such a counterbalancing factor: there are few goods which European countries can supply, but the United States cannot. If the reserve asset which is plentiful, the dollar, continues to be accepted internationally without restrictions, whereas E.E.C. countries permit its use within their own area only in combination with other, scarcer assets, settlements with and between those countries become 'harder'.

Among the scarcer assets there are their own currencies. Admittedly, E.E.C. countries are making them available to each other. But is what is being done adequate? 'Adequate' is an ambiguous word; however, in this context it is not difficult to make clear what in principle it should mean: namely, that E.E.C. currencies should not be to member countries in scarcer supply than the dollar – both actually and potentially.

This could be achieved in several ways. Official short-term dollar holdings could be largely funded, with a provision that each member country would receive, from its partners, E.E.C. currencies equivalent to the amount of dollars it had agreed to fund. The scope for settlements in E.E.C. currencies would thereby be amplified, without adding to total liquidity. Moreover, the international monetary system would benefit from the lightening of the burden on the dollar. If E.E.C. countries wish to have their currencies compete with, if not altogether replace, the dollar for intra-European transactions, what is needed is

fresh creation of Community liquidity, offset by the reduction
of 'international' or rather dollar liquidity.

Community liquidity is needed to 'Internalise' Intra-E.E.C. Trade

As long as payments imbalances arising out of such trade and
other internal transactions are to be settled by means of a
currency external to the group, because the Community is
unable to agree on ways to endow itself with its own sources of
liquidity, the Common Market will not be truly common.

The substitution of part of existing official short-term dollar
assets by E.E.C. currency holdings would help to 'internalise'
intra-E.E.C. transactions. With this end in view, an *ad hoc*
Community asset for official settlements, such as the one I
have hinted at in the final section of the previous essay, would
be more effective than consolidation of dollar balances within
the S.D.R.–I.M.F. framework. More especially, the task of
providing the periodic increases in liquidity, which will be
necessary once the problems pertaining to the appropriate
quantity and quality of the existing stock have been solved,
should be achieved through the creation and allocation of such
an asset or of the proposed new European currency, whereby
Community liquidity would be supplied for use in both official
settlements and market transactions.

If access to the United States money and capital market is
easy, any progress made in funding existing dollar holdings
could be swallowed by a new dollar inflow. *Ceteris paribus*, the
dollar will be in a stronger posture to play the role of international currency as a result of consolidation of United States
short-term foreign liabilities. Similarly to a business firm, a
country by consolidating its short-term debt increases its ability
to take up fresh debts. If access to the dollar is easier than to
European sources of finance, the potential supply of dollars will
be larger than that of E.E.C. currencies, thus reinforcing the
tendency to economise the latter and use dollars instead. Whereas monetary integration implies that the use of external currencies should be discouraged and that of internal currencies
promoted, we could find ourselves in a situation in which a
member country or region would (still) be so much more
dependent on external rather than on E.E.C. sources of finance,
as to configure a monetary union between the private sector

of a member country and that of a third country – a sort of Atlantic 'private monetary union', which in the end would threaten the working of European official arrangements based on the assumption of different monetary and financial circuits.

This is the rationale behind the controls on capital flows vis-à-vis third countries. The harmonisation of external exchange controls by E.E.C. countries is, in a sense, the equivalent of the common external tariff on imports of goods. If you eliminate internal barriers, you need common commercial and exchange (including exchange-control) policies towards the outside world.

Administrative Controls on Capital Movements and Monetary Unification

It might be argued that the case for this is less clear-cut for capital movements than it is for the movement of goods, not only because of the cosmopolitan nature of capital, but also because of the deep penetration of European money and capital markets by the dollar. Exchange controls could, however, be applied selectively, if in a more burdensome way, to cut down the inflow of dollars, originated both by United States capital exports and by European dollar creation, taking place in connection with intra-European dollar-denominated capital movements. If intra-European capital transactions are not to be much affected, these will however to take place in European currencies (and in the proposed common European currency) to a larger extent than has been the case so far.

The difficulties with exchange controls and their harmonisation are not only technical in nature. Those of an economic nature point to the question of whether we have a common market for capital as we know we have it for goods.

A factor requiring the effective unification of E.E.C. money and capital markets is that harmonisation of exchange controls is much more difficult to enforce along the frontiers of fragmented national markets. The smaller the markets, the larger the distortions produced by administrative controls and discrimination. Moreover, how can countries with differences in basic payments positions, which cannot be overlooked even under present conditions of dollar glut, be expected to stick to the same controls? When some of them run into payments difficulties again, how can they dispense with dollar finance, if they are not afforded the alternative of an equally easy access to E.E.C. money and capital markets?[1] That is why *it will be difficult over a period of time to maintain external unity, while remaining divided internally.*

To foster internal unity beyond the measure of integration attained through the dollar, not much has been done. Reciprocal credit-granting in connection with the implementation of the narrower margin agreement is for the time being very short-term; whereas by sticking to a fixed exchange rate with the dollar, at a time when the latter is inconvertible (and overvalued), European countries have implicitly accepted to grant the United States credit indefinitely.

As far as private sources of liquidity are concerned, the Eurodollar and, potentially, the dollar as such are more accessible and also better placed from the viewpoint of large-scale lending operations. European national markets, even in the case of countries which have progressed most towards freedom from exchange controls, continue to be shielded by official 'guidance' to the banks and other financial intermediaries, which usually discriminates against foreign borrowers. Moreover, countless regulations other than exchange controls are still enforced: regulations concerning *inter alia* the types of security that savings banks and other credit institutions are permitted to accept, the

[1] An intriguing aspect of last June's flare-up on exchange markets is that speculative attacks on currencies should have recurred at all when ample official reserve holdings could easily be increased by resorting to the very large credit potential of the international market. One is almost tempted to think that the outcome of such attacks might depend on the different determination with which that potential will be harnessed by the authorities in order to defend a parity, and by speculators endeavouring to defeat them. The latter, however, are at an advantage, since speculation against a currency can be financed by using the monetary asset most easily available, the dollar, which for official settlements in the E.E.C. is subject to the already mentioned limitations.
Besides the restrictive E.E.C. intervention and settlement rules a decisive consideration in the floating of the pound was, of course, the fact that faster inflation in the United Kingdom put in jeopardy the competitiveness of British output on the eve of the country's accession to the E.E.C. The lira, on the other hand, stayed put while Italy's reserve position was bolstered by engineering large medium-term borrowing operations on the Euro-dollar market by government-controlled institutions. Thus a well-tried pattern in Italy's external monetary policy could be confirmed.

G

categories of assets in which insurance companies may invest, the conditions to be met for issuing securities. With regard to these, it has at times been argued that uncontrolled freedom of access to national issue markets is not practicable. Markets simply cannot be relied upon – so the argument runs – to enforce the restraint on large borrowers (governments) from other E.E.C. countries that would be required in order to perform appropriately their allocative function. But surely, situations in which the excess of purely domestic demand for funds has threatened the collapse of capital markets are not unknown. They have been tackled through rationing the scarce resources available by national capital market supervisory bodies. A similar institution for the E.E.C., a European capital issues committee, could be set up to authorise issues at first by E.E.C. borrowers on other E.E.C. capital markets, later without discrimination, i.e. through regulation of the market as a whole. It would do so *only for issues exceeding a certain amount and in periods of marked tension.*[1] This instance shows that the unification of European money and capital markets does not necessarily imply freedom from all controls. What it does imply is a denationalisation of such controls as may be necessary from time to time. They, and tax provisions, which are so often used to discourage investment in foreign countries, should be applied without discrimination in the E.E.C. As Scitovsky has argued, 'an integrated capital market may discriminate among borrowers according to the nature and riskiness of their business, the size of their assets, their past financial record, and other such factors, but not according to the region where they operate' ([38] p. 88).

The abolition of discrimination based on the nationality or residence of borrowers and lenders or on the location of the investments, is laid down in Article 67 of the Treaty of Rome. That Article, however, prescribes the liberalisation of capital movements only to the extent required for the 'proper functioning of the Common Market'. Moreover, Article 73 introduces

---

[1] Coffey and Presley have listed among the measures for hastening the formation of a European capital market, the co-ordination of public authority bond issues through a capital issues committee. In this connection, they make a reference to the German experience with the central capital market committee since 1969 ([8] p. 91).

an escape clause for dealing with capital movements that upset the operation of a member's capital market. Protective measures can be taken against such movements, under certain circumstances without even prior consultation with the Community.

The escape clause has been resorted to on several occasions. In some cases the E.E.C. Commission has had to authorise exchange controls involving a retreat from the directives adopted in 1960 and 1962. Of course, this has happened mostly under pressures which practically had created a state of necessity. And it would not be realistic simply to ask governments to renounce for good any use of administrative controls over the flow of funds with member countries. Such a renunciation can only be envisaged if accompanied by the whole set of moves that belong to monetary unification: policy harmonisation, abolition of tax and other distortions, formal regulation of exchange-rate flexibility, creation of Community liquidity, centrally financed regional policies.

However justified the recourse to administrative controls may have been, monetary unification clearly cannot be achieved if the remedy for the payments imbalances which are bound to develop from time to time is sought in the maintenance of old barriers and the erection of new ones. It is indeed essential, in the troubled conditions created by the international monetary crisis, not to lose sight of the fact that the ultimate aim for E.E.C. countries is to ban the *power* of governments to enforce exchange controls and other discriminatory devices. The power to reintroduce controls is itself sufficient to cripple the functioning of a unified market. In recent years banks of countries in payments difficulties have raised their interest rates on Euro-dollar deposits, but have failed to attract funds because of the fear that their withdrawal might be restricted. This shows that the power to impose exchange controls can undo the market's unity, even when a common currency is used and therefore no exchange-rate risk is involved.[1] Sometimes the suspicion that exchange

[1] Keynes, with reference to that 'extraordinary episode' in the economic progress of humanity represented by the freedom of movement of goods and productive factors that obtained up to 1914, noted the following:

'The inhabitant of London . . . could at the same moment and by the same means adventure his wealth in the natural resources and new

controls might be introduced has further undermined confidence in the currency and triggered off a 'flight' from it. When a 'flight psychology' develops, the recycling of funds may be the only alternative to strict exchange controls. Recycling as a form of open-end monetary facility raises a number of problems, both of a technical and an economic nature. Their solution is difficult in a world-wide context, but less so in a group of countries moving towards integration, since in such a group the recycling facility would not be applied in isolation, but in combination with the many constraints put upon members by the mechanism of monetary unification. This also means that in the end the need for actually recycling funds would be less likely to arise (for purely economic reasons, in any case).

In conclusion, unimpaired freedom of circulation should be put beyond doubt. Precarious liberalisation of capital movements would continue to inflict upon us the disturbances they give rise to when markets are not unified, but are only allowed to communicate; whereas it would go on denying us a good deal of the benefits that large, truly unified, markets afford. Governments should renounce for good the power to introduce exchange controls simultaneously with the adoption of the whole set of measures agreed upon for achieving monetary union. This undertaking should also be embodied in the proposed European monetary convention. Moreover, national governments and Community institutions should help in a

---

enterprises of any quarter of the world, and share, without exertion or even trouble, in their prospective fruits and advantages; or he could decide to couple the security of his fortunes with the good faith of the townspeople of any substantial municipality in any continent that fancy or information might recommend. . . . But, most important of all, he regarded this state of affairs as normal, certain and permanent, except in the direction of further improvement, and any deviation from it as aberrant, scandalous and avoidable.' ([27] pp. 9-10)

It is instructive to contrast this with Nurkse's remarks about exchange controls and lack of confidence in currencies during the 1930s: 'It was lack of confidence that made exchange control necessary for the prevention of abnormal capital exports. But experience has shown that the introduction of control itself has tended to upset confidence further, increasing the urge to export capital and making it necessary to tighten the control and to scrutinise even commercial transactions more closely. The process may thus be self-aggravating to some extent' ([36] p. 163).

positive way to maintain freedom of circulation, unrestrained and undoubted. They should orientate the flow of financial resources over which they have, or will have, direct command in the direction appropriate to offset imbalances, lubricate the mechanism of intra-E.E.C. settlements and, over the longer term, secure the rate and regional pattern of growth acceptable to all concerned. If there is to be direction of financial resources, it certainly should not be done on a national basis, but within the Community-wide context and with the instruments which ought to be created for a policy of balanced growth.

The banking systems might also be encouraged gradually to diversify their lending activity as to embrace customers in other E.E.C. countries (this is of particular importance in cases where industrial financing is largely channelled through the banking system). Banks might be encouraged to lend more to the low activity regions, by the Community subsidising the payment of a fractionally higher interest rate. Financial institutions, belonging directly or indirectly to the public sector, which have provided and/or are providing finance for development purposes to regions in their own countries, or in third countries, could be requested to focus on the Community's needs, to help towards mitigating the financial and payments difficulties of the low-activity regions.

These are all steps whereby E.E.C. currencies could be prevented from becoming harder than the dollar to E.E.C. residents. In contributing to promoting a reliable flow of equilibrating capital movements, they would not only complement the regional credit policy of the proposed Multi-role European Bank, but also foster the formation of a truly European money and capital market.

From Communicating to Fully Integrated Markets

The unification of exchange rates, of external exchange controls, of central-banking systems and of monetary policies – in short monetary unification at the official level – can hardly be achieved and maintained without full integration of the national markets for money and capital. It would also be pointless if it did not raise those markets above their suboptimal dimension.

Given freedom of circulation, transfers of funds across national borders take place, which are prevalently connected with an excess demand (supply) of funds in a country being matched by an excess supply (demand) in another. These marginal transfers obtain as a result of a series of price and/or interest-rate adjustments, through which a pressure is brought to bear, although less and less directly, on the wide range of claims that form the various national stocks of monetary and financial assets, to adjust to equal yields for similar risks. Thus elimination of controls tends to lead to a uniform demand–supply relationship in the same way as in a system of communicating water-pipes a liquid finds a uniform level. But the bulk of transactions continues to unfold in much the same way as before the elimination of controls; in other words, the markets, although communicating, go on largely as separate entities.

As against this type of marginal unification a more pervasive one should be aimed at, which one could perhaps more appropriately call *integration*. In fully integrated markets there would no longer be a strong prevalence of transfers of funds motivated and enacted by lenders and borrowers at the margin of the national demand and supply curves, or beyond. There would be instead an intensification of transactions among infra-marginal lenders and borrowers, who would interblend irrespective of national frontiers using a much more developed network of bank and other financial linkages. One would be justified in using a single demand and a single supply curve for representing conditions on what would be truly one market.

The aggregation of the sets of national demand and supply curves into one Community set would mean that the distinction between domestic assets and external assets would be fading away: more types of assets and liabilities would join the group of those having Community-wide currency; and the gap with those still outside would tend to shrink. As already hinted, contact points would not just connect the markets at the tip of the transaction icebergs. As the network of contacts and linkages hardened into a system of banks and other financial intermediaries stretching over several member countries, the maze of monetary and financial relations intertwined across state boundaries would become harder to undo, so that communications with any one (national) section of the Community money and capital market would be less likely to be obstructed. Unification of the markets would rest, and be seen to rest, on more solid foundations than has been the case hitherto. In addition, the unhampered circulation of a common European money, simultaneously with national currencies, would gradually grow into an instrument for the thorough interpenetration of the markets.

Integration in this sense would create conditions in which not only would the monetary union be unlikely to be called into question, but the performance of the market would also be more efficient than under conditions of *unification at the margins*. Markets which are said to be unified only, or mainly, because they communicate through a few selected points tend to concentrate in the short end the excess of demand and supply, which is in fact generated in their different sections. Commercial banking systems traditionally have the lion's share in the process of matching excess demand and supply on the international market, both because they are better equipped for it and because controls are easier to enforce through them. The national systems of commercial banks not only tend to clear debit/credit positions within themselves; they are, albeit to different degrees, instrumental in clearing positions between the various sectors of the markets for loan funds. This is one reason why pressures to equalise interest rates build up mainly in the short end of the markets, while for medium- and long-term finance discrepancies *tend* to be more persistent.[1]

A demonstration *a contrario* is provided by the United Kingdom. The City of London, having been the monetary and financial centre of the world up to 1914, and of the sterling area since the 1930s, is the most open and diversified financial centre, especially as concerns the network of linkages with overseas, as well as the amount and types of operations which are carried out for foreign account. Large stocks of United Kingdom gilt-edged securities are owned by, and actively traded for account of, residents in other sterling countries. As a result, these securities have been a source of 'external' liquidity to the United Kingdom, but has shrunk the latter's freedom to deter-

---

[1] Of course, the pressures to equalise interest rates reach the medium- and long-term sections of the credit market, if only indirectly, because of the interaction between the different sections of domestic markets.

mine the structure of interest rates even on the stock of domestic medium- and long-term paper. Had the United Kingdom not suffered a relative loss of economic weight in the last few decades, it would now be in a better position to influence the level of interest rates all round; so that again, interest-rate discrepancies with and between thoroughly integrated markets would be small.

The fact that at present final users of credit, such as industrial companies, tap sources outside their own countries points to progress towards integration, as distinct from marginal unification. However, not all industrial borrowing from 'foreign' sources of capital is a sign of financial integration in the sense used here. There have been instances in recent years of industrial and other companies, mainly government-controlled, which have borrowed funds abroad primarily upon advice received from their monetary authorities, whose balance of payments forecasts and the ensuing foreign borrowing decisions can be assimilated to a global *ante litteram* clearing of internal demand and supply of resources.

Markets which, although communicating at the margins, are not fully integrated tend in more ways than one to behave, especially in the medium and long ends, as separate markets. As far as the bulk of transactions is concerned not a great deal is changed, from the viewpoint of size and cost, by establishing a marginal communication with other markets. The financial needs of large companies cannot be catered for smoothly. Security turnover is sometimes so small as to reduce substantially the marketability of the securities involved On the other hand, markets which are integrated in a way that enables them to match *global* demand for funds against *global* supply behave virtually as one large market and thereby achieve substantial economies of scale. They are more efficient, cheaper and more competitive. While investors will be willing to pay a higher price for securities which are equivalent in all respects but are more easily marketable, borrowers will get the higher price and in addition often save on the issue costs.

In order to second the process of Europe's industrial integration and improve the prospect of standing up to the dollar's competition, we need to push the interpenetration and unification of the financial infrastructure much further than has so far been achieved, even taking into account developments prompted by the growth of Euro-markets.[1]

The immobility of those financial resources, which in truly unified markets respond to changes in fundamental economic factors, is still too high in the Community; particularly so in those very countries which would otherwise be in a position to release the resources – and with them the entrepreneurial skills – needed elsewhere for narrowing the gap between over-capitalised and undercapitalised countries and regions. Moreover, the 'direction' of credit flows, to the extent necessary to support a policy of regionally balanced growth, would itself be facilitated, in several respects by the ease with which funds can be made to move within unified institutional structures. This would more than offset the increase in the risk of leakages inherent in a policy of differentiated credit availability.[2]

A Ring of E.E.C. Financial Centres

The formative process of a common monetary and financial market implies changes in the set-up now obtaining inside each member country, and in intra-E.E.C. relations as well. But are the changes going to be, and should they be, of the type which would lead to the emergence of a Community financial super-market, a single giant market-place, where wholesale monetary and financial transactions would be concentrated?

As in so many other respects, in this case too the long existence of separate national markets in Europe and the strength of the centrifugal forces make people inclined to advocate a larger measure of centralisation than is in fact needed. More generally, biased thinking in favour of concentration of large-size transactions in one dominant centre often overlooks the fact that a number of alternative market structures have been made possible *inter alia* by the progress of telecommunications and the formation of international banking groups with a decentralised

[1] Lamfalussy argued some time ago that the development of dollar, unit-of-account and other currency loans was not 'tantamount to the development of a European capital market', but simply superimposed a new layer on national markets ([32] p. 27).

[2] In the Annual Report of the Banca d'Italia for 1971, it is argued that the unity of the monetary framework, on a national basis, is necessary in order to allow the flow of financial resources between the various parts of the country, such as posited by regionally balanced growth [1].

structure. The notion of a financial centre has for a long time already had little significance for exchange markets. Their operations, international in nature, are carried out with the help of telex machines and international direct-dial telephone;[1] the network of these contacts stretches around the globe.

The exchange-market pattern has had to be borrowed for the organisation of a secondary market for Euro-bonds. The geographical dispersion of participants in that market and the complex settlement procedures, in which delivery of the bonds, and payment for the same, have often to be made in different countries, and these in turn may not be the countries of residence of seller and buyer, have made it difficult for any one stock exchange to centralise trading. Notwithstanding the benefits which can be derived from listing when it comes to selling the bonds, the role of stock exchanges in Euro-bond trading has tended to decline.[2]

If markets can be integrated without having to concentrate orders to buy and sell in a single location, then the argument in favour of the formation of a financial super-centre falls. In fact, one wonders what good integration could bring, if one centre were to crush all competition and finally downgrade the others to the status of local markets, which in the end would communicate among themselves not directly, but through the intermediation of the super-centre. Local markets would form and gravitate around the two or three major centres in each country. Each centre would develop the links with the Community super-centre; but those with other centres, both within the same country and in other member countries, would get thinner.

This set-up would clearly favour marginal unification of what would remain basically distinct markets, rather than their thorough integration in a way that would go beyond the concept and essence of communicating markets. In my view, the markets would be better served if, instead of one super-centre, there emerged a ring of half a dozen or so closely integrated financial

[1] To co-ordinate daily interventions on exchange markets, in accordance with the E.E.C. narrower margins agreement, a 'conference telephone' system has been installed to connect simultaneously the participating central banks. Such a device might be of great help to European multinational credit institutions with a decentralised general management.

[2] Listing requirements are a guarantee to investors. Also, listing is often necessary to make the bonds eligible as an investment for certain categories of institutional investors.

centres with a leading position in E.E.C. business. In each and all of them the major European credit and financial institutions would be represented at general management level; they would be able to bid for deposits or otherwise raise funds; make loans and investments; match orders to buy and sell securities; have a share in the wholesale credit business to which the multinational companies are parties; and carry out any business originating anywhere in the Community without having to funnel them through one super-centre. They would maintain instant and constant communication with one another and work as institutions of one market.

A polycentric structure of the markets would, of course, not be a novelty. Among Continental European countries, Switzerland offers the closest approximation to it, and within the E.E.C. itself, the Federal Republic of Germany has the 'big three' commercial banks with the general management decentralised in three major financial centres – Frankfurt, Düsseldorf and Hamburg. In Italy, the market has a bipolar structure, with Rome and Milan showing a measure of specialisation.

Decentralisation would have to be accompanied by a deployment of the banks' general management that would allow coverage of all the major financial centres in the ring. It is, however, worth noting, in this respect, that the many foreign banks which during the 1960s have come to London, mainly on account of the Euro-dollar business, have had their operations headed by a senior officer (in the case of the United States banks, a vice-president or senior vice-president) with sufficient delegated responsibility. With possibly a few exceptions, the need to post a member of the general management in London has not been felt, at a time when London was asserting herself as the leading centre for Euro-market business. Not one has had on this account to move its head office there.

Within a polycentric structure, no single centre would dominate in the way in which, say, New York has for so long dominated the United States scene. There would be competition among the principal financial centres to lead in one sector or another. And of course, a few would try to establish a lead over the others in most, if not all, sectors of activity.

Not much is known about the hierarchies of money and capital markets and how they are established. We know from history that financial centres grow stronger in places enjoying prosperity and fast growth. In fact, as these latter shift from one country or region to another, the location of the leading financial centres tends to follow. Thus, in the Renaissance, the great city-states in Tuscany and northern Italy also dominated the world scene as centres of banking and finance. Thereafter prosperity moved northwards and the Hanseatic cities became the new centres of world finance, until in the nineteenth century London took over, with Paris and Berlin as strong competitors. After the First World War, the rise of New York as the world's financial hub was another sign of Europe's economic and political decline. This latter lasted nearly uninterruptedly till after the end of the Second World War, when the trend was finally reversed. Having staged during the 1950s its powerful economic comeback, in the 1960s Europe successfully challenged the dominant position of New York in international finance.

Historical observation, however, also suggests that there is no absolute set of requirements that have to be met in order to gain financial ascendancy. In fact, even the general rule that financial centres follow prosperity seems to admit of exceptions. London has risen to primacy in the 1960s while the United Kingdom economy was growing sluggishly; the economic decline of the United States relative to Europe in this post-war period was mainly due to the high rates of growth attained by most *Continental* Western European countries.

What can be stated more safely is that there are several conditions which favour the relative position of financial centres. While no single one could be regarded as essential, the larger the number of requisites that a centre can satisfy, the better its chances of achieving dominance. The fact that there is no single condition that *must* be met works towards the establishment of a market structure based on a plurality of financial centres, such as advocated here.

Among the conditions favouring a financial centre, the degree of its external orientation and of accessibility would have to rank high. To attract business from all or most areas of the Community, a financial centre must be outward-looking. If it is geared preponderantly to financing local (national) industry and trade, it will not be able to make an important contribution to the creation of a Community-wide market for loans. Financial leadership in the Community can hardly be reconciled with parochial attitudes. The inclination to think of money and capital markets as more or less automatic mechanisms leads to underrating the weight of psychological attitudes and long-standing habits of isolation. Even in the absence of restrictive regulations and of an inward-looking institutional organisation, access to a market can *de facto* be limited by attitudes biased against 'foreign' borrowers.

Outward-looking centres will have to rely on men of vision. Vision is needed to accept and foster acceptance of the new European currency; to cater for a clientèle which will have to be attracted from outside one's traditional purview; to judge the risks which in the short term may appear forbidding in a region or a country, because of an unsettled social or political outlook.

As a rule, access is easier in market-orientated centres, where there are a large number of participants, actual and potential, as suppliers and demanders of funds. These centres tend to be more open and more competitive than those dominated by a handful of lenders. In some European countries, capital markets are tightly controlled by the major banks; a large chunk of investment finance for companies in the private and public sectors is provided directly in the form of loans by a few commercial banks and medium-term credit institutions.

A set-up of this kind may be a source of strength from the viewpoint of the individual country, but it is a hindrance for integration and for global efficiency. Mobility is reduced to an unduly high degree in order to keep financial resources within a national domain, which is not necessarily conterminous with an optimum currency area. The balance of payments will tend to show surpluses when financial markets are inward-looking.

Within this framework, it is relatively easy for the few to make or break habits and fashions, to call the tune generally and, in the end, control the markets; in short, the market structure is more strongly oligopolistic. In some cases it is the governments that have seized the opportunity offered by ease of control and have used the mechanisms of capital markets as well as of bank credit as tools for directing the flow of loan funds in accordance with the objectives set in a national economic plan or programme. This management of the market has implied control over access to it, as well as over interest rates. The link between internal and external interest rates has been weakened and communications with other markets have been restricted.

Attitudinal and institutional openness can, of course, be restricted through exchange controls. True, we have witnessed some remarkable feats in the exercise of reconciling domestic control with external freedom, and with an important role in international finance. But, to take the case of the United Kingdom, this achievement was made possible perhaps mainly by the use of a third currency – the dollar – which already led over all others in the many private and official roles that an international currency must fulfil. Moreover, the two-layer structure of markets was well suited to the degree of co-operation and policy harmonisation which governments were willing and able to accept. But if economic and monetary union is the aim, crop-sharing with an external currency and the separation of domestic and external operations and prices will have to go, as far as intra-E.E.C. transactions are concerned.

A centre which by hypothesis had to dispense with the use of the domestic currency could adopt another E.E.C. currency or, indeed, the proposed European currency. Still, it would be at a loss vis-à-vis another Community centre where exchange controls were minimal or non-existent. For instance, London's financial expertise and infrastructure could well succeed in attracting Euro-mark trading, but competition would very likely be stiffer than in the case of the dollar, fettered by interest-rate regulations on bank deposits and, in the 1960s, by controls on capital movements. It is worth noting that in the last two years London has lost ground to the Continental centres roughly in correspondence with the advance of Continental currencies in the total volume of Euro-currency dealings. Thus there would be a built-in interest in abolishing exchange control entirely; this would have to be done anyway as part of the formation of monetary union.

If domestic savings formation is weak relative to internal demand, a centre may still attempt to develop with an entrepôt function. But to compete all along the line, the generation of an exportable savings surplus would help. Among other things, it would lend a centre more credibility if it wanted to compete for the secondary market in European securities. To make that market and assure investors of its continuing existence and functioning under less than favourable circumstances, the centre must be in a position to inject domestic savings and money, should flows from other sources dry up.

This applies to the initial or preliminary stage; but that is when centres will try to gain a decisive lead in the race to a position of dominance. Once full freedom of circulation and mobility of funds have been achieved, the concentration in given centres of financial know-how and of the ability to make savings available to the most efficient users will grow more important than the location of the savings-generation process. An illustration of this is offered by the experience made in several Continental European countries. There, savings banks have become the largest savings and liquidity reservoirs mainly as a result of their institutional vocation to cater for the smaller customers, as well as of the tendency of income shares to move in favour of labour. This, however, has not given them the key position in the national credit and financial systems, a position that is held by the commercial banks, to which the surplus funds of the savings banks largely flow.

On the other hand, the ability directly to tap savings where they are formed is strengthening the position of the savings banks to the point where they now compete both for the types of operations and the class of customers which earlier were firmly within the grip of commercial banks.[1]

While the picture is already mainly one of competition, it is likely that the scope for the latter would be considerably increased, if somehow or other it proved possible to establish a polycentric structure, such as suggested above. Competitiveness is another attribute which will help centres to lead. Markets are established to serve customers – savers, traders, industrialists, local authorities, governments; the more competitive they are, the better placed will they be to perform that function. Competitive markets work on finer margins; they offer better rates and are thereby able to attract business. This in turn enables them to achieve economies of scale, which again enhances their competitiveness.

Competitiveness does not only influence cost and price performance. A posture of aggressive competition will make a

---

[1] Similarly, in the United Kingdom the clearing banks, which possess placing power, are challenging the dominant position in the issue market of the merchant banks, which possess more expertise.

centre more sensitive to changes; will put it under stronger pressure to adapt; will make it quicker to seize new opportunities, devise and offer new services, than a centre with a fundamentally defensive stance vis-à-vis thrusts by other centres into what it may regard as its more or less private preserve. Thus a competitive centre will also offer a wider range of services –and do so with a flexibility which company treasurers do not fail to appreciate both as borrowers and as lenders.

The pressure of competition is bound to be felt also from outside the Community, once the improvement in the United States balance of payments finally makes the American authorities scrap existing controls over capital movements; then New York will in its turn be in a position to challenge European financial centres.

A Suggested Specialisation Pattern for E.E.C. Financial Centres

The attitude towards the mixed economy will also count. I think that it is safe to build on the assumption that Western European countries will remain for as far as can now be foreseen anchored to the mixed-economy system. There are, and will be, occasional thrusts by one sector to the detriment of the other, but in general policies seem to aim basically at maintaining a *competitive equilibrium* between the private and public sectors, the vitality of both being regarded as necessary to secure dynamic efficiency and fast growth. To be sure, the institutional structure does, however, slowly evolve; but not necessarily in the direction of either the preponderantly private or preponderantly public economy: a *tertium genus* may eventually emerge. If this is the prospect, an unprejudiced outlook will be an asset.

Not long ago it was thought unlikely that a government-controlled company – and a bank at that – might join a multi-national group of companies for other than a loose form of co-operation in the conventional way. That view may be exploded by the link-up between the Banco di Roma, the Commerzbank and the Crédit Lyonnais. A link-up is not exactly a merger; but then it is unlikely that we shall find acceptable solutions for our own problems if we work in the narrow groove of textbook patterns. Businessmen and bankers, just like politicians, are groping their way towards new formulas, apt to reconcile the advantages of large size with the need to preserve the deep-felt national and regional heritage.

The attitude towards private enterprise and ownership is part of the mixed-economy outlook. At a time when the share of labour in the national income is the largest and personal income after tax is sufficiently high to allow for a considerable part of it to be saved, a financial centre operating in a socio-political environment likely to inspire confidence to individual savers and to the financial intermediaries catering for them will be in a better position to attract the funds needed to meet the demands of industry and trade. Finally, a key role will be played by the confidence which a centre will be able to inspire, as concerns its ability to protect savings against the risks of mismanagement, of predatory inflation and, possibly, of what has come to be regarded in some cases as quasi-confiscatory taxation.

Clearly, no E.E.C. centre meets all these conditions; and they do not exhaust the list of those likely to foster financial leadership. Some centres, however, meet a larger number of conditions than do others. On this basis, one would have to rank uppermost the City of London. The financial know-how and infrastructure which the City inherited from its past as the world financial centre have been reinvigorated and developed as it has risen to the position of principal Euro-currency market.[1] To

[1] J. E. Nash, a City merchant banker, has very aptly described the sort of know-how that a borrower has available in London:

'Take the example of a substantial capital investment needed for a new large industrial facility. . . . Once the decision of principle was taken, the feasibility of the operation, in the City of London, would then depend on a multiplicity of advisers and financial intermediaries having some influence on the final resulting action.

'Even if a merchant banking issuing house is put in charge of the operation, considerable consultation will take place with the clearing bank involved, with the stockbrokers retained, with institutional investors whose support is needed, with the reporting accountants – even with public relation specialists within and without the institutions involved, and possibly even with senior financial writers. The terms of the issue, and the timing of the issue, would overwhelmingly depend not only on the judgement by experts of the resulting (and existing) financial structure of the borrowing company, but largely on the multiplicity of judgements on the attitude of "the market" to the issue, and on likely market action, both generally and in the case of the specific security, over the relevant period. The resulting opinions of the terms on which an issue is possible would decide whether the project is possible or not, and what its profitability is likely to be in market terms (i.e. technically calculated pay-back in relation to market cost of resources needed).' [35]

contend with the City will require a very determined effort on the part of other financial centres, and even perhaps some political propping (however much one may desire that the context be decided on the merits of the participants). To remain in the race, Continental financial centres should already now be intensifying the contacts between themselves. If banks and other financial intermediaries on the Continent open branches or otherwise establish a foothold in the City, but not in Continental financial centres, the gap between the latter's importance and the City's will grow. The monocentric pattern will be strengthened, each Continental centre being linked to the City and only communicating with one another through it.

The opening of branches by Continental banks in Continental centres is needed not just from the viewpoint of competition between financial centres, but also to attain the depth of integration posited by monetary union. This aim can be achieved within a reasonable time horizon by pursuing all suitable lines of action, including the formation of bank consortia and linkups.

Multinational bank consortia have known a great success in recent years, largely owing to the persistence of a 'Macmillan gap' on a European scale, while the quickened pace of obsolescence of production plant and equipment was increasing the demand for *medium-term* credit.[1] Technically, the attraction of consortia springs from the fact that member banks are enabled to take on commitments which they could not do individually. Furthermore, banks without prominent experience in the field improve their chances of joining the international circuit of lucrative underwriting business. On the other hand, banks forming a consortium keep their independence as well as their freedom of initiative in fields such as deposit raising, where very large size is not essential, or in territories where the agreement is not meant to apply; thus banks competing in one country form consortia to operate together in others. Although this would appear to confirm that competition and co-operation are not necessarily incompatible, a number of consortia have

---

[1] A point made by the Macmillan Committee, over forty years ago, was that the British financial system was not 'as fitted as it might be to supply industry (i) with intermediate credit and (ii) with long-dated capital' ([10] esp. pp. 161-74).

experienced difficulties due to conflicts of interest between sponsoring banks. In some cases there has been resistance to making services reciprocally available; in others, the chances for the consortial bank to pursue lucrative business propositions have been pre-empted by competing actions on the part of the founding houses themselves. In several instances, however, bank consortia continue to function to the satisfaction of all concerned.

I regard bank link-ups as a potentially powerful instrument for the unification of the Community's money and credit infrastructures. Although not outright mergers, they may ultimately have similar results. In principle, the solidarity of interests is pursued over the whole range of the banks' activities, not just in one sector. The relaxation and final abolition of exchange controls would significantly increase the scope for managing their joint resources as a unified pool; in fact, the formation of a number of such link-ups would exert a rising pressure towards liberalisation. On the other hand, one should again not lose sight of the fact that the outcome will depend largely on the attitudes of the personalities involved. Link-ups are also taking place between banks within the same country; there are no exchange-control barriers to overcome, but that *per se* is no guarantee of success.

Bank link-ups must still prove their worth; but if their potentialities promise to materialise and convincing progress is made towards monetary unification at the official level, many large and medium-size banks might find link-ups the most suitable way of coping with the challenge. It would allow them to grow into truly European credit institutions, instead of risking falling into the class of local banks. Banks more jealous of their autonomy, which they also value as a guarantee of their continuing adherence to the business philosophy and style they may have developed over centuries-long activity, might seek congenial society in other member countries. They would attempt to form groups balanced also as to the size of the participants. Although a *primus inter pares* position might emerge, the balance of power would be such that no single head office could be regarded as the exclusive centre of decision.

There is no inescapable necessity for such groups to be less efficient than those with a monocentric structure of general management. In fact, given the conditions of diversity we are starting from, it may be a distinct advantage to have a decentralised general management, which would meet at regular intervals and between meetings keep in touch through 'conference telephone' and otherwise. Men are needed, who can forcefully assert their own regional and national experience and interests, but who also realise that the fruits of integration cannot be reaped, and identity cannot in the end be saved, without allowing for competition and change. Exchanges of staff, all the way up to general management level, would foster interpenetration and cohesion between banks in a link-up.

Finally, there will also be cases of very large banks deciding to 'go it alone'. They might, however, be tempted to link up with smaller banks, in which case the operation would be more akin to a take-over and would represent a short-cut to the otherwise slow creation of a multinational network of branches.

A big reshuffling of banking and finance is likely to take place during the present and the next decades in Europe. As a result, the deposit banks' network of branches will no longer be conterminous with a country's territory – or part of it. Indeed, many existing banks may become the national arms of new European banking groups. This would allow banks to attain the optimum size posited by the current scale of industrial and commercial business without weakening competition – or at least without further reducing the number of banks operating in *each* member country.

In view of the prominent place which economic and financial questions have in today's politics, it is unlikely that the latter would keep outside the game. If political 'guidance' cannot be dispensed with, a helpful task for it might be to orientate the reshuffling so as to allow each country to have one of its banks in a position of *primus inter pares* in a proportionate number of European banking groups. This task would be both easier and more beneficial if it was pursued with a view to favouring specialisation among the main financial centres, according to their experience and endowment. The City of London, with the wealth of its international contacts, its acceptance houses, its overseas and foreign banks, might lead in the Community's foreign business. The City's institutions might take the initiative for link-ups with similarly orientated Continental banks. The

City would find allies and competitors especially in Amsterdam, with its long-standing experience in international money arbitrage.

On the other hand, the financing of European industry would gravitate mainly to those Continental European centres that have already tested the formulas that are bound to be more widely applied in future. Financial centres in the Federal Republic of Germany would be well placed to attract this business, given among other things the close links between banking and industry.[1] The French and Italian banking systems, on the other hand, have respectively made a unique contribution in Western Europe, in directing the flow of funds towards the fulfilment of the aims of the national economic plan, and in the financing of the public sector, as well as of industrial conversion and regional development programmes. The formulae are controversial; but if the mixed-economy assumption is correct, France and Italy would have a special contribution to make as to the ways and means of financing industry belonging to the two sectors. Moreover, a surplus of savings being by and large a feature of Continental financial centres, they would have a differential advantage, at least at the start, for dealing with the long-term financial needs of European industry.

Finally, the position of Continental Europe will also be bolstered through the activity of the Community itself in this field. On the basis of present indications, Belgium and Luxembourg are likely to be the seat of the institutions that may be formed in order to carry out monetary unification such as it is now being pursued. But when it finally comes to the creation of a European bank on the scale proposed for the M.E.B. in the previous essays, that bank should have its own skeleton network of branches – at least one branch in each of the main economic regions of the Community, where the European bank might have to be lender or borrower of funds. There would be distinct advantages in establishing direct Community contacts and not having *all* the local work done for the European bank

---

[1] Here are a few lines from the evidence given by a German expert to the Macmillan Committee: 'The relationship between a bank and an industrial or trading company commences with the latter's foundation. Scarcely a single important company in Germany has been founded without the collaboration of a bank' ([10] p. 163).

through the agency of other banks and institutions. The management of each branch would be assisted by an advisory board, on which would sit representatives of local economic interests.

These suggestions are offered, of course, only as an exemplification of the pattern that might be aimed at for Europe's money and capital market. Together with the other suggestions made in this book, they may perhaps help to build a Europe of free and gifted equals.

REFERENCES

[1] BANCA D'ITALIA, *Assemblea Generale Ordinaria dei Partecipanti – Anno 1971* (Rome, 31 May 1972).

[2] BANK FOR INTERNATIONAL SETTLEMENTS, *Annual Report for 1971* (Basle, June 1972).

[3] BANK OF ENGLAND, 'The Euro-currency Business of Banks in London', *Bank of England Quarterly Bulletin* (Mar 1970).

[4] BELL, P. W., *The Sterling Area in the Post-war World; Internal Mechanism and Cohesion, 1946-1952* (Oxford: Clarendon Press, 1956).

[5] CARLI, G., 'The Euro-dollar Market and its Control', address at the Swiss Institute of International Studies, Winter Program 1971-2: Lectures on 'Inflation and the International Monetary System' (Zürich, 14 Feb 1972).

[6] CARLI, G., 'Adapting to E.E.C. System', *The Times*, 24 May 1972.

[7] CASSELL, F., 'The Role of Sterling in the E.E.C.', *Bankers' Magazine* (May 1972).

[8] COFFEY, P., and PRESLEY, J. R., *European Monetary Integration* (London: Macmillan, 1971).

[9] COLLIN, F., 'Towards a Stable Standard of Value', in *The Unit of Account in the European Capital Market* (Brussels: Kredietbank N.V., 1970).

[10] COMMITTEE ON FINANCE AND INDUSTRY (Macmillan Committee), *Report* (London: H.M.S.O., 1931).

[11] COMMITTEE ON THE WORKING OF THE MONETARY SYSTEM (Radcliffe Committee), *Principal Memoranda of Evidence*, vol. 1, Memorandum no. 7, 'Sterling as an International Currency', by the Bank of England (London: H.M.S.O., 1960).

[12] CONAN, A. R., *The Sterling Area* (London: Macmillan, 1952).

[13] COOPER, R. N., *Sterling, European Monetary Unification and the International Monetary System* (British–North American Committee, London: Mar 1972).

[14] DE LATTRE, ANDRÉ, 'The Euro-dollar Market: A French View', in H. V. Prochnow (ed.), *The Eurodollar* (Chicago: Rand McNally, 1970).

[15] DESPRES, E., KINDLEBERGER, C. P., and SALANT W. S., 'The Dollar and World Liquidity – A Minority View', *The Economist*, 5 Feb 1966.

[16] DEUTSCHE BUNDESBANK, *Geschäftsbericht für das Jahr 1971* (Frankfurt a.M., 1972).

[17] ECONOMIST, THE, 'The World is a Market', 15 July 1972.

[18] EINAUDI, L., 'Galiani Economista', *Atti dell'Accademia Nazionale dei Lincei*, anno CCCXLVI (1949), Serie 8, *Rendiconti, Classe di Scienze Morali, Storiche e Filologiche*, vol. IV (Rome, 1949).

[19] EINZIG, P., *A Dynamic Theory of Forward Exchange* (London: Macmillan, 1961).

[20] ELSASSR, F., 'Pour une Union Monétaire Européenne dès 1973', *Chroniques d'Actualite*, tome VI, no. 2 (Feb 1972).

[21] EMMINGER, O., 'The Dollar and the International Monetary System', *Euromoney* (Dec 1971).

[22] EMMINGER, O., 'Was Wird aus dem Dollar?', interview with the Vice-President of the Bundesbank, *Wirtschaftswoche der Volkswirt* (Frankfurt a.M.), 14 July 1972, as reported in *Auszüge aus Presseartikeln*, published by the Deutsche Bundesbank.

[23] FLEMING, M. J., 'Dual Exchange Rates for Current and Capital Transactions: A Theoretical Examination', in *Essays in International Economics* (London: Allen & Unwin, 1971).

[24] FRIEDMAN, M. 'The Euro-dollar Market: Some First Principles', *Morgan Guaranty Survey* (Morgan Guaranty Trust Company of New York, Oct 1969; reprint).

[25] HABERLER, G., 'Prospects for the Dollar Standard', *Lloyds Bank Review* (July 1972).

[26] HIRSCH, F., 'The Politics of World Money', *The Economist*, 5 Aug 1972.

198   EUROPEAN MONETARY UNIFICATION

[27] KEYNES, J. M., *The Economic Consequences of the Peace* (London: Macmillan, 1920).
[28] KINDLEBERGER, C. P., *Power and Money* (London: Macmillan, 1970).
[29] KLOPSTOCK, F. H., *The Euro-dollar: Some Unresolved Issues*, Essays in Internation Finance, no. 65 (International Finance Section, Princeton University, Mar 1968).
[30] KREDIETBANK, 'Unit of Account Bonds: Situation after the Washington Monetary Agreement', *Kredietbank Weekly Bulletin*, 31 Dec 1971.
[31] KREDIETBANK, 'New Paths for the Unit of Account', *Kredietbank Weekly Bulletin*, 4 Aug 1972.
[32] LAMFALUSSY, M. A., 'Towards a European Capital Market?', in *International Monetary Problems* (London: Federal Trust for Education and Research, 1965).
[33] MACHLUP, F., 'Changes in the International Monetary System and the Effects on Banks', in *Banking in a Changing World*, Lectures and Proceedings at the 24th International Banking Summer School held in Chianciano (Italy), May 1971 (Rome: Associazione Bancaria Italiana, 1971).
[34] MUNDELL, R. A., 'World Inflation and the Eurodollar', in *Note Economiche, Monte dei Paschi di Siena* (Mar–Apr 1971).
[35] NASH, J. E., *The Future of Financial Centres in a European Monetary Union* (Tilburg: Société Universitaire Européenne de Recherches Financières, 1972).
[36] NURKSE, R., *International Currency Experience: Lessons of the Inter-war Period* (Geneva: Economic, Financial and Transit Department, League of Nations, 1944; reprinted 1947).
[37] OSSOLA, R., 'The European Economic Community at the Crossroads', in *Essays in Honour of Thorkil Kristensen* (Paris: O.E.C.D., 1970).
[38] SCITOVSKY, T., *Economic Theory and Western European Integration* (London: Allen & Unwin, 1958).
[39] U.S. GOVERNMENT, *Economic Policies and Practices*, paper no. 3: *A Description and Analysis of Certain European Capital Markets*, Materials Prepared for the Joint Economic Committee, Congress of the U.S. (Washington: U.S. Government Printing Office, 1964).
[40] VINER, J., 'Clapham on the Bank of England', *Economica* (May 1945).

European Monetary Integration

Introduction

One of the principal decisions reached by the Heads of State of the Six, at their conference at The Hague in December 1969, was to proclaim the goal of converting the European Economic Community into an economic and monetary union. The subsequent history of this ambition has not, so far, been happy. A committee chaired by M. Pierre Werner, the Prime Minister of Luxembourg, was created to advise on how the goal might be achieved. Its report (the Werner Report) provoked considerable controversy and criticism; even some of the modest first steps that were ultimately agreed on have never been implemented, being among the casualties of the Dollar Crisis.

The unsettled state of the international monetary system may increase the difficulties of constructing a European monetary area, but it increases the importance and urgency of the task even more. It is the aim of this Report to develop a strategy that will enable the drive toward monetary integration to be resumed, whatever the outcome of the Dollar Crisis. This strategy involves filling some of the gaps that were left by the Werner Report, notably with regard to the intermediate stage of partial monetary integration. But it differs from the Werner approach

Text of the report prepared by a Federal Trust for Education and Research working group, of which the present author and Professor J. Williamson were joint rapporteurs. First published by the Federal Trust in Feb 1972 (London).

in that the latter envisaged integration solely as a process of the convergence of existing currencies (especially with regard to exchange rates), while the present Report argues that integration could be facilitated by the early creation of a new currency, which is provisionally called the 'Europa'.

The general political outlook of the Group responsible for this Report is one of sympathy for European integration coupled with a desire to retain the rich diversity that history has bequeathed to contemporary Europe. Integration is desirable, not as an end in itself, but because there are some fields in which nation-states are too small to be viable decision units in the present age. In some cases this is because efficiency demands a larger market than the nation can provide; in others because spillovers beyond national boundaries have become critically important; and in others because the small nation-states of former ages carry little weight on the world scene unless they act together. Where such factors as these indicate the desirability of centralising decision-making, integration should be pursued. But where no such rationale exists, centralisation should be resisted and individual countries, or regions, should be encouraged to develop in their own individual way.

I. *The Meaning and Rationale of Monetary Integration*

Full monetary union implies a single currency circulating throughout the union and managed by a single central bank system. Monetary union may be taken as virtually complete when individual currencies, though still existing, have been irrevocably locked together by the total abandonment of independent parity changes, the suppression of the margins, and the establishment of complete convertibility.

A state of economic union exists when all the principal levers of economic policy, and not just the monetary levers, are centralised. This includes, in particular, fiscal policy, incomes policy, planning, and regional policy.

One may distinguish four economic advantages of creating a monetary union:

(a) The increased efficiency resulting from simpler transfers and calculations and the elimination of exchange risk.

(b) The elimination of traditional-style balance-of-payments problems through increased capital mobility (although of course developments that now create payments problems could still give rise to regional problems).

(c) The economies in reserve-holding provided by pooling of exchange reserves.

(d) The possibility of re-establishing European control of European monetary conditions.

In so far as monetary integration was successful in achieving these advantages, it would contribute to creating the political conditions for progress in other spheres where a functional need for integration exists.

Conversely, however, the cause of European integration would be retarded if monetary integration were to be pursued but the attempt were to fail. The potential dangers of monetary integration stem from the loss of the power of altering the national exchange rate; such a loss could threaten the more stable countries with excessive inflation and/or the more inflationary countries with a loss of prosperity that would be the more intractable precisely because it would be manifest as a regional problem rather than a balance-of-payments problem. This danger is particularly acute in the European context because different national traditions and institutions could give rise to inconsistent trends in unit costs in different national 'regions'. This development would be so disastrous, if realised, that it would inevitably lead to the destruction of monetary union.

The advantages of monetary integration can only be completely realised through full monetary union, so it is desirable to retain this as the ultimate goal, even though prudence may demand that moving to this goal be delayed until one has confidence that conditions have been created under which the potential dangers of monetary integration will not materialise. But there is considerable scope for realising the advantages of integration by a more limited measure of integration, involving the creation of a European monetary area with its own currency, even before these conditions have been created. This intermediate stage of monetary integration would be feasible in the near future. The next three sections of this Report are therefore concerned with developing proposals for the intermediate stage, while Section V discusses the conditions necessary for transition to full monetary union.

II. *Outline of a New Plan by Stages*

It is proposed that the *final* stage of monetary integration would be a state of full monetary union, as envisaged in the Werner Report. Prior to this there would be an *intermediate* stage; this would be of indeterminate duration, since transition to the final stage would await realisation of the conditions needed to ensure that the danger of inconsistent cost trends did not materialise. The intermediate stage would be characterised by limited intra-European exchange-rate flexibility (as compared to that between European currencies and the rest of the world), the active use of the Europa to serve as international money and circulate in parallel to existing European currencies, and the abolition of intra-European exchange controls. Since the Europa would serve as the intervention currency during the intermediate stage, it would not be practicable to change directly from the present state of affairs to the intermediate stage. There would need to be a *preliminary* stage to launch the Europa and build up its use as a market asset. It is envisaged that this preliminary stage should be brief.

(1) *The Preliminary Stage*

The programme of monetary integration would be inaugurated by the founding of a European Bank. This Bank would perform the functions that have been assigned to a European Reserve Fund or Stabilisation Fund in previous proposals, but it would not be limited to these. In particular, it would be responsible for launching the Europa and encouraging its adoption as a monetary unit by those engaged in international transactions.

Existing intervention arrangements would not be altered drastically during the preliminary stage, since it is desirable that this be as brief as possible in order to obtain the benefits of moving to the intermediate stage quickly. If the dollar was still being used as intervention currency and it was desired to have an intra-European band that was less than twice the European/dollar band, this could be achieved by concerted intervention as proposed by the Werner Committee (the 'snake in the tunnel').

It would also be desirable to commence the steps towards policy harmonisation and liberalisation of capital flows that the Werner Report advocated for the first stage. (However, in Section V it is suggested that policy harmonisation should be primarily concentrated on monetary rather than fiscal instruments, and this difference in emphasis would apply *a fortiori* to the preliminary stage.)

(2) *The Intermediate Stage*

The transition from the preliminary stage to the intermediate stage would be made as soon as the Europa was sufficiently widely held in private hands to permit the dollar to be replaced by the Europa as the intervention currency. The national central banks would have the responsibility of intervening to defend the rate between their national currencies and the Europa, while the European Bank would defend the Europa/dollar rate. There would be a narrow intra-European band coupled with a wide band between the Europa and the dollar.

Maintenance of a narrow intra-European band would require conjunctural harmonisation within Europe. However, the intermediate stage would be practicable before the total suppression of divergent trends in unit costs, because intra-European parity changes would still be permissible. The wide band between the Europa and the dollar would enable Europe to regain a greater measure of freedom from U.S. monetary policy, although it could not insulate Europe from the effects of any future American fundamental disequilibrium. The existence of the Europa would make it possible for the exchange rate between the dollar and European currencies to vary in any imaginable way (including floating) without disrupting intra-European relationships. Other advantages of Europe moving jointly against the dollar include the greater ability of the whole European area to absorb hot money without being overwhelmed, as compared to a situation in which the whole weight is concentrated on the strongest individual European currency (e.g. the Deutsche Mark in May 1971); and the reduction in the subsidy that central banks pay to international companies who switch their funds from one financial centre to another to take advantage of sequence of parity changes.

(3) *The Final Stage*

This would involve full monetary union with a common currency. The transition from the intermediate to the final stage would be contingent on satisfactorily overcoming the problem of divergent cost trends. This would require, among other things, a fair measure of centralisation of economic policy, since automatic fiscal transfers and a centralised regional policy are among the factors that contribute to enabling a monetary union to dispense with internal exchange-rate changes. Although a measure of fiscal unification would be desirable and necessary, this certainly does not mean that total centralisation would be needed (as, for example, the American experience of state fiscal autonomy demonstrates). When the interlocking of the economies and the construction of an economic union had provided the necessary conditions for proceeding to the final stage, national currencies would be withdrawn and replaced by Europas.

III. *The European Bank and the Europa*

It will be evident from the preceding outline that the Europa constitutes a central feature of the proposed strategy, and that the European Bank is being assigned a key role in fostering monetary integration. It is appropriate to sketch the rationale of these strategic proposals.

The case for creating a Europa stems from the practical need for an international money and the unsuitability of the alternatives. In recent years the dollar has been the dominant form of international money, and the Euro-dollar market has grown up primarily in response to the desire of those engaged in international business to hold international money. The Euro-dollar market has in fact constituted the nearest approach to a common European money and capital market, and has in this capacity been a potent factor favouring financial integration within Europe. But it has suffered from the embarrassment of also being closely linked to the U.S. money market, thus serving to transmit American monetary policies to Europe. Since American monetary policy is (understandably) determined with reference to the U.S. domestic situation, the result of this arrangement has been to impose monetary conditions on

Europe that were at times strongly at variance with local conjunctural needs. So long as the dollar remains the international money, any European country attempting to insulate itself from American monetary policies will also insulate itself from its European partners either by exchange controls or by exchange-rate flexibility.

One could seek to replace the dollar by adopting one of the European currencies as the international currency. This, however, would tend to reproduce the same kinds of difficulties, since the country whose currency was selected would naturally wish to determine its monetary policy with a view to domestic rather than pan-European conditions; the problem would be mitigated only to the extent that a European country would prove more susceptible to its partners' representations than the United States has proved to be.

Since S.D.R.s were specifically designed to be only an official international money, while the need is for a private international money, it is necessary to create a new unit in view of the disadvantages of using a national currency. This solution may be regarded as a compromise between the positions of the 'monetarists' and the 'economists'. It endorses the 'monetarist' view that common monetary arrangements need to be developed in the short run and not merely after lengthy experimentation with harmonisation, but it also incorporates the 'economists' view that premature commitments to rigid exchange rates need to be avoided.

The case for a European Bank, performing the functions of an embryonic reserve bank, is twofold. First, it is necessary to create an institution charged with developing and managing the Europa. Secondly, the policy harmonisation that is a precondition for the transition to full monetary union can best be furthered by the creation of an institution with significant powers to influence the member countries and a vested interest in promoting harmonisation.

The Bank would be formed on the general lines that Triffin has long advocated for founding a European Reserve Fund. That is, countries would pay in to the Bank a specified proportion of their reserves plus a quota of domestic currency. The latter would be sufficiently large to have the effect of reproducing the support facilities that E.E.C. members have agreed to provide under the Barre Plan. Countries would receive in return deposits denominated in Europas. These deposits would count as a part of countries' reserves and could be drawn on in the event of a payments deficit.

The European Bank would be managed by a Board of Governors, which might comprise the governors of the national central banks together with a chairman appointed by the Council of Ministers of the European Communities. The Board would be responsible to the Council of Ministers. In order to ensure that the Council was able to exercise effective control of the continuous policy-making that would be involved in determining European monetary policy, it would be necessary to eliminate the right of individual nations to exercise a veto in this limited area. The effective and speedy administration of those policy weapons that were specifically placed at the European level would only be feasible on the basis of majority voting.

The European Bank would have the following responsibilities:

(a) It would act as a European Reserve Fund from the date of its inception.

(b) Once the preliminary stage had given way to the intermediate stage, it would intervene to stabilise the Europa/dollar exchange rate.

(c) It would recommend changes in the parity of the Europa in terms of gold/S.D.R.s to the Council of Ministers.

(d) It would control overall European monetary policy, and would attempt to ensure consistency between the general Community policy and the policies being pursued in individual states. (This would include supervision of intra-European exchange rates.)

(e) It would nurture the growth of the Europa as a private monetary asset, principally by acting as a central bank to commercial banks operating in the Europa market.

The parity of the Europa would be defined in terms of the international monetary unit, which at present consists of gold and S.D.R.s rigidly linked together. The parity would be changeable by a decision of the Council of Ministers, who would be advised on this subject by the European Bank. The governing principle in determining parity changes between the

Europa and the rest of the world would be that of maintaining the Bank's external liquidity at a level sufficiently high to safeguard the pursuit of a high rate of balanced growth in the Community, but not so excessively high as to involve a waste of resources, and embarrassment to third countries.

The Europa would serve as a reserve medium for the European central banks. (Unless present trends away from the reserve-currency system are reversed, one would not expect it to become a reserve currency held by non-European countries.) Above all, however, the Europa is envisaged as a private asset able to function as a pan-European money. If it succeeds, it will fill the role that the Euro-dollar has performed for the past decade in acting as an instrument for the creation of unified European money and capital markets. In due course the Europa could be expected to displace the Euro-dollar, at least so far as European borrowers and lenders are concerned. This would have the advantages of helping to insulate intra-European relationships from instability emanating from the other side of the Atlantic, of enabling Europe to exercise some measure of control over this important component of the effective European money supply, and of permitting Europe to exercise flexibility against the rest of the world without disrupting the stability of intra-European exchange rates.

It has often been stated that monies grow naturally and that attempts to impose a new money artificially are bound to fail. There is much truth in this contention. If the Europa is to succeed, it will only be because it is an asset with more desirable properties, from the viewpoint of the prospective holders, than the dollar. In large measure success breeds on success; once an asset has become firmly established, this fact in itself will enhance its position, because of the ease of using the asset as a means of payment and of the resiliency, breadth and depth of its financial markets. The difficult part of the problem is to win initial acceptance of the Europa as a unit for denominating market assets. There are, however, a large number of measures that could be taken to stimulate the establishment of the Europa as a market asset. Some of these measures might initially involve a slight element of additional cost to the authorities, but this would disappear (and might well be reversed) as soon as the Europa had become thoroughly accepted. The measures that could

H

be adopted to foster the establishment of the Europa are as follows:

(1) The issue by Community institutions, such as the European Coal and Steel Community and the European Investment Bank, of Europa-denominated assets.

(2) A Community requirement that some proportion of the national debt of each member state be issued in Europa-denominated assets.

(3) The imposition of an obligation on commercial banks to hold some proportion of their assets in Europa-denominated assets. (This might involve the banks in either running an unbalanced Europa position, which should be acceptable if parity changes were always small, and offset by interest rates, or else in covering their Europa position forward, which the European Bank might assist by providing any necessary support in the forward market.)

(4) A willingness by national goverments to accept taxes in Europas.

(5) The European Bank providing clearing-house facilities for Europa transactions.

(6) The European Bank making a secondary market in Europa-denominated Treasury Bills.

(7) Once the intermediate stage had been reached, the European Bank could take the responsibility of acting as lender of last resort in the Europa bill market.

(8) The attractiveness of the Europa would also be enhanced by the exchange-rate provisions that are envisaged (see Section IV), since these would minimise the fluctuation of European currencies in terms of the Europa while making them relatively large in terms of the dollar.

It is sometimes supposed that, because the growth of the Euro-dollar market was fed by a prolonged U.S. deficit, there would be an analogous need for a European deficit in order to support the growth of a Europa market. This is erroneous. A European deficit would assist in turning the Europa into a reserve currency, and it would no doubt be helpful in developing the Europa as a vehicle currency for use by parties external to the Europa area, but it is irrelevant to the establishment of the Europa within Europe.[1]

It is of interest to examine the way in which the European Bank would perform its functions. Its balance sheet would contain the following items:

BALANCE SHEET OF EUROPEAN BANK

Liabilities	Assets
Capital and reserves	Gold, S.D.R.s, national
Europa deposits by central banks	currencies
	Europa-denominated bills
Europa deposits by commercial banks	Europa-denominated loans

The Bank would engage in the following types of operations:

(a) It would intervene in the Europa/dollar market; for example by selling dollars from its portfolio and debiting the accounts of the commercial banks on which the Europa cheques to pay for the dollars were drawn.

(b) It would deal with non-European central banks; for example, by exchanging gold and S.D.R.s for dollars (so as to maintain appropriate dollar working balances), by engaging in swap transactions, and by making purchases (or re-purchases) from the I.M.F.

(c) It would deal with its member central banks; for example if a member acquired excessive Europa deposits, because of a payments surplus, these might be extinguished by the country repurchasing some of its Europa-denominated bills held in the Bank's portfolio.

[1] This can be seen by considering a typical Euro-dollar position, e.g. a 3-month Euro-dollar deposit, representing the proceeds of exports to the U.S. by a German firm, with a Euro-dollar bank in London; and a 3-month loan by the Euro-dollar bank to a Dutch firm which proceeded to convert its borrowings into guilders. Suppose that, at the end of the 3-month term, both the German and Dutch firms wished to roll forward their loans for a further 3 months, but that the greater exchange-rate stability between their respective national currencies and the Europa (as opposed to the dollar) led them to want the loan to be denominated in Europas. There would be nothing to prevent the Euro-dollar bank re-denominating both loans accordingly at the prevailing exchange rate, in which case a switch to the Europa market would take place without any movement of funds at all.

(*d*) It would engage in open-market operations in the Europa bill market, buying or selling bills with a resultant impact on the Europa deposits of commercial banks.

The terms on which the European Bank would deal with non-European central banks are bound to depend upon the form of the global monetary system that emerges from the dollar crisis. The examples given in paragraph (*b*) above assume, as seems probable at the time of writing, that this will be a universal, I.M.F.–centred system in which S.D.R.s become the principal reserve asset and are used to fund outstanding balances of reserve currencies in excess of working balances. (If this does not happen, and the world polarises into a set of defensive monetary blocs, dollar convertibility will presumably not be restored and it will not be possible to maintain dollar balances at the required working level through transactions with the Federal Reserve or the I.M.F. The result would no doubt be a floating Europa/dollar rate, with Europe gradually disposing of its excess dollar holdings. Another probable consequence of such a development would be the emergence of the Europa as a reserve currency, which would involve non-European central banks holding Europa deposits at the European Bank on essentially the same terms as those envisaged for commercial-bank deposits.)

One important purpose of replacing Euro-dollars by Europas would be to establish a measure of control over this important constituent of the effective European money supply. Such control requires that it should be relatively difficult to switch between Europas and Euro-dollars, since otherwise any attempted monetary policy could be side-stepped through a transfer of business to or from the Euro-dollar market. There are two ways of counteracting a tendency for undesired switching. One is to allow significant fluctuation in the Europa/dollar exchange rate; this would lead to any one-way movements being nullified by rate changes. The other method is to surround the Europa area by an effective exchange-control barrier. This might involve forbidding residents of the area to borrow or hold short-term externally-denominated assets without permission. The best policy would probably involve moderate recourse to both techniques.

In the past Euro-dollar assets have often been more attractive to hold than national assets, as a result of the lack of regulation of the Euro-dollar market. In order to allow Europas to displace Euro-dollars it would be necessary to avoid regulating the Europa market so soon, or so severely, as to make Europas unattractive to hold relative to Euro-dollars. No doubt the dollar crisis will help to mitigate this particular problem by reducing the attractiveness of the dollar as a vehicle currency, so that some influence on the Europa market could be exercised by open-market operations from an early stage. In due course it should prove possible to establish additional leverage by introducing moderate reserve requirements: indeed, if this were not done there would be a danger of the Europa making excessive encroachments on national money markets. Once the Europa is firmly established and there are effective monetary walls insulating the Europa area, it might well prove more important to align Europa reserve requirements with those in the national states rather than with those in the remnants of the Euro-dollar market, especially since one hopes to operate with minimal exchange-control barriers between the Europa and individual European currencies.

IV. *Exchange Rates during the Transition*

The proposed arrangements regarding exchange rates during the transitional stages before full monetary union are motivated by three convictions. The first is that the 'economists' are right in arguing that monetary locking cannot force a harmonisation of cost trends; it would be foolhardy to lock parities in the belief that this alone would produce a convergence of costs. The second conviction is that the 'monetarists' are right in arguing that a harmonisation of conjunctural policy can be induced by locking exchange rates together. The third conviction is that, other things being equal, it is desirable to limit flexibility with a view to reaping the gains that were discussed in Section I.

(1) *Intra-European Parities*

The above principles dictate that parities remain changeable until such time as inconsistent cost trends in different national regions cease to be a problem sufficiently acute to require offsetting by parity changes.

H*

Necessary parity changes should be executed promptly and with as little disruption as possible. They should be small and timely rather than large and delayed; precisely how small the steps would need to be would depend upon the size of the threshold that would provoke disruptive speculative movements in an environment of minimal exchange control between national currencies and the Europa. National differentials in interest rates can play a major role in limiting speculative flows, provided that parity changes are modest in size; it is envisaged that interest rates would be allowed to adjust in an appropriate way.

It would be important to create an environment that would promote speedy implementation of necessary parity changes. It would not, however, be advisable to try to construct some automatic formula to determine parity changes, because (a) this would make it easier for speculators to anticipate impending changes; (b) there is little prospect of constructing a formula that would be of much help, because of the variety of factors that are relevant to determining whether a parity change is desirable; and (c) when an apparent need for a parity change emerges, it would always be desirable to examine whether some other policy change(s) might not be more appropriate. A more hopeful approach than that of seeking automatic formulae is to provide that the periodic Community-level reviews of national economic policies regularly include discussion of exchange-rate policy. Although in practice the final responsibility for determining parity changes would no doubt remain at the national level, one might recognise the Community interest by formally providing that changes in the parities of national currencies in terms of the Europa could be proposed by either the country or the European Bank and would require the approval of both.

It is envisaged that the prices fixed under the common agricultural policy, like all other prices fixed by Community organisations, would be determined in Europas. There would be no need for special transitional relief measures after parity changes (such as those which followed the devaluation of the French franc and revaluation of the Deutsche Mark in 1969) so long as parity changes were small, since the changes in domestic price levels would only be modest. Limited parity flexibility (unlike floating or big parity changes as practised in recent years) is, in fact, quite compatible with the aims of the common agricultural policy.

(2) *The Width of the Bands*

While the necessary extent of parity flexibility is principally determined by the need to offset differential cost trends, the width of the band is primarily determined by the extent of parallelism in conjunctural policy. If one is seeking to minimise exchange-rate variability, then the band should be as narrow as is consistent with the needs of anti-cyclical stabilisation. This criterion leads to very different conclusions regarding the desirable Europa/dollar band and intra-European band. U.S. reliance on monetary policy as its main anti-cyclical weapon has in recent years resulted in European policies being strongly distorted when the cycles between America and Europe were out of phase, especially since the United States determined its monetary policy unilaterally and with scant regard for the spillover effects on other countries. To insulate Europe from these spillover effects it is clearly necessary to envisage a significantly wider band than existed prior to the dollar crisis. In contrast, the co-ordination of monetary policy within Europe that would be needed to ensure a narrow intra-European band would be both feasible (although it would require more active fiscal policies in some countries, notably Germany and Italy, to compensate for the loss of the monetary tool for internal stabilisation purposes) and politically acceptable (since monetary policy would be determined by a consensus rather than being dictated by a single country).

During the preliminary stage a wide Europa/dollar band could only be reconciled with a narrow intra-European band by concerted intervention policies of the sort proposed in the Werner Report (the 'snake in the tunnel'). During the intermediate stage, however, this problem would be handled automatically by having the European Bank defend the Europa against the dollar within a wide band while the national central banks defended their individual currencies against the Europa within narrow bands.

(3) *Europe/Rest of World Parities*

During the preliminary phase there would be no special mechanism for a concerted European move. One of the advantages of the intermediate phase is, of course, that this would cease to be true. In the intermediate phase the parity of the Europa in terms of gold/S.D.R.s could be changed according to whatever rules were normal for I.M.F. members, and any such change would result in a joint move by all the European currencies. Decisions on varying the Europa parity would be made by majority vote in the Council of Ministers and would be guided by the liquidity position of the European Bank in terms of external assets.

V. *The Non-monetary Conditions for Transition to Monetary Union*

Creation of a European monetary area as proposed above would re-establish European control of European monetary conditions while strengthening economic integration. But European economic integration will fall short of that found within nation-states until monetary integration is consummated by the creation of a monetary union. This ultimate step poses problems and dangers that are altogether more profound than those involved in limited integration, because national governments would be deprived of the instrument of exchange-rate policy which has up to now provided an ultimate escape from the need to conform to the price trends in the Community as a whole.

Governments can scarcely be expected to give up this autonomy unless they are satisfied that the common pattern to which they would have to conform would be reasonably consistent with their set of policy objectives. Since inflation has been a perennial (and increasingly troublesome) problem in the post-war period, it is natural for those countries that have enjoyed the greatest price stability to fear the inflationary potential inherent in pooling their external reserves and monetary policies with countries whose record of inflation leaves more to be desired. Conversely, the more inflation-prone countries may fear that their growth and employment policies would be jeopardised by tying themselves to countries whose greater stability seems to be largely explicable by a more favourable unemployment-inflation trade-off rather than by different priorities regarding objectives. It is clear that monetary union would not be worthwhile if it led either to a levelling-up in rates of inflation or to a check to growth in significant parts of the Community. Indeed, either of these developments would be so disastrous that it is doubtful whether a monetary union that led to their emergence could hope to survive.

The important question that requires discussion is whether the automatic results of increasing economic interdependence, reinforced by conscious attempts at policy harmonisation, can be expected to ameliorate these problems to the point where they become amenable to a feasible and politically-acceptable regional policy.

Interpenetration

In principle, a country can move into payments deficit, or a regional problem can emerge, either because its prices become uncompetitive or because of an adverse structural shift in demand. In practice, however, regional problems within nations generally have structural causes. It seems that, within nations, there exist inherent forces that limit divergent cost trends: the resulting interregional wage rigidity serves both to hinder depressed regions recovering their prosperity but also to prevent regions actively bidding up local wage rates to a point that jeopardises their prosperity. It is therefore important to establish whether similar forces are likely to develop on a European scale as a result of integration.

There are in fact a number of reasons for expecting the increasing interdependence of the European economies to promote a growing convergence in economic performance. Ever-increasing trade flows will tend to sharpen competition and make it more unlikely that the competitiveness of one country will fall badly out of line with that of its partners. The growth of multi-national corporations will tend to make productivity performance more uniform. The emergence of transnational unions would reduce the probability of an isolated wage explosion undermining the competitiveness of one country. The adoption of a common monetary policy would eliminate the possibility of divergent price trends arising from differing monetary policies. As price trends converge, so will price expectations: hence this important source of pressure for differential wage increases will tend to be eliminated. The increase in labour mobility is likely to help check divergent wage trends, especially when it is reinforced by common policies in such fields as vocational training. Indeed, the adoption of common policies in a wide range of diverse fields – e.g. with regard to research, energy, transport, and competition – seems likely to promote a convergence in price performance.

For such reasons as these it seems unlikely that an inter-dependent and monetarily-unified European economy would experience cumulative divergences in cost trends. It is more likely that Europe would experience a particularly acute form of regional problems of the character that have been manifested within nation-states, where regional problems generally seem to reflect either natural disadvantages, the decline of old-established industries, or an initial position of underdevelopment. Even if this is true, of course, it is no cause for complacency, because there would remain an urgent need to ensure that geographical variations in unit costs were such as to promote regionally-balanced growth.

Harmonisation

The automatic effects of increasing interdependence can be reinforced by the deliberate harmonisation of economic objectives, policies and institutions. Such harmonisation will necessarily play a central role in the attempt to create the conditions for monetary union.

A natural first step in any programme of harmonisation is agreement on a mutually-consistent set of objectives for all member-countries. The Community has, in fact, already agreed on harmonisation of medium-term objectives, and specific targets have been laid down.

The harmonisation of objectives is only a first step. In itself it fails to answer the really difficult question of what should be done when it becomes apparent that the objectives will not be attained – a question that is particularly acute when the reason for failure is that the set of objectives accepted by a country turn out to be mutually inconsistent, or when the objectives of different countries prove to be incompatible. It is reasonable to suggest that a country which discovers that it is unlikely to achieve its targets should automatically have its strategy re-examined at Community level. Hopefully, this will sometimes lead to constructive suggestions regarding the resolution of apparent policy conflicts, or else to a consensus regarding the priorities that the country should attach to conflicting objectives. No doubt such a procedure would exert pressure on the member countries to pursue effective incomes policies, since these are potentially a substitute for exchange-rate changes.

Nevertheless, the lag between the implementation of policy changes and the consequential changes in the values of the policy targets is such as to limit severely the effectiveness of Community control which is limited to discussion *after* it has become apparent that agreed targets will not be achieved. Because of this lag problem, effective harmonisation must extend to the *instruments* of economic policy as well as to the *targets*. Within a full monetary union there is a built-in mechanism which makes for harmonisation of monetary policy, either because only one monetary policy exists or else because monetary spillovers are so strong as to render independent monetary policies impracticable. During the transitional stages this mechanism would become increasingly effective, and monetary policy in the individual states would increasingly be determined by the policy being pursued by the European Bank. In contrast, there are abundant historical examples of monetary unions that have flourished despite the maintenance of independent fiscal policies by the constituent units (e.g. the Latin Union, Belgium– Luxembourg, Switzerland and the United States). This suggests that harmonisation of policy instruments should be centred on the harmonisation of monetary policy. Fiscal policies might well be left to the control of the individual nations (subject, of course, to the need for enough tax harmonisation to permit the total dismantling of frontier barriers), to be used for purposes of local stabilisation when the conjunctural needs of a particular area run counter to those in the Community as a whole.

Regional Policies

Even if the growing interpenetration of European economies, reinforced by the deliberate harmonisation of economic policy, has the expected effect of limiting the extent to which unit costs diverge in different areas of the Community, it would be unrealistic to expect balanced growth throughout the Community unless deliberate regional policies were adopted. It

follows that an effective regional policy is of the utmost importance in creating the conditions for monetary union.

It would be a mistake to leave regional policy to be entirely a
national responsibility. There are three reasons for this. The
first is that in the absence of central control there is a real
danger that regions will compete with one another in offering
incentives to attract industry, the net result of which will be
to increase industrial profits without achieving any systematic
effect in steering industry toward the less prosperous regions. It
is for this reason that the Community has already imposed a
limitation on the sums that can be spent on subsidising investment in the 'central area' of the Community. The second reason
is that fiscal transfers constitute one of the most powerful factors
tending to maintain income within a region of an economic and
monetary union which experiences a decline in demand for its
output. As countries lose the opportunity of compensating for
a decline in demand by altering the exchange rate, they will
require the Community's fiscal powers to be exercised in a way
that acts as a substitute. A third reason is that the decrease in the
regional multiplier will make an injection of central funds more
essential. Within the framework provided by Community rules
and Community fiscal and credit policies, it is desirable to maximise local participation in the detailed implementation of
regional policy.

Some of the Community's existing fiscal instruments (e.g.
expenditure on restructuring agriculture) tend to have a re-
distributive impact that is regionally favourable. These effects
could usefully be reinforced by transferring the unemployment
insurance programme to the Community level. This would
result in an automatic and immediate redirection of fiscal transfers towards regions where prosperity was ebbing.

The fiscal instrument which would seem best suited to the
objective of promoting balanced regional growth is a regionally-
differentiated payroll tax/subsidy. It is desirable to relate the tax
and subsidy payments to payrolls, rather than to investment or
value-added, so as to provide the strongest incentives for labour-
intensive industries to move to areas of labour surplus. (It may
be worth noting that labour-intensive industries are not necessarily the same as low-wage, low-efficiency industries; economic
development is of course best advanced by introducing modern

industries which nevertheless have high labour requirements.) The tax rate (in the prosperous regions) or subsidy rate (in the less prosperous regions) should clearly be related to the unemployment percentage, so as to provide the appropriate incentives for industry to choose the less prosperous regions unless there were sufficiently compelling reasons to justify location elsewhere. There is also much to be said for increasing the tax rate in areas where wage-rates are high, and increasing the subsidy rate in low-wage regions. This would make a direct contribution to equalising incomes throughout the Community, and it would also provide a helpful incentive to unions to recognise that regional wage differentials can materially contribute to an equalisation of prosperity. If, for example, the unions in one country were to push wages above the level justified by productivity and thereby induce excess unemployment in that area, this formula would relieve the rest of the Community of the obligation to subsidise that region through the mechanism of the payroll tax. The payroll subsidy would, in effect, only be available to regions that were prepared to contribute to their own growth by exercising moderation in income claims.

The effectiveness of regional policies could be further enhanced by utilising credit policy in parallel with fiscal policy. Easier access to (subsidised) credit for investment in the less prosperous regions would prevent any desire to invest in those areas as a result of the fiscal incentives being frustrated by lack of finance, as well as creating an independent incentive to increase activity there.

Even in countries that have long been unified, policies based on national aggregates alone have been found inadequate. The business cycle does not coincide in space with national boundaries, but rather with the economically-homogeneous regions. Disinflationary policies which do not discriminate between economic regions, according as to whether or not they are actually affected by excess demand, inflict an unnecessary damage to the weaker regions, where 'overheating' is often the result of cyclical conditions external to them. And yet the impact of restrictive policies tends to concentrate there. When credit is cut, most casualties are to be found in these regions, since they have a larger share of smaller firms, and banks as a rule find it more convenient to reduce lending to such firms. A differentiated credit policy should, on the one hand, make possible a more effective stand against inflation in the regions where demand for productive factors tends to exceed supply; on the other hand, it should help to shield the weaker regions from the jolts of 'stop–go'.

These considerations should be taken into account when determining the Community's monetary policy. But this field would also appear to offer scope for direct action on the part of the Community. More specifically, a European credit institution endowed with large enough resources and powers might contribute to the pursuit of regionally-differentiated policies. It is a matter for consideration whether this task would best be accomplished by an adequate expansion in the European Investment Bank or by the proposed European Bank adding a Development Division to function in parallel with its central banking activities. In favour of the former solution is the traditional separation of monetary activity from finance for development purposes, but the latter might be best suited to maximise results in terms of the impact which overall credit conditions throughout the Community would have on economic trends in the weaker regions. Moreover, because the European Bank, as proposed in a previous chapter, would go beyond the concept of a reserve fund, whose activity is mainly confined to official settlements, and would thus deal directly with commercial banks and other bodies, the steps required to give its activity a regional orientation would not be too many. The process and machinery of monetary unification would in this event be harnessed to bring about a more even pattern of demand and economic activity, and to raise rates of growth. This would help to overcome the reservations that prudence engenders towards divesting national governments of their powers in the field of money, capital and exchange-rate policies.

Political Conditions

The preceding sections have argued that the preconditions for a successful monetary union include growing interpenetration of the European economies, deliberate harmonisation of economic objectives and of monetary policy instruments, strong regional policies (including the subsidising of the less prosperous by the prosperous regions, and the deliberate direction of cheap credit to the less prosperous regions), and a Community fiscal policy with automatic transfers of income on a significant scale. It is scarcely possible to conceive of these substantial powers – in addition to the control of European monetary policy resulting from the control of the European Bank – being exercised without some development in the Community's system of political control.

There are many other considerations that will be relevant to any changes that may be made in the Community's political or administrative organs. So far as the control of monetary and economic policy is concerned, the need might be met by a strengthening of the Commission's powers and therefore its accountability to the European Parliament, in parallel with the direct election of the Parliament. Or the Council of Ministers might remain the forum with final authority in these areas, but the Council might be strengthened by introducing one or more 'European Ministers' (who might, for example, be appointed by the European Parliament) charged with specific responsibility for formulating and expressing the general European interest, to supplement the national Ministers whose primary loyalty is to their respective national governments. Be that as it may, the powers involved in the economic control of a monetary union are so important that some method of strengthening political control is essential unless democracy itself is to be threatened.

VI. *Conclusion*

The preceding Report suggests that a new initiative for European monetary integration should be based on the early creation of a European monetary area. This area would be characterised by minimal internal exchange-control barriers, narrow bands between the currencies of the members, the widespread use of a new monetary unit (the Europa) to facilitate financial integration and replace the Euro-dollar in the role it has come to occupy as a pan-European currency, and the creation of a European Bank to further monetary integration, particularly by promoting and managing the Europa. Since the Europa would circulate in parallel to the existing European currencies, this intermediate stage would be consistent with the maintenance of limited exchange-rate flexibility within Europe and could therefore be adopted even before success in harmonising cost trends has been achieved.

Creation of a European monetary area, especially if reinforced by a wide band between the Europa and the dollar, would be an important achievement which would permit the re-establishment of European control of European monetary conditions. It will be more difficult to proceed to the final goal of full monetary union with a common currency as envisaged in the Werner Report. Realisation of this ambitious goal would pose considerable dangers in the absence of strong interpenetration of the economies, effective policy harmonisation, strong regional policies, and supporting political developments, all of which would be necessary to overcome the problems that are posed by inconsistent cost trends. It is not at present possible to predict the time that will elapse before these problems are solved and full monetary union, with its inevitable abandonment of internal exchange-rate flexibility, becomes feasible; but the best way of accelerating that time is to make a speedy start to the construction of a European monetary area.

Index of Authors

*Pseudonym

Index of Subjects

London, as financial centre, 181, 186,
191

Macmillan gap, 192
Mobility
factor, 51; policy for, 59
of labour, 14; occupational, 52
'Money illusion', 39, 104
Money-supply policy, 124
Multinational banks, 192; industrial
managements, 101
Multi-role European Bank (M.E.B.),
1, 29-32, 74, 80, 121, 160, 179;
see also European Bank

National propensity to inflation
(N.P.I.), 10, 13, 62-72; and
passim
Non-monetary conditions for monetary union, 214-15
Numéraire, problem of the, 154 ff.

Openness, of optimum currency area,
48
Optimum currency areas, 43 ff; and
N.P.I., 66; size of, 75
— rate of price changes, 69
Organisation for European Economic Co-operation (O.E.E.C), 7

Parity ratios, 3, 113-19, 168-73, 211-212
Payroll tax or subsidy, 218
Phillips curve, 12, 16, 61
Productivity, 64

Quality of life, 56

Recycling, 178
Rediscount facilities, 124, 128
Regional employment premium, 79

Regional policies, differentiated, 13,
217; see also Regions
United Kingdom, 15
Regions, 19
high-activity: with low inflation
propensity, 91; with high propensity, 94
low-activity, 22, 86
nodal, 91
Regulation Q, 141

Seigniorage gains, 123, 166
Semi-integrated and fully merged
economies, 8
Smithsonian agreement, 163, 170
Special Drawing Rights (S.D.R.s),
34, 129 ff., 169, 205
Speculation, 115, 119
Stabilisation policies, 59, 70, 89

Tax on congestion, 88
Taxation, 22
Tourist trade, 127
Trade unions, 63
Trade-off relationships, 12, 13

United Kingdom
balance of payments, 73
inter-war problems, 58
regional policy, 15, 79, 87
United States
and exchange control, 156
dollar tap, regulation of, 153
Federal Reserve system, 145, 148
inter-district clearings, 34
Value-added tax, 4

Werner Report, 2-4, 9, 30, 36, 97,
116, 199 ff.
decisions on, 5
attitude of France to, 5